Lesbian Romance
Novels

ALSO BY PHYLLIS M. BETZ

Lesbian Detective Fiction: Woman as Author, Subject and Reader (McFarland, 2006)

Lesbian Romance Novels

A History and Critical Analysis

PHYLLIS M. BETZ

McFarland & Company, Inc., Publishers
Jefferson, North Carolina, and London

LIBRARY OF CONGRESS CATALOGUING-IN-PUBLICATION DATA

Betz, Phyllis M. (Phyllis Marie), 1953–
   Lesbian romance novels : a history and critical analysis / Phyllis M. Betz.
       p.   cm.
   Includes bibliographical references and index.

   ISBN 978-0-7864-3836-5
   softcover : 50# alkaline paper ∞

   1. Lesbians' writings, American — History and criticism.
   2. Love stories — History and criticism.   3. Lesbians in literature.   I. Title.
   PS153.L46B485   2009
   813'.085093526643 — dc22   2009022074

British Library cataloguing data are available

©2009 Phyllis M. Betz. All rights reserved

No part of this book may be reproduced or transmitted in any form or by any means, electronic or mechanical, including photocopying or recording, or by any information storage and retrieval system, without permission in writing from the publisher.

Cover images ©2009 Shutterstock

Manufactured in the United States of America

McFarland & Company, Inc., Publishers
   Box 611, Jefferson, North Carolina 28640
       www.mcfarlandpub.com

Once more for Joan
and
Mildred J. Betz

Acknowledgments

I first want to thank Jennifer Fulton, Karin Kallmaker, and Radclyffe, three romance writers, who graciously allowed me to impinge on their time and submit a list of questions asking them their views on lesbian romance novels. Their answers not only provide the content of Chapter Five in this study, but have given the theory substance.

Again, I must thank my colleagues for their support and sufferance during the writing of this study. Roz Miller must also be thanked for reading the draft.

As always, to Joan and my family for the best support of all, believing it could be done.

Table of Contents

Acknowledgments — vi
Preface — 1
Introduction: Reading Lesbians Reading Romance — 5

One: From Stephen Gordon to Molly Bolt — 21
Two: Speaking the Unspeakable — 55
Three: Coding the Erotic — 79
Four: Erotic Achievement — 111
Five: Practicing Romance — 138
Six: Reading Between the Sheets — 169

Conclusion: Escape Clause — 194
Chapter Notes — 199
Works Cited — 209
Index — 217

Preface

Popular texts, despite increasing critical respect for some genres, are still considered literature's bastard children, accepted only if an appropriate lineage can be discerned. Yet sales figures from *Publishers Weekly* and other industry sources constantly show that more money is spent by readers on just these popular genres that cause academics to wring their hands about the intellectual decline of civilization. Of course, this does slightly exaggerate critical reaction, but the underlying premise that popular works offer little beyond a temporary escape and, that beyond the skill of popular writers in manipulating the formula, such works have little intrinsic value, remains a common view. I am one of a growing number of critics and commentators who do not share this negative position on the value of popular literature, and in the pages that follow, I offer my analysis of one of the most prominent of the popular genres — the romance novel — and discuss how lesbian authors utilize and adapt the form for their particular audience.

Romance, of all the popular genres, typically receives even less critical acknowledgment than that afforded to mystery, science fiction, or horror; it's seen as the literary equivalent of eating empty calories. Contemporary criticism of the romance, however, has begun to consider these works more seriously, looking at how they embody the specific cultural, social, and emotional demands of their readers. Romance writers, themselves, have also become the focus of serious critical study especially given the close relationships they deliberately establish with their audience. A clear shift in the perceived limitations of the romance is taking place, but the focus of such criticism remains centered on mainstream writers and texts. My discussion, while not the first to examine specifically lesbian works, positions lesbian romance within the dominant critical frameworks and expands their application by tracing the various ways the lesbian romance also reflects the particular cultural, social, and emotional interests of its community of readers.

The lesbian reader expresses the same fantasies of love, acceptance, and intimacy as heterosexual readers. She wants to see her desires given a recognizable and honest representation within the pages of the novel. By describing the ways in which lesbian romance writers not only incorporate the conventions of the romance but adapt them to the desires of their readers, I intend to demonstrate the flexibility of the popular form to accommodate a new audience. For me, the ability of popular literature to respond more quickly, and often more accurately, to social change represents its real value. From the pulp novels of the 1950s to the most recent romance, the variety of lesbian experience has been described in rich detail, and this, most importantly, allows the lesbian reader to see women like herself achieve the same romantic fulfillment heterosexual women take for granted. In spite of the visibility of out celebrities, like Ellen DeGeneres and Melissa Etheridge, and television shows like *The L Word*, most lesbians still live on the margins and must still confront the homophobia that prevents them from fully participating in their society. Within the pages of her romance novel, the lesbian reader finds a range of models for romantic behavior; she also is given the opportunity as the narrative develops to play out the processes of searching for and finding the appropriate romantic partner. She can learn what might prevent a successful outcome as well as how to achieve the desired happy ending.

My study of lesbian romances began, like many authors and critics, with reading the books for pleasure; I wanted to see if it were possible for two women to discover their mutual feelings, act on them, and come out winners in the pursuit of love. Since my critical interests include popular culture and literature, pursuing my interest and enjoyment in these works in a more formal manner seemed logical. It also provided a justification for buying more romances, since one needs primary material to illustrate the theory. Standard critical examinations of the romance are available, from surveys of the genre to histories of the form, including the studies of Tania Modleski, Janice Radway, Carol Thurston, and Pamela Regis. The majority of these discussions, however, focus on mainstream, heterosexual narratives and their readers; lesbian-authored works or audiences are mentioned only in passing. Criticism on lesbian romance texts and writers tends to concentrate on the pulp novels of the 1950s and early 1960s or is limited to discussions of Jane Rule's *Desert of the Heart*, Isabelle Miller's *Patience and Sarah*, Radclyffe Hall's *The Well of Loneliness*, and a small handful of other texts. Such treatments, though, generally use them to illustrate historical, cultural, and other theoretical approaches; often, too, the literature itself is subordinated to an author's major critical focus, for example Judith Roof's utilization of Rule and Rita Mae Brown to illustrate her discussion of the absent mother and its impact in the development of lesbian identity in *A Lure of Knowledge: Lesbian Sexuality and Theory*. Not surprisingly, many critics of lesbian literature overlook and undervalue popular lesbian romance, concentrating instead on the identification and examination of a more serious canon of lesbian writers and texts. Such work, of course, is necessary and important as it reveals a much more complex portrait of lesbian identity, activity, and creativity than the stereotypic concepts provide. My particular emphasis, however, also helps to expand the ways through which lesbians are given the means to re-imagine themselves and their relationships with their own communities and the wider world. In my analysis I first place contemporary lesbian romance novels within an historical framework that includes the pulps, Hall, Miller, Rule, and others to suggest that recent romances build on or correct the images and experiences presented in these earlier works. My subsequent intent centers on detailing the ways in which these texts embody key aspects of lesbian romantic behavior and expectation, looking at the way lesbians talk, construct, and perform love.

Since the reader's role in the experience of the text is vital to its impact, I consider the implications of lesbians reading romance. While Radway's and Thurston's analyses are built on extensive surveys of romances readers, their samples reflect mainstream, heterosexual ideas and expectations. With no such material available for my study, I went to the web pages of the three lesbian romance writers, to whose work I give full critical attention. As is typical, these sites allow readers to contact the authors with their reactions, criticisms, and questions. The answers open up the authors' writing processes, as well as their comments on issues such as the role of sex and the value of the work to its audience. These sites also facilitate the creation of a self-defined community as the authors include personal anecdotes or offer comments on current events, all of which invite a reader to feel more invested in the novels. This shared experience becomes particularly important, especially given the stress each writer places on what she sees as her responsibility to present an affirming, supportive representation of lesbian life and love.

Although popular romance's portrayals of the pursuit of love face ridicule or dismissal, after all the novels rely on clichés and stereotypes, exaggerations and coincidences, they provide a valuable service: where else can a woman, whose sexuality pushes her to the edge of social interactions, see her life and her desires described and celebrated?

Introduction: Reading Lesbians Reading Romance

> This process of seeing oneself in print in a mass-market format provides a kind of identification which carries the mark of a subcultural identity and the authority of a mass-cultural reality. Lesbians describe this event variously as making them feel joyful or "quite cold and frightened." The image is there, widespread and readily available material for the process of lesbian identification. The process by which we react to that image is highly variable, but nevertheless, an identification.
> — Meredith Miller, "Secret Agents and Public Victims: The Implied Lesbian Reader"

> "But she's the most incredible person I've ever known and she *likes* me. She makes me laugh, and think, and feel. Can you understand what that means to me?"
> — Maggie Ryan, *The Deal* (italics in text 197)

Romantic fiction is, perhaps, the most maligned of the popular genres, despite the fact that is outsells most other fiction — popular and literary.[1] This paradox becomes the crux of most critical commentary and analysis of these works, as critics attempt to answer why the romance appeals to so many different types of readers regardless of the genre's reliance on standardized plots and conventional characters. Is reading romance novels a harmless pastime, allowing the reader a chance to fantasize about being swept off her feet by an incredibly handsome, wealthy, powerful hero, rescued from a mundane life? Or is reading a romance novel a trap that seduces the reader's expectations by creating idealized, and therefore unachievable, concepts of love and the trajectory of the romance? Or does the romance novel allow the reader to *practice* romance, by engaging the reader in the variations of relationship and encouraging her to respond to such situations? Each position has its advocates and detractors, and the debates over the value of romantic fiction seem to bring strong ideological, even emotional, responses from its critics.

Trash or treasure? The major participants in the debates over the romance novel always begin from this question. It is important to note that the division of response breaks according to the writers and readers of romance and the academic commentators and critics of romance, who emphasize the negative qualities of the genre, the clichéd characters and situations, the unrealistic narrative progression, the happy ending. Most critical examinations, if not implying hostility to the work and its advocates, frequently take a benign position. Leslie Rabine's comment typifies such a view: "Romantic love, *although a myth that does not exist in daily experience*, remains the ideal model for interpersonal relations.... It is *supposed* to give meaning to an otherwise drab existence, and allow us to transcend daily life to a higher plane" (*Reading the Romantic Heroine* vii, emphasis added). This quotation appears to suggest a separation of ideas about romantic love — ideas that find the widest range of representations in various popular and literary media — and the possible ways of expressing it in an individual's actual experience. The quotation almost suggests that any translation of romantic dreams to lived experience does not, indeed cannot, take place.[2]

Not surprisingly, writers of romance novels, and at this point my analysis focuses on heterosexual romances and their authors, constantly confront these accusations. They defend their work and its value and champion their readers' ability and expertise in selecting and enjoying these works. Jayne Ann Krentz, a very popular contemporary romance writer, in the Introduction to a collection of essays on the romance typifies this response:

> Critics and readers who fail to comprehend the complexity and subtlety of the genre frequently dismiss the books as poorly written or unimaginative, when the simple truth is that they just don't understand the encoded information in the text.... The problem was inevitable due to the inherent difficulty of explaining any type of fantasy experience to those who do not grasp it intuitively. Thoughtful readers of the essays will have to abandon some of the conventional critical assumptions in favor of other perspectives if they wish to comprehend much of what is said here about the nature of the appeal of the romance novel [*Dangerous Men and Adventurous Women* 8].

Krentz stresses that reciprocity between reader and writer is essential for the success not only of a specific book, but for the genre itself. This relationship is a continually expanding one, as readers become writers and writers continue reading others' work. The authors of the essays in *Dangerous Men and Adventurous Women* are all well-known popular romance novelists, and each reiterates the importance of being a reader of the genre before she attempted writing such texts. This self-sustaining relationship between reading and writing is not as frequently seen in other genre fiction, although some fans of other genres will produce such a text.

Most detective novels are not written by professional investigators nor is most science fiction written by astronomers, yet most people experience some form of romantic relationship. This widely held notion, that everyone knows what true love is, for some detractors of the romance novel, becomes the central argument. How can a narrative whose readers can all claim expertise in offer insight into the human condition? Characters must be diminished into stereotypes, events stripped of their intensity, meaning diluted to the most common denominators. The writers simply repeat a narrow set of formulas that easily satisfied readers unthinkingly consume. Such views position the romance as the worst kind of popular text, one that homogenizes the expectations of the reader by offering a set of pre-determined formats which are mass-produced. The outcome of such material is the creation of a passive audience, receptive to the manipulations of the publishing industry. Scott McCracken, in *Pulp: Reading Popular Fiction*, summarizes this viewpoint by referencing the work of Hall and Whannel whose ten points stress the dominance of industrial/media production, the coercion of the audience to consume without thinking, and the mediocrity of cultural artifacts (25).

However, some critics do defend the romance novel, seeing it as artifice and art.[3] The romance has a long history that can be traced from ancient Greek prose romances, through medieval tales, Renaissance dramas, and the major eighteenth-century novels.[4] From these precursors come the standardized narrative, conventional characters, and dominant thematic stresses seen in their contemporary practitioners, but, according to critics, simply stringing clichéd stories and actors together does not produce a successful genre romance. As Anne Kaler asserts, "Romance, despite presumptuous assumptions that it is froth and frills, is a sturdily constructed form whose component parts must be correctly mixed to achieve its intended effect" ("Introduction," *Romantic Conventions* 4). Like other genre fiction that also relies on conventional formats, romance novels work best when writers are able to stretch the limits of the genre without breaking them.

Their discussions, too, stress the importance of the link between the romance writer and the reader. The most important critics — Janice Radway, Pamela Regis, Carol Thurston, Suzanne Juhasz, among others — consistently note the intersections between what happens in the text (the story) and what happens in the (to the) reader of that story. Whatever emphasis the critics offer in the analysis of the genre, they all take care to include the reader as an active participant in the creation and development of the romantic narrative. As contradictory as the preceding sentence seems, for many novelists, readers do help shape the content and outcome of the romance story. The All About Romance website (www.likesbooks.com) is one example of the linkages between audience and writers: besides publishing articles and reviews on romance novels, the site offers message boards, online discussions, links to author and other related websites, and feedback and FAQ sections. This site also takes a yearly poll of reader preferences, tabulates and ranks the responses, and publishes the results on the site. Romance writers also contribute articles and commentary to the site. The increasing number of such online, as well as traditional, methods of interaction with authors reinforces this extraordinary relationship. Diana Palmer puts it more bluntly in her article included in *Dangerous Men and Adventurous Women*: "[These women] are my family, my fans, my friends. I know many of them by name. They write to me and I write back. I remember them in my prayers at night. I never forget that it is because of them that I am privileged to be a successful writer. I owe my career, my livelihood, and my loyalty to them" (157).

The supportive critics share a basic assumption of the value of the romance, although they differ in their opinions of that value. The range of the critical responses include an emphasis on the transformation of the sexual awareness and behavior of the heroine (Thurston), to the expanded position of the heroine within her society (Regis), to the connections between finding love and discovering one's self (Juhasz). The one topic that all commentators do share centers on the definition and nature of the fantasy element that the romance narrative embodies. Whether that fantasy involves "believ[ing] in the possibility of transcending the divided self" (Modleski, *Loving with a Vengeance* 37) or provides a temporary "self-interested pursuit of individual pleasure" (Radway, *Reading the Romance* 96) or enables the final achievement of an "idea of recognition, of unconditional and nourishing care" (Juhasz, *Reading from the Heart* 10), the romance depends on the ability of the text to encourage the reader's interest in and involvement with some type of fantasy. At the heart of the fantasy is the articulation of some kind of desire, and many romance novels attempt to provide a frame of reference for defining that desire. Here is the point where author and reader collude in the making of meaning: through the conventions of the genre, especially the creation of the heroine and hero, the romantic narrative presents a pattern of dreams and behavior that are seen as achievable.

Qualifying the nature of desire, then, opens any discussion of the romance novel to its fundamental question: What is a romance? As with every other component of this genre, the answer first combines the expectations of the reader and the ability of the authors to meet them while expressing their own vision. In March of 1999 the editors of the All about Romance website asked popular romance novelists this question. A small sample of their replies highlights key technical and ideological aspects. Jo-Ann Power says that the romance is an "exploration of how two people who have the potential to love fully, find each other, conquer whatever problems stand between them, and make a decision to continue with each other." Rebecca Sinclair stresses the two influences — the writer who "breathes life into two endearing characters who were meant to be together" and the reader who puts the "emphasis on the romance, or way these two people's lives intertwine." Jennifer Cruise focuses on "the heroine's quest for self-actualization," while Stoble Piel asserts that romance describes "people's dreams and values overcoming circumstances and obstacles, and that love matters, people matter, and that two people who love each other can live an adventurous, successful life." What these definitions share is the importance of the relationship of the heroine and hero; without the tensions of attraction and rejection felt between these characters there is no story. The narrative itself provides the framework on which the relationship is built, and while the progression of the narrative follows a standard pattern, its variations reveal the flexibility of the formula. Romance novels are categorized as historical, Regency, Georgian, Victorian, Edwardian, contemporary, suspense and/or mystery, gothic, and family saga. In addition, many romance novels — called category romances — are published by specialty houses; Harlequin, Silhouette, Dell, and Avon some of the best known.[5]

Throughout *Dangerous Men and Adventurous Women* romance novelists offer more formal definitions of their work. What these offer are clarifications and interpretations of the basic concepts stated above. Linda Barlow, for example, asserts that

> the romance novel is an emotional coming-of-age story. At some subliminal level, the narrative teaches a woman how to reconcile the various aspects of her own psyche that may be at war with one another so that she can feel herself to be a truly integrated, competent, and emotionally whole individual

who is able to perform her various functions in the world ["The Androgynous Writer: Another Point of View" 46].

For many writers, the essential attraction of the genre centers on the development of the heroine; her transformation — and the ways in which she will change varies according to the type of romance, the time of writing, and the nature of the hero's character — is traced through some kind of journey. During this process the heroine discovers an awareness of herself and her abilities, all of which are focused on the achievement of a newly articulated desire. This recognition that she has needs both emotional *and* sexual marks the starting point for many romance narratives. As the story progresses the heroine will be tested, and her growing confidence leads to the successful outcome that is the hallmark of the romantic story.

The happy ending, which many negative critics find most questionable, must be achieved if the narrative is to succeed. As Pamela Regis points out, the ending of the romance does not essentially require marriage. In her analysis, Regis stresses the ending is important for its signaling of the heroine's victory over the "barriers" that stand in the way of her self-awareness: "Seeing the barrier overcome is for many readers and writers the focus of the book.... In overcoming the barrier, the heroine moves from a state of bondage or constraint to a state of freedom. The heroine is not extinguished and the reader is not bound. Quite the contrary. The heroine is freed and the reader rejoices" (14–15). The romance writers themselves emphasize the importance of the happy ending. Jo-Ann Power states that the happy ending "reaffirms that it *is* possible to find someone to love and have someone to commit to you." Throughout the March 1999 forum on defining the romance, writers constantly use words like promise, optimism, happiness, devotion, commitment when describing the ending of their novels (www.likesbooks.com). The other requirement of the happy ending is the heroine's eventual union with another; the couple that appears at the conclusion of the romance represents the fulfillment of her efforts and desires. No romance novel ends with the heroine not in a relationship. In fact, until she moves into (or back to) some social environment that approves of and supports the couple, the heroine's journey is not complete.

Of course, since these authors are, presumably, heterosexual women writing for an assumed heterosexual audience, the happy ending always involves a couple made up of a man and a woman. Even though the story concentrates on the heroine's development, the narrative must link her own movement toward self-awareness with a similar process of discovery in the main male character. Several of the romance writers included in Krentz's anthology focus emphatically on the role of the hero in the romance story. Susan Phillips' view is typical: "In the romance novel the domineering male becomes the catalyst that makes the empowerment fantasy work" ("The Romance and the Empowerment of Women" 56). The hero typically is represented as a mystery that must be solved if the desired happy outcome is to be achieved. Traditionally, the perceived gulf between heroine and hero appears so great that the possibility of union becomes what compels the reader's attention. This apparent imbalance in status, ability, and power between these characters also underlines the importance of the happy ending; what the heroine achieves at the end of the narrative is not only her own growth, but also the stability of the hero's love.

Over the course of the genre's recent history, the positioning of the hero within the narrative has also become the focus of much of the critics' analysis. The earlier version of the hero, a dark, brooding individual who shuns any social contact, is one that emphasized the potential for violence, especially toward the heroine. Some critics even called the heroine's eventual surrender the culmination of a rape fantasy.[6] Feminist critics, particularly, saw the heroine's concessions to male demands as a devaluation of her own sense of self and agency. More recent evaluations of the hero indicate an emphasis on males who express vulnerability, especially in the area of their emotional lives, and a willingness to accept the heroine's strengths. Most important in recent romantic fiction is the hero recognizing the value of mutuality for their relationship to flourish:

> Individualism is no longer shown as healthy. Heroes are unhappy, miserable, and ultimately weak because of their emotional isolation. Heroes are saved by acknowledging their need for other humans and entering into a relationship. Relationships are no longer based on sexuality and male dominance but on mutuality and equality. In turn, this emphasis on mutuality further changes the meanings of sexual relations, as well as gender and gender roles [Heinecken, "Changing Ideologies in Romance Fiction" 165].

Whatever the make-up of the hero, however, the paradigmatic couple remains heterosexual.

Sexuality, itself, remains conservative and traditional within the romance genre. A difference between implied and explicit sex must be noted; often depending on the sub-genre of the romance or its date of publication, actual physical intimacy is omitted from the narrative. However, many times the descriptive language of the narrative — euphemisms for the body, verb choices that suggest the sex act — clearly indicates the direction of the couple's initial contacts. Certain characteristics of the romantic heroine, particularly her verbal ability, replace actual sex. While there may be explicit sex scenes present in some romances, these tend to portray standard sexual performances by both hero and heroine. Sexual experimentation is limited, except in those romances that specifically situate themselves as erotic and spend much of the narrative describing the sexual encounters of and between the heroine and hero.[7] Sexual encounters, of course, are divided into good sex and bad sex, but this should not only be read as judgments of the couples' performance. Rather, sex becomes the signal of the hero and heroine's compatibility and indicates that their relationship will evolve to include the intangible qualities like emotional openness. "Sex," according to Heinecken, "is no longer the 'climax' of a relationship, but is part of an evolving relationship. Furthermore, within the act of sex itself, the emotional states of the hero and heroine are in a constant process of transformation. Sex is thus no longer a mere physical act, but is understood to be an expressive form of communication..."(168). Sex used purely for shows of power or for physical release dead-end this movement to the development of a mutual connection between the couple. More often than not, though, it is the male whose sexual practices must shift from such limited expressions to more fulfilling ones. Even the modern sexually aware and competent heroine tends to maintain a more traditional sense of restraint.

Sexual intimacy, particularly when it works to bring about the happy ending, must spring from the heroine's desires for such a fulfillment. Desire, then, becomes the critical reference point for her and, ultimately, his behavior. Within the pages of the romance novel, however, the definition(s) of desire are fluid, referencing physical, emotional, and psychological wants and needs. The writers in Jayne Ann Krentz's *Dangerous Men and Adventurous Women* identify this desire in many ways: to be cared for, to be swept up by feelings never before experienced, to find and keep the perfect partner, or to achieve self-sufficiency. The heroine will often express her want for any or all of these goals, and the narrative movement illustrates how and why she finally attains these desires. Further complicating the definition is that this desire appears not only in the text, but between the text and the reader; most writers and critics of the romance novel emphasize the importance of desire as the motivation for the narrative and the attraction of the work for its audience. Interestingly, while the heroine does achieve complete satisfaction, the reader, for many of the critics, is left having to balance what happens in the text with her own experience. Janice Radway's analysis focuses on the reader's uneasy relationship with the narratives themselves and the purchase of them:

> When Dot and her customers insist that they have a right to escape and to indulge themselves just as everyone else does, they are justifying their book purchases with arguments that are basic to a consuming society.... However, when they subsequently argue that romances are also edifying and that reading is a kind of productive labor, they forsake that ideology of perpetual consumption for a more traditional value system ... romances are valuable to this system because they enable the reader to accumulate information, to add to her worth, and thus to better herself [118].

Scott McCracken sees the reader of romances as continually involved in a process of adaptation; with each new novel, the reader confronts a new heroine undergoing the repeated journey of "transformation" and "comprehension." While no firm or final resolution is experienced by the reader, she is able to recognize the heroine's story and "negotiate" its individual meaning for herself (Chapter Three, "Popular Romance").

Such contradictory characterizations still dominate critiques of the romance novel and still open the genre to negative comments, bringing this preliminary discussion back to the key questions: since women continue to read romances, what value(s) do they find within their pages? And more importantly for my particular focus, what changes within the romance itself and in the audience when the producers and readers are lesbians?

Because lesbians do read romances and read them often.[8] And lesbians have been reading romances, and particularly lesbian-authored and populated romances, for much of the twentieth century. The history of the lesbian romance novel, however, does not follow as clear a trajectory as the heterosexual romance novel, but the recent work done on lesbian pulp novels as well as studies of early twentieth-century lesbian writing has begun to fill in the gaps. (An overview of this history will be presented in a subsequent chapter of this study.) As with any adaptation of a genre work, my intention in this examination is to discover if lesbian romances differ from their straight counterparts. If they do alter the standard narrative, character, and thematic stresses, how are those changes made and how are they incorporated into the romantic fictional framework? The last set of issues I hope to address centers on how lesbian romances may impact their readers. What values are incorporated into the pages of the romantic story and what images of lesbian relationship, society, and sexuality find representation in these works?[9]

Because the formula of the romance novel, like all genre fiction, remains the essential component of any adaptation, examining the ways in which lesbian-authored books adhere to these guidelines is necessary.

Like their heterosexual counterparts the lesbian romance presents a story of discovery for its main *characters*; here is the first point of difference. In traditional straight romances there is only one heroine who seeks fulfillment through her eventual connection with an appropriate male. Most lesbian romances double this basic narrative movement by having two women looking for this relational completion. The variations of the couple do echo the dominant models of heterosexual romances, particularly in the creation of the "hero," but where in traditional romantic narratives the viewpoint reflects the heroine, in lesbian romances both women's internal experience and response are presented. This is due, to a large extent, to the romance's reliance on third person narrative; unlike other genre fiction, like the detective story, the heroine rarely tells her own story.[10] This insistence on an objective narrator may account for the romance reader's ability to insert herself into the story and/or the heroine's position.

This encouragement of two women to imagine and eventually explore the romantic possibilities of their coming together, of course, is the most radical difference between straight and lesbian romance. The foundation of the romance rests on the expectation that the heroine's quest ends in a heterosexual union — one man and one woman — as several authors on the All About Romance website assert. Changing this essential dynamic sets up the potential for a re-imagination of what becomes acceptable romantic behavior: if two women can follow the assumed "normative" trajectory of romance, and discover the same intense, passionate intimacy as straight couples, this alters social perceptions and response about love. I find Thomas Wartenberg's notion of the "unlikely couple" extremely helpful in both articulating and expanding the idea of the lesbian couple as potential vehicle for social change (*Unlikely Couples: Movie Romance as Social Criticism*, passim). Although Wartenberg analyzes film in his study, his definition of the unlikely couple and its role on and beyond the screen can be applied to fiction.

In brief, the unlikely couple is comprised of individuals who do not belong together; in fact, their eventual union contradicts multiple levels of social expectation and approval. The couple's connection may cross class, race, age, ability, sexual orientation, and other perceived barriers and is considered "inappropriate because its composition violates a social norm regulating romance" (2). However, the filmmaker's (or author's) positive viewpoint acts as a counterweight by "setting the love the two partners share above the conventions it violates" (2). During the development of the narrative while confronting the anxieties and prejudices of the dominant society, the couple, by not only declaring, but actively working to sustain their love, becomes "a vehicle for social critique" (3). The film, just as the popular text, becomes a way to reconcile the transgression embodied in the unlikely couple with social beliefs. What occurs, then, is the "familiarization" detailed by Philip Fisher in *Hard Facts: Form and Setting in the American Novel*, the "process by which the unimaginable becomes, finally, the obvious" (8).

In addition to this radicalized outcome, the lesbian romance offers its lesbian readers versions of ways of being and behaving. Here, like heterosexual narrative, the fantasy element is a prominent feature. Standardized physical traits and personalities are found in any romance — lesbian or straight: The characters are extremely attractive, physically adept, intelligent and witty. Both male and female characters tend to have upper level careers or are successful entrepreneurs, and they usually move within the upper tiers of their social world. This scenario can be seen especially in contemporary romance novels. In other sub-genres, class distinctions and work are presented as initial obstacles to the developing romance. Lesbian romances are no different in their utilization of these conventions; both main characters are stunningly attractive, although there tends to be a reliance on some variation of the butch/femme dyad common in lesbian literature. (The ways in which lesbians are imaged within the pages of the romance will be examined in a later chapter.) Like heterosexual romances lesbian romance narratives are situated within an exaggerated environment, where the focus and direction of the plot center on the progress of the romance. Finding love, maintaining that love through trials, and the consummation of that love dominate the energies and efforts of the couple. Passion becomes the *sine qua non* for everything that happens within the book's pages.

However similar some fantasy components are between lesbian and heterosexual romances the essential distinction is that the imagined lover and desired sexual fulfillment are experienced by two women. Suzanne Juhasz in "Lesbian Romance Fiction and the Plotting of Desire: Narrative Theory, Lesbian Identity, and Reading Practice" describes this desire for and process of relationship as "feminosociality," a network of "maternal, sororal, and homoerotic relationships and institutions" that operate beneath the surface of a heterosexual/heterosexist society (70). Discovering this community becomes an important part of the lovers' story, as both women must come to terms with their sexuality — individually and jointly. It should not be surprising, then, that a high percentage of lesbian romances have one woman coming out, either by acknowledging her lesbian identity for the first time or by accepting that identity and "de-closeting" herself. More recent lesbian romances do not concentrate on the coming out aspect of the couple; instead both major characters are personally and publicly comfortable with their sexuality. This romance narrative emphasizes the couple's interactions within a specific social circle made up mostly of other lesbians; the story traces the various levels of connections, tensions, and influences among the group and typically ends with the properly suited lovers establishing their commitments.

The essential romance convention that lesbian authors keep is the happy ending, although, of course, the united couple is made up of two women. Just as in the heterosexual narrative the couple is (re)united after undergoing a series of trials and separations that test the suitability of the pair and the quality of their commitment. The implications of the happy ending for lesbians point not only to traditional notions of the importance of love in human relationships, but also the validation of the love between women:

> A narrative trajectory of discovery is plotted for both heroines that is both social and psychodynamic in nature, having as a goal the development of a full and mature identity for each. Even as social structures define the possibilities and limitations for identity, so psychodynamic structures, the network of desires and responses forming the mental world of each individual, affect how social experience is allotted meaning. Identity is at issue, lesbian identity, because the foremost fantasy explored by the text is that a person could *be* in such a way as to function usefully and satisfiedly in the life that she lives [Juhasz, "Lesbian Romance," 74].

In other words, the lesbian romance asserts the right of women to love each other and to actively seek such a relationship; it models ideas of romantic behavior — how to woo, how to compromise, how to be wooed; it provides temporary assurances of the value of a woman's loving relationship with another woman; it offers scenes of sexual experience and fulfillment. In spite of its reliance on the techniques and conventions of heterosexual romantic fiction, lesbian romances are, to use Jill Ehnenn's phrase, "doubly dangerous" because they allow, perhaps encourage, their readers to dream and enact the possibility of a satisfying passion and connection (126).

In the chapters that follow I explore the intersections of lesbian and straight romance fiction that have been sketched here. Chapter One will lay out the historical foundations of this fiction, discussing texts that, at first, may seem inappropriate to this analysis. Most studies of lesbian genre romance begin with the pulp fiction of the 1950s and early 60s, and I will also examine how pulp novels established and stretched the conventions.

However, the pulps did not spring fully articulated or independent of influences. I hope to link these works to earlier twentieth century texts that I believe provide points of reference and response for the pulps and later novels. Radclyffe Hall's *The Well of Loneliness* and Mary Renault's *The Friendly Young Ladies* will be examined as precursors to the contemporary lesbian romance. Chapter One will end with a discussion of Patricia Highsmith's *The Price of Salt* which is seen by many critics as the dividing line between the more limited representation of lesbian life of the pulps and the modern romance narrative. In addition, I will consider two novels that have also been seen as the first to present lesbian love — its pursuit and outcomes — within the conventional romantic frameworks. Both Isabel Miller's *Patience & Sarah* and Rita Mae Brown's *Rubyfruit Jungle* have achieved the status of classics, due, in part, to their transforming of the pulp narrative from tragic to comic.

Once the background of the lesbian romance has been described, my focus will shift from history to content and the ways traditional heterosexual concepts of romance are transformed by lesbian authors. Chapter Two will concentrate of the language of the romance, considering the essential issues of how lesbians talk about love, particularly when that language has, in a sense, been co-opted by the dominant culture. If all the words available to lesbian lovers are also the property of straight couples, how can lesbians assert the distinction of their passion? Do meanings change with the context or does meaning depend on who articulates desire? The importance of speaking love cannot be overlooked, especially for a community that has often suffered the cultural and social silencing of their speech. In addition to speaking, romance involves a whole range of behaviors, and in Chapter Three my analysis will center on the consistencies and alterations in the "look" of love and lovers. As with their heterosexual counterparts, lesbian romances portray their characters' ages, clothing, living situations, careers, recreation, and entertainments according to time and place. This includes historical romances, but also reflects alterations within lesbian experience and communities. For example, variations in the butch/femme dynamic can be seen particularly with a toning down of the stone butch to a more androgynous body type or both partners conveying a femme sensibility and presence.

Once the speech and look of the lesbian romance have been delineated, I will discuss how the sexual content functions in the lesbian romance in Chapter Four. How do lesbians behave when they're in love; how do they recognize and reciprocate those feelings? What do they do both in and out of bed? Sexual intimacy must be addressed here, because either implicitly, more often explicitly, the narrative trajectory aims towards physical intimacy. Sex is seen as the key moment in the identification of the couple's feelings, functioning as the initiation from isolation to relationship. This initiation does take the standard form of the experienced member of the couple bringing out the other partner's understanding of her lesbian identity, but this also signifies a willingness in each partner to be open emotionally. Couples, however, do not only behave in private but must act in the public sphere. Focusing on this aspect of the story will deal with how the lesbian couple is integrated into a set of wider communities: how "out" can the couple be, as a couple and as individuals; how do the couple's families react to the declaration of love; what are the wider implications of moving from the private to the public?

In Chapter Five my analysis will center on three lesbian writers — Karin Kallmaker, Radclyffe, and Jennifer Fulton — whose extensive literary output illustrates the variety of ways the romance, as re-imagined, encourages a lesbian reader to participate in the creation of the romantic narrative. Each of the authors has written in the romance genre for many years, utilizing the conventions and adapting them to her audience. Kallmaker, for example, has been writing under this and two other pseudonyms for more than twenty years, and in that time has produced novels that range from the comic to the Gothic. Likewise, Fulton and Radclyffe have produced works that illustrate a wide range of romantic situations and expressions, from the fairly traditional narrative to explorations of more dangerous sexual passions to expanding the focus of the romance story to include more than one pair of lovers. Over the course of their writing careers, each author has also recorded changes in the representations of lesbian life, from what the characters do, where they might live, and how they look. Their novels also have characters confront serious social issues, industrial pollution in Kallmaker's *Car Pool*, loss of jungle habitat in Fulton's *More than Paradise*, or remaking families in Radclyffe's *Turn Back Time*.

The last chapter of my study will consider the impact of the romance on its lesbian reader. Throughout Chapter Six I will offer suggestions about the impact of the portrayal of lesbian passion and relationship in a positive light. This is an important component of any critique of the romance genre; in fact, most studies of heterosexual romances begin with the question of how these works affect their readers. Two of the most important studies of the romance — Janice Radway's *Reading the Romance* and Carol Thurston's *The Romance Revolution*— include copies of the surveys the authors gave to romance readers and the statistical analyses of those responses. One cannot talk about romances without bringing the reader directly into the discussion. As mentioned earlier, romance writers themselves take great care in responding to their audience. Of course, the nature of the reader's response will vary. Some readers cultivate a self-conscious relation to the narrative being read; they are aware of the limitations of the genre and often treat their reading simply as a way to fill time. Other readers, like Radway's Smithton group, take their reading seriously, make their selections carefully, and look for a clear sense of value. Can the same observations be made about how lesbian readers might view their romance novels? Do lesbians read any differently from straight women once the form and operation of the genre itself has been understood?

The clichés of romance have been thoroughly intertwined in our social and cultural consciousness through a myriad of popular media. Movies, television, and, perhaps most importantly, novels have offered us forms of expression and behavior; in one sense, they have taught us how to pursue, accept pursuit, and build relationships. We like to think that these notions of love and passion erase the numerous distinctions and tensions that operate in our daily lives. Unfortunately, in the world beyond the romance novel, those differences frequently overwhelm our desire for shared experience and meaning. Lesbian love is impossible, because lesbian passion must remain unexpressed, because the idea of two women becoming a couple cannot be imagined. Yet, within the pages of the lesbian romance novel, however temporary the fantasy, the reader "enacts a performance of affirmation" (Ehnenn 126). Love, it seems, can conquer all.

Chapter One

FROM STEPHEN GORDON TO MOLLY BOLT

> Lesbian novels have been formula fictions constructed out of the heterosexual plot and according to the same patterns whether they were written by heterosexual women, by straight or gay men, or by lesbians; whether they were produced by reputable writers and published by respectable presses, or written anonymously and published as pulp paperbacks; whether they were intentionally derogatory, intended to titillate, or self-conscious pleas for understanding. The history of the lesbian novel is a history of refinements, extensions, and challenges to a formula.
> (Julia Abraham, *Are Girls Necessary?* 4)

> She'd tried rereading her favorite romances to get the right mindset but every time the hero growled or the heroine swooned Carolyn either burst into laughter or felt vaguely sick. Romance no longer gave her a thrill on any level, and so Carly Vincent had nothing to write about. Carolyn was now at a stage where she felt that if she left her writing alone long enough a new twist might occur to her — something she could believe in again.
> (Karin Kallmaker, *Paperback Romance*, 9–10)

Lesbian romance novels did not spring fully formed from the pen of the first lesbian romance novelist. Like any other literature, popular lesbian romance has a history of practitioners, influences, and adaptations, and like any other literature, this history does not follow a straightforward, causal trajectory. Finding the patterns of influence for the development of lesbian popular romance also requires the teasing out of recognizable romantic situations between women within the pages of the text. Before this can be attempted, though, some attention must be given to an essential concern — what exactly do critics mean when they identify a text as a romance?

A key issue in framing the definitions of the romance text whether lesbian or heterosexual, it seems to me, stems from articulating the distinction between a novel in which romance serves a distinct, but limited, narrative function or focus and a genre text where the fulfillment of the romance embodies the essential narrative purpose. The first category may include texts as diverse as *Wuthering Heights*, *Middlemarch*, *The Great Gatsby*, or *The Portrait of a Lady*: the second ranges from Elinor Glyn to Georgette Heyer to Jayne Anne Krentz. The first group of texts garners critical praise for the complexity of narrative development, characterizations, and thematic intent while the second is more often relegated to a second class status. In *A Natural History of the Romance Novel*, Pamela Regis addresses this important matter of definition; as she notes, the meaning of a romance depends, first, on how the text may be categorized, a medieval prose tale of Arthurian chivalry or a contemporary novel. In each case the expectations of what will appear in the text to portray the romance differ. The term also takes its meaning from the thematic implications and/or purpose of the narrative, which generally focus on "what is depicted — an idealized world — and how — non-mimetically — and on that depiction's status in the minds of authors and readers — fantasy" (20). Regis asserts, however, that such definitions do not necessarily separate any romance from what she identifies as a romance novel, or what I am calling a genre text. To clarify the difference completely, Regis adds that a third way of identifying a romance novel is its utilization of specific "narrative elements," the heroine's courtship, engagement, and happy ending (an actual or implied wedding) (22). Unless these events are present to organize the development of the heroine's story, the text is not, according to Regis, a romance novel.[1]

Most histories of literature illustrate the importance of making this distinction about the nature of the romantic situation that appears in the pages of the text. Examinations of the novel place such work within cultural, aesthetic, psychological, and other frameworks; the romance may be discussed as plot device, a reflection of specific social norms and expectations, or as a vehicle for some kind of ideological commentary. The inclusion of the romance, as well as its prominence in the text, addresses a multitude of authorial purposes, from providing serious analyses of gender to comic representations of social mores. It may be peripheral to the main narrative action or the central component of the story; it may only involve secondary characters or become the vehicle for the representation of the primary actors' behavior and feelings. Whatever the position of the romance within the plot, the expectations of its progress remain consistent; the lovers will be identified, their attraction described, and the outcome — positive or negative — detailed. Of course, this oversimplifies an extraordinarily complex range of responses to such literature, and many discussions of this work do treat the importance of the romance itself according to the particular emphasis of the critique.

Genre romance is separated from fiction that includes a romance by its perceived subordination of context, characterization, and ideology to the establishment and development of the passionate connection between individuals. Paradoxically, the concept of grand passion seems to be viewed as too complex to find successful representation in the pages of a popular romance, in spite of the fact that the entirety of the technical and thematic decisions that control the production of a popular romance are directed toward an assumed shared interest between the author and reader in the creation and maintenance of a love story. The conventions have a consistency that supports a continued engagement of the reader with the text, yet, at the same time, they encourage a reader to look for adaptations that keep her engaged in the development of the particular relationship being presented. After all, while the reader expects to encounter innovation, for instance, new settings or career opportunities for the characters, she still expects to engage with the familiar progress on the romance. If this renewed connection does not occur between the reader and the story, she will most likely reject the text. As Radway states, "The point of the experience is the sense of exquisite tension, anticipation, and excitement created within the reader as she imagines the possible resolutions and consequences for a woman of an encounter with a member of the opposite sex and then observes that *once again* the heroine in question has avoided the ever-present potential for disaster because the hero has fallen helplessly in love with her" (65, emphasis added). The security of the conventional framework provides the reader the opportunity to imagine and re-imagine her sense of what being in love means. Popular romance encourages such identification between reader and heroine because the reader is able to figuratively put herself in the heroine's place. The heroine — her appearance, her public role, her emotions — are recognizable. Most heroines of non-genre romances, say Catherine Earnshaw, or Anna Karenina, or Lily Bart, are not: for these characters there is no romantic fulfillment or permanence nor is there a sense of compatibility between the reader's experience and the characters. Tragedy may be emotionally cathartic, but not something most would wish to imitate.

I realize that the above paragraphs do not settle the issue of definition, nor are they intended to. The frustration and attraction of the romance narrative rests on its ability to blur the lines between serious and popular literature; whether the text offers deep insight into the complexities of human relationships or provides a brief hope of creating a fantasy connection, the idea of romance remains a mainstay of the fictional world. Lynne Pearce opens her analysis of the cultural position of romance in literary history by highlighting the dual nature of romantic representation:

> Indeed, what the condition of being in love *conceals*, romance — I would contend — *reveals*. And the fact that what it reveals is not the messy "truth" of the condition but its spectacular, fantastical "other" is the reason it provides us — as readers and as subjects — with such limitless pleasure; why it inclines us, moreover, to "fall in love" ourselves and to produce stories every bit as spectacular, fantastical and pleasurable to account for the traumatic moment that has seemingly redefined us [3, emphasis in text].

These stories, then, become the focal point for considering the impact that the various configurations of the romantic relationship have on their readers. Another important concern becomes the contexting of these stories and the adaptations that have been made to this most basic of narrative frameworks over time.

Of course, this opens the investigative process to those basic questions of what makes the romance text specifically lesbian and what makes the relationship in the text specifically romantic.[2] Lesbian popular romance novels, like their heterosexual counterparts, have a history, although tracing the descent of lesbian centered romances requires separating out the fictional texts from other written texts. Emma Donoghue has noted in her survey of the culture of lesbians in seventeenth and eighteenth century Britain that women's relationships with other women were identified in numerous ways and published in a variety of written forms, including criminal and medical proceedings, biographies of well-known women of the periods, newspaper reports, and poetry. Purely fictional texts, both sentimental and erotic, also appeared during this period. More provocative in her discussion are Donoghue's assertions that women who loved other women had a language to describe themselves and their relationships, had access to the production and reading of writings that offered descriptions or attempted explanations of their lives, and received wider social acknowledgement of their experiences, both positive and negative ("Introduction"). Donoghue's notion of an identifiable lesbian culture contrasts with the more common emphasis, offered by Faderman and Castle, among others, that passion between women was — had to be — disguised due to the ingrained homophobia of time and place.

However, these more traditional histories of lesbian life and literature also indicate that, despite the social, legal, religious, psychological biases, lesbians were able to find ways of representing themselves. Castle's image of the "ghost," for example, serves both a signal of what has disappeared from a text or a literary history — the lesbian; yet, at the same time, what is not represented has a way of haunting the pages of the text. The ghost has a way, according to Castle, of constantly reappearing, of reasserting herself into the consciousness of author and reader, causing a reevaluation of her purpose to the text:

> The spectral figure is a perfect vehicle for conveying what must be called — though without a doubt paradoxically — that "recognition through negation" which has taken place with regard to female homosexuality in Western culture since the Enlightenment. Over the past three hundred years, I would like to suggest, the metaphor has functioned as the necessary psychological and rhetorical means for objectifying — and ultimately embracing — that which otherwise could not be acknowledged [60].

For Faderman, lesbian representation cycles through a series of stereotyped images — the exotic, the seducer, the New Woman, the romantic friend, the invert — and each type calls up a set of institutional responses that attempt to position the lesbian as deviant and therefore outside social margins (*Surpassing the Love of Men*, passim). Yet, in the face of such attempts to deny lesbian existence and silence her experience, Faderman in *Odd Girls and Twilight Lovers* traces the ways that lesbians transformed the dominant social constructs of their lives: "However, once they became a part of the category the nineteenth-century sexologists had established, they altered it continually by their own lived experiences of love between women. And they thereby helped to demonstrate the large extent to which sexuality is often a social construct..." (308). This conundrum of lesbians' cultural and social positioning keeps the delineation of the subject matter of lesbian romantic fiction fluid because determining the outlines of actual lesbian experience cannot be pinned down. Is it enough that two unrelated women share a household, for whatever length of time? Must the couple present themselves according to the heterosexual model of relationship, with one the "man/husband" and the other the "woman/wife"? What is the nature of intimacy for the lesbian partners, simply emotional or is physical contact essential (and how far does such bodily intimacy go)? Do the women need to call themselves lesbians to be lesbians?

Complicating any answers to these questions, of course, is another problem of language, specifically the moment in history when the word lesbian became the commonly accepted name for women loving women. Emma Donoghue suggests that, although infrequently used, the word with its attachment to an erotic meaning, appeared as early as 1732 (7).[3] By the end of the nineteenth century, as the standard histories of lesbian experience assert, lesbian became the term most commonly used. Besides a name, merely an identifier, the word signifies a particularized set of behaviors that marks the woman as deviant. The nature of such deviance depends on the reference points of propriety, legality, or custom sanctioned by time and place. Again, it is Donoghue whose cultural history points out the range of terms used to describe women loving women, many of which referenced certain physical acts (tribade), appearance (tommy), or relationship (romantic friend). The more generic terms applied to homosexuals — gay and queer — slip in and out of common usage, finding their way into Radclyffe Hall's *The Well of Loneliness* (1928) as well as the pulp novels of the 1950s and 1960s. However, usually these words carry the burden of negativity, even when used by specifically gay or lesbian characters. The language of the community, the words lesbians call themselves — butch/dyke/femme — also connects to and amplifies not only the outward signals of being lesbian (appearance, career, relational behaviors), but also the identity the individual takes on herself. Assuming the name provides recognition and, depending on the particular historical moment and social milieu, meaning. Other words that are shared by the heterosexual and gay communities, like friend, roommate, sister, become coded, charged with nuances that are understood differently depending on who is using and listening.

Given the difficulties of identification and articulation of the subject of a lesbian romance novel, delineating the history of such texts would seem to present difficulties, the most serious being the accusation of misinterpretation. An affectionate gesture does not always indicate a possible lesbian attachment. Yet, there is a history, although not one that can be as readily identifiable as heterosexual romance literature. Obscenity trials and control of content by publishers to insure sales, for example, meant that authors were silenced or be willing to face legal and social conflict and restrictions on their creative endeavors. In spite of such constraints women managed to produce work that conveyed *a* reality of lesbian life for their audiences. There is also a progression towards the application of mainstream romantic conventions for specific lesbian readers of genre fiction.[4] Throughout the twentieth century, starting with novels like Hall's and Mary Renault's *The Friendly Young Ladies*, through the pulp fiction of the 1950s and early 60s, lesbian writers manipulated the standard romance narrative to produce, within the demanded industry frameworks, stories that achieved the description and recognition that lesbians existed and expressed common human desires. By the last two decades of the twentieth century, lesbian genre romance has gained a noticeable proportion of space on bookshelves.

Lesbian romantic fiction in the early years of the twentieth century, however, does not fall as easily into the dominant categories of popular romance and novels with romance, particularly in those texts written by recognized lesbian authors. Most histories of lesbian literature also concentrate their analyses on authors and texts that form, what can be called, the "official canon" of lesbian writing: Virginia Woolf, Willa Cather, Djuna Barnes, and Gertrude Stein, among others. Most of these novels deal with complex representations of the human condition that position them beyond the requirements and constraints of genre expectations. Woolf's *Orlando*, for example, does contain a romance, indeed at least two major romances: the first occurs during Orlando's Elizabethan years, as a young man, the second during the Victorian period when the female Orlando expresses desire for Shelmerdine. In both situations the gender of the partners remains heterosexually framed, even though the exploration of social constructions and responses to gender is one of the dominant thematic stresses explored throughout the text. In *Mrs. Dalloway* Woolf frames Clarissa's romantic and erotic memories of Sally Seton within the novel's examination of the nature of personal relationships and the responsibility individuals have in and for them. The potential for a fully committed lesbian relationship between Clarissa and Sally is thwarted by the social interests of heterosexuality, represented by the desire of both Richard and Peter for Clarissa, and by her choice of those social norms through her eventual marriage to Richard. Many of the lesbian authors of the late nineteenth and early twentieth centuries, in fact, did not even treat overt romantic relationships between women. For instance, the majority of Cather's novels focus on characters who establish heterosexual connections or remain celibate; the sexuality of her characters is either left undetermined or centered, however tenuously, on male characters.

When two female characters express strong feelings and attachments for each other, they are generally framed within the context of the romantic friendship as defined by Carroll Smith-Rosenberg and Lillian Faderman. Elizabeth Stuart Phelps' *The Silent Partner* and Mary Wilkins Freeman's *The Country of the Pointed Firs* typifies this situation. In both novels the major female characters — Perley Kelso and Sip Garth from Phelps's book and Mrs. Todd and the narrator in Freeman's — develop strong emotional connections that grow and strengthen over the narratives. However, these relationships never cross the line from emotional to physical intimacy, except for chaste kisses or embraces. Usually some impediment, class, age, ethnicity, or the like, keeps the women from redefining their relations. This is not to suggest that these women do not gain from their intimacy. Perley Kelso, for instance, becomes more aware of the economic injustices involved in the life of the laborers who work in her family's mills and makes efforts to correct them. Sip Garth, through Perley's interest, gains knowledge and the courage to become the literal and figurative voice for the mill workers. Interestingly, at the end of *The Silent Partner* both Perley and Sip are presented as remaining unmarried as they pursue their moral crusades. It is the narrator in Freeman's *The Country of the Pointed Firs* who gains most from her time spent with Mrs. Todd; she learns to appreciate the simple life of and wisdom of the people of Dunnet, Maine. The narrator expresses deep regret at having to leave Dunnet and especially Mrs. Todd, who has given her the opportunity to find a sense of peace and self. Not all female characters find themselves in such rewarding intensely emotional friendships. Some relationships have no deeper implications; the women's engagements remain neutral in terms of the emotional component. Some, as in Nella Larsen's *Passing*, have tragic outcomes.

The above brief description obviously begs the question as to whether texts like these can be considered lesbian at all. If subject matter is the touchstone, then many of these works cannot be seen as presenting lesbian experience at all, while others allude to same-sex attraction without carrying it to a complete outcome. If the author's sexuality is the determining factor, then these texts can be seen as lesbian, since it can be argued that the work may be seen as embodying a particular approach and sensibility to the content. What such texts cannot be called, however, are romances; the narratives focus on ideas and issues that supersede the development of any intimate relationship. Even in those texts where a romantic attraction can be discerned, the primary emphasis of the story is directed to more far reaching thematic implications. The love story, if the plot details even support such a name, remains subordinate, usually included to highlight other meanings. For example, while Larsen's *Passing* can be read as an exploration of lesbian desire between the main characters, the novel is more frequently read within the critical and social contexts of race. Where, then, does the lesbian romance novel situate itself becomes the key question.

Recognizable popular lesbian romance begins with Radclyffe Hall's *The Well of Loneliness*, originally published in 1928 and continuously in print since then. Hall's novel establishes key character types and narrative movements that became the conventional strategies of later works, especially the pulps. These include the stereotype of the mannish lesbian or, to use the language of the sexologists, the invert, the pairing of this figure with a very feminine partner, the discovery and joining of a community of lesbians, the inability of these women to achieve a satisfactory relationship, and the ultimate separation of the couple. In many ways, the story of Stephen Gordon's recognition and acceptance of her lesbian identity and her search for love actually contradicts the standard definitions of popular romance, particularly in its most important requirement of the happy ending. Yet, the novel must retain its place as the foundation for subsequent romantic stories because Hall deliberately set out, according to her biographer Sally Cline to connect with two audiences, "a middle-class heterosexual audience *whose attitudes she wished to change,* and an audience of guilty and voice-less inverts *whose suffering she hope to reduce*" (230, emphasis added). Hall explicitly created Stephen and her story to present the actual experiences of the sexual invert to evoke understanding and sympathy for these individuals. In doing so, Hall exposed her own sexuality to public scrutiny, particularly during the obscenity trial that the novel faced in the same year as its publication.[5]

Typically, critical evaluations of *The Well of Loneliness* focus on the psychological frameworks, since Hall herself read the works of Havelock Ellis, Richard von Kraft-Ebbing, and others. Ellis, himself, wrote a brief "Commentary" that introduces the novel and asserts that it "presents, in a completely faithful and uncompromising form, one particular aspect of sexual life as it exists among us to-day." More recent critical assessments, in addition to acknowledging the psychosexual themes and issues, examine Hall's work as embodying the "values of imperial ideology" prevalent among the more conservative fiction writers of early twentieth century Britain, which included "its patriotic representation of a prewar pastoral England, its eugenicist insistence on motherhood, and its final melodramatic repudiation of lesbianism" (Wachman 152). Hall's novel is also discussed in relation to the practices and conventions of heterosexually framed narratives; interestingly, though, these critiques do not usually position the novel as a popular romance.[6] I have found only one critic who compares the novel to other popular romantic narratives of the period. Jean Radford's essay, "An Inverted Romance: *The Well of Loneliness* and Sexual Ideology," identifies three points of similarity: the titled family and setting of the aristocratic estate, which will be lost; the deliberate use of "linguistic archaisms, syntactical inversions, adjectival insistence and exclamatory style"; and the struggle of the lovers to overcome a range of obstacles (108).

Even the unhappy ending, the separation of the couple, and the religiously based concept of noble sacrifice show up in earlier heterosexual romances. Radford points out that Hall's inversion of these romantic conventions, while denying the specific fulfillment of the romance provides a larger general audience with some sense of a positive future. However, Radford's major emphasis in her analysis is focused on the multiple levels of popularity that Halls' text embodies; these include its reputation, due mainly to the obscenity trial and its outcome, the conscious inclusion of the current theories of sexual inversion, its positive appeal to lesbian readers despite the negative portraits of homosexual life, and the narratives outcomes.

I am left with the questions, then, that given the varied interpretations of Hall's novel, can *The Well of Loneliness* really be read through the prism of the popular romance, and, if so, how? What Hall's novel offers my study of lesbian romance is a set of thematic and technical choices and responses regarding the representation of an intimate relationship between two women, and while the dominant narrative and, I would argue, emotional outcomes are negative, Hall establishes a paradigm that late authors will expand and contract, accept and contradict. My terms — pathology, intentionality, and ambiguity — can be found in the way lesbian writers, particular those whom this chapter considers as illustrations of a proto-popular romance, coordinate the technical requirements of plot, setting, and characters. In addition, these concepts can be found in the response of readers as well as critics. It must be stressed that every text does not embody all of these approaches in its pages at the same time or to the same degree, and that these positions should not be seen as necessarily engaging with one another. For example, while Hall deliberately framed her novel to present the life of the lesbian in a sympathetic manner, she also accepted and incorporated the sexologists' belief that "homosexuality was diseased" (Cline 228). Yet, for many lesbian readers, particularly the generation that followed Hall, *The Well of Loneliness* offered a portrait of a community that, however bleak, provided a limited recognition of themselves.[7] It must also be noted that the majority of lesbian romance novels published in the 1980s and 90s do not reference these concepts, whether through the characters' behavior or response, with the same stresses or intent. Much of the shame or denial or despair evinced in the proto-romances has disappeared, and although some of the characters may initially express fear of being labeled a lesbian, over the course of the narrative they will come to understand and accept that identity.

From the beginning Stephen Gordon feels out of place, even her name signifying this sense of dislocation. Wanting a son, but having a daughter, Sir Philip tells his wife that, "'we've called her Stephen so long, ... that I really can't see why we shouldn't go on —'" (13), so the child is christened Stephen Mary Olivia Gertrude, a juxtaposition of masculine and feminine identifiers that will haunt Stephen's sense of her self and position throughout the early books of the novel. As Stephen grows up, she develops an increasing awareness of her difference, feeling more comfortable with her horses, developing interests and ability in masculine activities, such as hunting and fencing, and preferring the solitary pursuits of learning and writing. The local social engagements which require Stephen to appear womanly become torturous for her. Stephen's only sense of belonging and connection is to Morton, the family estate: "The spirit of Morton would be part of her then, and would always remain somewhere deep down within her, aloof and untouched by the years that must follow, by the stress and the ugliness of life. In those after-years certain scents would evoke it — the scent of damp rushes growing by water; the kind, slightly milky ordour of cattle; the smell of dried roseleaves and orris-root and violets..." (35). At a pivotal point in the narrative, after her affair with Angela Crossby has been discovered, Stephen is exiled from Morton; she will only return for periodic visits, and by the conclusion of the novel any hope for going home permanently seems unlikely.

Her parents also feel this sense of estrangement from their daughter: Sir Philip, wanting a son, raises Stephen as a son, encouraging her athleticism and further education. In return Stephen idolizes him and attempts to be the boy he desires. Yet, Sir Philip is aware of Stephen's innate differences; he is often shown observing her behavior and responding to the pain and confusion he sees. But, he seems incapable or unable to offer Stephen any guidance, although he does placate Anna when she becomes angry or upset about Stephen's behavior. After her father's accidental death, Stephen will discover that he has read the work of the sexologist Kraft-Ebbing and made comments in the margins linking what he has read with Stephen. This sympathy, though, is not strong enough to prevent Sir Philip from anticipating the possibility of an engagement between Stephen and Martin, a visitor to the area: "He could not quite keep the great joy from his eyes, not the hope from his heart. Had he been mistaken? Perhaps after all he had been mistaken — the hope thudded ceaselessly now in his heart (97). When Martin does propose, Stephen rejects his offer, and in an attempt to understand why, she goes to her father. After describing her feelings and actions, Stephen asks the question her father fears: "'Is there anything strange about me, Father, that I should have felt as I did about

Martin?'" (105). Sir Philip sacrifices the truth, partially to protect his daughter, but also to protect himself; he identifies her questioning as "foolish fancies" and offers to send her to Oxford (107). Father and daughter will not have any further opportunity to confront Stephen's questions; soon after this exchange Sir Philip will die from a fall.

Lady Anna cannot offer Stephen any emotional support, and, as the novel develops and she becomes aware of Stephen's sexual identity, Lady Anna ultimately cannot overcome her sense of dismay and confusion. Stephen's lack of femininity, in her appearance and behavior, embarrasses and disturbs Anna. However, until the scandal of Stephen's affair with Angela, Anna's involvement with Stephen is somewhat superficial; neither seems able or willing to break through a self-imposed wall of superficial affection. Once Stephen's behavior becomes public knowledge, Anna's reticence crumbles:

> "'All your life I've felt very strangely towards you'; she was saying, 'I've felt a kind of physical repulsion, a desire not to touch or to be touched by you — a terrible thing for a mother to feel — it has often made me deeply unhappy. I've often felt that I was being unjust, unnatural — but now I know that my instinct was right; it is you who are unnatural, not I...'." [200].

Stephen accepts the label of unnatural until the moment her mother calls her feelings for Angela "unnatural cravings of your unbalanced mind and undisciplined body" (201). Hall allows Stephen to articulate the first of the novel's calls for the legitimacy and right to express her love for women: "'As my father loved you, I love. As a man loves a woman, that was how I loved — protectively, like my father. I wanted to give all I had in me to give ... It was good, good, *good*...'" (201). Neither woman can reconcile the other's assertion and their separation is managed to appease both private and public propriety.

Once away from Morton, Stephen begins to establish and accept her identity; she moves to London where she meets Jonathan Brockett, a gay man who recognizes Stephen's sexual difference. He introduces her to the artistic community — Stephen's first literary effort, a novel, has become a critical and financial success — and encourages her to leave England for Paris; there he will introduce Stephen to the lesbian salon of Valerie Seymour as well as the city. Eventually, Stephen buys a home and establishes herself in Paris, but has little interaction with Seymour and her friends, focusing on her writing. The outbreak of war will alter this life; Stephen becomes an ambulance driver for the allies, performs heroically, being wounded and receiving the French Croix de Guerre, and falling in love with Mary Llewellyn, a younger member of the ambulance corps.

The relationship between Stephen and Mary highlights the intersection of pathology, intention, and ambiguity which I have identified as key characteristics of these early models of romantic possibility. Stephen's earliest romantic feelings have always been directed towards women, a maid and a governess at Morton, which were considered childish crushes. Her passionate desire for Angela Crossby brought Stephen to the realization of her difference. In the confrontation with her mother Stephen acknowledges this feeling of otherness but also asserts that she feels no shame in her feelings. This sense of courage, interestingly described by Hall as Stephen "[finding] her manhood," helps her accept her exile from Morton (202). However, this self-assurance is short-lived; just before leaving she discovers her father's annotations in Kraft-Ebbing. Her response highlights the contradictory position Stephen feels she embodies: "...there are so many of us — thousands of *miserable, unwanted people, who have no right to love no right to compassion because they're maimed, hideously maimed and ugly...*" (204, emphasis added). She then picks up a Bible which opens at Genesis and the marking of Cain as an outcast. Once Stephen leaves Morton she will return again and again to a belief in and acceptance of her own, and others like her, flawed nature. Repeatedly in the novel, Hall has Stephen Gordon and other homosexuals identify themselves as flawed, as things, as incomplete and therefore incapable of achieving real satisfaction in their lives and relationships.

Throughout the novel Stephen fluctuates between positively claiming her difference and rejecting any identification with it. The head of the ambulance corps senses Stephen's growing attraction to Mary and suggests they spend less time together, and although she accepts their separation, Stephen cannot deny her feelings. After the war she brings Mary to Paris and determines to maintain the relationship despite social criticism: "There was many another exactly like her in this very city, in every city; and they did not all live out crucified lives, denying their bodies, stultifying their brains, becoming the victims of their own frustrations. On the contrary, they lived natural lives ... they had their passions like everyone else..." (299). Discovering that her desires are reciprocated, Mary and Stephen set up their household and live as a couple for several years. Stephen, however, keeps Mary isolated from any social contacts, which strains the relationship. Stephen's friend Jonathan Brockett rightly accuses her of "shun[ning] your own ilk as though they were the devil!" (346). After acknowledging the truth of Jonathan's statement, the couple becomes part of the lesbian circle of Valerie Seymour. This brings the couple into contact with other lesbian couples as well as exposes them to social derision and ostracism and the terrible emotional pain such responses inflict on these women: lose of family and home, poverty, alcoholism, and promiscuity. Yet, Stephen finds solace and comfort in the company of Seymour and her friends, because here Valerie has "created an atmosphere of courage [where] everyone felt very normal and brave when they gathered together" (353).

Such moments of acceptance, however, are quickly undercut by Halls' introduction of scenes and situations that emphasize the strangeness and despondency of the homosexual community. In a scene that becomes increasingly perverse, Stephen and her friends visit a series of gay bars where one proprietor "collects" homosexual customers, where Stephen experiences an increasing disgust for the effeminate men, where she momentarily considers rejecting any connection to such people. Hall introduces at this moment the character of Adolphe Blanc who articulates the belief that, even though such degradation seems to be the only course open to the sexual invert, a time will come when these people will call for the recognition and acceptance of their right to exist (390). The final chapters of the novel, unfortunately, work against such a hope. One of their friends becomes ill and dies, and her lover, distraught, commits suicide. Martin Hallam, the man who proposed to Stephen many years ago, comes to Paris, meets Mary, and falls in love with her. Intent on winning Mary's affection, Martin and Stephen engage in a test of wills; Stephen seems on the verge of succeeding until she overhears two women commenting on her appearance. After that moment Stephen devises a plan to convince Mary that she has had spent the night with Valerie Seymour and that Mary will be better off marrying Martin. Mary's departure sets off an hallucinatory experience for Stephen; a vision of her lesbian friends, of the effeminate men from the bars, of hundreds of the sexually outcast who crowd in on her demanding that she plead their cause with God and the world: "'We are coming, Stephen — we are still coming on and our name is legion — you dare not disown us!'.... They possessed her.... They would turn first to God, and then to the world, and then to her.... And now there was only one voice, one demand; her own voice into which those millions had entered.... "'God,' she gasped, 'we believe; we have told You we believe ... we have not denied You, then rise up and defend us. Acknowledge us, oh God, before the whole world. Give us also the right to our existence!'" (437). Forced to give up her own right to happiness, Stephen takes on the burden of becoming the spokesperson for tolerance of the sexually different.

The tragic ending of *The Well of Loneliness*, with its increasingly insistent religious imagery and idea of sacrifice, moves the romantic story to the periphery of the narrative. Stephen Gordon's desire for her right to love and for that love to be acknowledged becomes analogous to a crusade, as she takes on the task of representing the invert community and offers her own suffering as atonement/expiation for these individuals' very existence. In her biography of Hall, Sally Cline states the Hall recognized the limitations within which she positioned her narrative and gave them the ending that society would accept:

> She allowed herself to write openly about her lesbian heroine Stephen and the other homosexual characters in Paris; she allowed her women to desire each other; but that was as far as she allowed the narrative to go.... In a profound sense her inverts *are* doomed; it is a narrative of damnation. And this for highly pragmatic reasons: she believed the law would allow no more than this, if indeed even this was permissible [230, emphasis in text].

The novel, then by its very publication offers a forward-looking representation of lesbians despite the dominant internal emphasis on the irreconcilable differences between the dominant society and this particular community.

This ambiguity of response follows the novel from its first appearance to the present. Within the text itself, Valerie Seymour illustrates the paradox of establishing a satisfactory identity in a world that finds one disgusting. She sympathizes with Stephen's need to be free to express her love, but also cautions patience and believes Stephen and others "should learn to be proud of their isolation. She found little excuse for poor fools like Pat, and even less for drunkards like Wanda" (406). She recognizes the dual influences on Stephen's character—her sexual difference and the heightened awareness it contributes as well as her ties to the traditions of the English gentry—and urges Stephen to "bring the two sides of your nature into some sort of friendly amalgamation and compel them to serve you.... The question is, can you ever bring them together?" (407–08). When Stephen asks Valerie to agree to the ruse devised to send Mary to accept Martin's proposal, Valerie points out these contradictions in Stephen's character again, but agrees to help. However, whether Stephen has managed to integrate the two aspects of her personality as Valerie recommends is left unanswered. Stephen's acceptance of the role of martyr, which has the potential for a positive outcome, also carries with it the real possibility of a series of private and public losses. But whatever next steps Stephen takes, with her ceding of Mary's love to Martin, she moves beyond the range of romance.

In an afterward written for the 1984 reprint of *The Friendly Young*

Ladies Mary Renault tells of reading Hall's *The Well of Loneliness* and finding the book "irresistibly funny" because of its descriptions of "an impermissible allowance of self-pity, and its earnest humourlessness" (281). Renault compares the despondent quality of Hall's novel to the works that incorporated homosexual characters and issues with lighter techniques published around the same period and finds Hall's representation to be curiously limited. During the composition of *The Friendly Young Ladies* Renault felt "it becoming to refrain from needless bellyaching and fuss" (282). The resulting fictional treatment of a lesbian relationship presents the couple — Leo (Leonora) and Helen enjoying a successful balance of the demands needed for sustaining that intimacy, at least until the ending. At the conclusion of the novel, Leo's relationship with Joe Flint, a deep friendship based on shared ideas and behaviors rather inexplicably turns into an apparent romantic one. The novel ends with Leo, after having had sex with Joe, beginning to pack up her things from the houseboat she and Helen have shared in preparation for leaving. The last picture of Leo offers a somewhat ambiguous indication of her new emotional position, showing her lying across the bed weeping "the tears of a woman" (279). The implication appears to be that Leo has matured into an acceptance of heterosexuality.

Until this unsatisfactory ending the relationship between Leo and Helen has been portrayed as positive and successful; they have been together seven years and have created and maintained a relationship that balances their differing personalities and demands. They clearly know one another's strengths and weaknesses and accommodate one another's desire (need) to stray beyond their own commitment. Sexual exclusivity, in fact, seems non-essential for Leo and Helen. Leo will have sex with Peter, an obnoxious young doctor who is prone to psychoanalyze everyone he comes in contact with, in order to protect her younger sister, Elsie, from being hurt. She will also seduce Peter's girlfriend in front of him. Attractions for others, whether male or female, are accepted because both women return to the central intimacy and understanding they have created for themselves. An extended conversation at the end of Chapter XIII highlights their ability to reconcile tensions: Helen has been asking Leo about her attraction for Joe and what at first seems to reveal her jealousy ("You like him five times as much as any of these people you've picked up and dropped. And I should think you could have had him years ago if you'd done the first thing about it.... At first I thought I'd mind, but then I knew I wouldn't..." [133]), simply becomes an acceptance of Leo's deep friendship for Joe. However, this balance is broken with the intrusion of Elsie and her misguided ideas of love into Leo's and Helen's life.

Elsie has run away from home, believing that her immature romantic feelings for Peter are reciprocated. Elsie's concepts of love have been shaped by contemporary popular romances which cause her to misread Peter's professional interest in her health as something more, or to imagine Leo in stereotypic, exotic (hetero)sexual situations. When she confronts the reality of Leo's and Helen's living situation, Elsie is unable to interpret it correctly. She readily accepts that Helen has given up her own room to Elsie and will share Leo's in spite of the obvious indications — the room's contents and the shared bed — that two people live there. Elsie's belief that she and Peter will become lovers insinuates itself into the daily lives of the others and eventually brings underlying tensions to the surface. Her naïve understanding of human relationships and sexual/romantic desires precipitates Peter's interference in the lives of Leo and Helen. Peter can be seen as Renault's satiric response to Hall's acceptance of the psychological definition of homosexuals as flawed. Peter espouses a belief in his ability to diagnose the real causes for his patients' physical illnesses as rooted in sexual repression (his treatment of Miss Perkins is typical). However, his methods are somewhat unorthodox, as he pretends a romantic interest which, when he feels progress has been made, is withdrawn. When asked if his specialty is psychology, Peter says, "Not officially. But it's indispensable, of course, in any branch. Unfortunately far too few people can be got to realize that" (175). Not surprisingly, his successes are only with female patients, and when Leo addresses his methods, his response is, first, offense, and, second, to defend his practice as ultimately beneficial to the woman. Leo, sensing that Elsie will become Peter's next victim, engages in a brief sexual liaison to divert his interest. Peter seems incapable of taking people or events at face value, everything must have a deeper meaning that he feels his duty to uncover and comment on; it is not surprising to learn that he keeps a file of interesting case studies.

Peter's "scientific" interest forces him to probe Leo's and Helen's relationship. In both the night he and Leo spend together and an afternoon spent with Helen, he makes sexual advances, first kissing, then checking the response, then advancing the sexual overtures. Helen, particularly, is unresponsive, which sets Peter to take the *"interesting alternative of verbal attack"* (emphasis added, 216). During this exchange Peter specifically asks about their relationships, trying, apparently, to get Helen to acknowledge fears or doubts. She, however, refuses to rise to his leading questions: "I expect most relationships are unusual when one knows enough about them. We're pretty well used to ours; it seems quite ordinary to us" (217). Peter keeps pushing his interrogation and finally, through an insinuation of censure, does provoke Helen to reveal a deeper emotion. He achieves a similar reaction from Leo when he accuses her of treating Elsie like a child for wanting to hide all indications that they have just finished having sex. The end result of Peter's probing is not to have Leo or Helen deny their intimacy but to facilitate its ending. In effect, Elsie and Peter, with their assertions of heterosexual expectation and their claims that others acknowledge them, set up a chain of events that results in the collapse of Leo's and Helen's partnership. Helen, as she leaves Leo for the last time, calls Elsie "our little Trojan filly; she looked so harmless and forlorn, standing outside the gates on the windy plain, but she brought her Ulysses sure enough.... Oh well" (269). The metaphor suggests deliberation and Peter can be seen as consciously manipulating his words and actions to produce a desired outcome; Elsie, through her naïveté, assumes that the desire is expressed only within the framework of conventional heterosexual romance. By trying to protect Elsie's innocence, Leo tacitly agrees with them and allows them to influence her decision to accept Joe as a serious lover. This, in fact, is the essential dividing line; any other dalliance, whether with a man or woman, did not disrupt Helen's and Leo's commitment to one another. But, the night spent with Joe tips the balance against Helen; in the letter he leaves for Leo in which he tries to explain and justify his feelings and behavior, Joe also includes what can only be called a rather traditional love poem. The last verse conveys the clichés of their love as new beginning, of their passion as the reconciler of opposites:

> Seek not the end. It lies with the beginning,
> As you lie now with me,
> The night with cock-crow, lust with the light unsinning,
> Death with our ecstasy [277]

Surprisingly, it this that pushes Leo to move towards the heterosexual ending that Elsie had believed Leo left home to find.

Renault's *The Friendly Young Ladies*, in several ways, can be seen as an antidote to the negative portrayal of lesbian relationships found in *The Well of Loneliness*. Neither Leo nor Helen feels in any way psychologically or physically abnormal, and neither feels their relationship diminishes their ability to engage with the wider world. Most of the social interactions described in the novel, in fact, show both women comfortably maneuvering among a variety of people — the doctors and nurses with whom Helen works, the river residents and pub patrons, and other writers and editors who work with Leo and Joe. Just as important no one seems to object to

Leo's and Helen's affection, except for Peter's apparent intention to pathologize it. Notable, too, is the fluidity of sexual expression throughout the novel. As noted above, both Helen and Leo have extra-relational affairs that are accepted, even encouraged, and which have no lasting impact on their intimacy. Stephen's desires are frequently described as painful; she expresses doubt and fear as well as an unbearable longing for romantic fulfillment. The only instance in Renault's novel where a character expresses such doubt occurs at the conclusion of the novel as Leo must choose between Joe and Helen: "Suddenly she flung her other arm across her eyes, and, standing as she was in the middle of the room, began to cry; hard sobs with struggling pauses between, painful and ashamed and resisted..." (278). Such flexibility anticipates what Lillian Faderman identifies as standard postmodern queer theory: "Renault," Faderman asserts, "questions easy assumptions about the connection between gender identification and sexual orientation" and in the character of Leo "presents a fine illustration of Judith Butler's concept, central to queer theory of the performativity of gender" ("Afterward," 292). Unlike Stephen, who feels trapped in her identification as invert, Leo and Helen feel no compunction to behave in ways they would see as ridiculous. In their engagements with Peter, the reader sees how both women understand and play with his psychological notions and efforts to analyze them.

Yet, the ending of the novel still separates the lesbian couple, leaving open the question of the ability of a lesbian couple, finally, to withstand the pressure of society's demand for the dominance of heterosexual romance. So even though the romance of Leo and Helen is portrayed as affectionate and convincing and they experience intimacy in their physical, as well as emotional, relationship, they appear to take it for granted. While the romantic/sexual needs and actions of the other characters are discussed in detail, neither Leo nor Helen speaks of their own needs or desires. However, both will examine these concerns in great detail with Joe and Peter (Helen, interestingly, does not have such conversations with Joe). While both women do not see themselves as pathological, they do accept their final separation as reasonable. Whether Leo will be happy with Joe is left unanswered at the novel's conclusion, and Helen's next step is also left undetermined, although she appears to articulate an understanding of Leo's decision and makes a determination to maintain what might best be called a lesbian orientation:

> So now I know. But, of course, I've know for years ... That's a long time to go on telling oneself the same lie ... I got all this over before we met each other; if not, I might have been the one. It's luck, it's a shape that makes

sense. It's perfectly fair. Whatever happens, that's the thing to remember. To see things straight, not to arrange them round oneself; if one keeps that, one keeps everything in the end [269].

The last image the reader has of Helen is of her calling for the ferry on her way to work, a signal that her life will continue.

Between 1950 and the mid–1960s the dominant format for descriptions of lesbian relationships was the paperback pulp novel. In its pages, readers found portraits, melodramatic as well as realistic, of women experiencing and expressing a desire for other women. These books ran the gamut of representation and technical skill: many were authored by men, deliberately providing prurient, unrealistic portrayals; those written by self-identified lesbians described a more believable picture of the positive and negative aspects of lesbian life during this time. Some writers were hacks, following publishers' scripts; others created strong, recognizable characters and devised credible stories. The success of lesbian pulp fiction rests on several factors: the explosion of the paperback publishing industry that produced a constant demand for original material; the distribution and availability of these books in venues other than the traditional bookstore — places like drugstores, grocery stores, bus and train terminals; and an avid reading public, whose purchases resulted in several of these works reaching sales in the millions.[8] Identifying the readers of these novels and determining the impact they had has been the focus of most of the criticism of pulp fiction. Critics have discussed these texts in terms of their representation of lesbian identities, as cultural markers of broader notions of gender, as examples of the impact of the mass-market publishing industry.[9] Some of these evaluations present positive readings of pulp fiction for their embodiment of a set of beliefs and behaviors that could be named lesbian; other view the texts as flawed or limited due their position within their particular historical period and its ideas regarding homosexuality in particular and women in general.[10] Very little critical attention is focused on the technical and stylistic components of these novels, except to establish that most could not be considered "good" writing. Some authors, Ann Bannon, Valerie Taylor, or Vin Packer, did create compelling characters and narratives, but they are considered the exception rather than the rule. (See Keller, Nealon, and Walters.) The majority of this critical attention is concentrated on Ann Bannon and the five novels that make up the Beebo Brinker series; one major reason for such attention stems from the continued reissuing of these texts, not only by small houses which emphasize the work of lesbian writers (Naiad and Cleis), but also by *The New York Times* book publishing division Arno Press and their selection by the Quality Paperback Book Club, a division on The Book of the Month Club. Another reason for the critical emphasis on Bannon's work can be found in Bannon's building her stories around a limited set of characters — Laura, Beth, Beebo, and Jack — who are positioned within a limited geographic space — Greenwich Village in New York City. This enables Bannon to present fuller biographical detail and allows her to expand the development of their private lives and personal interactions.

Despite all of the critical attention and commentary given to the pulps in the last thirty years, very little concentrated analysis of these works as romances appears. While the critics, like Foote, Walters, and Hamer, bring into their discussions brief references to the ways in which pulp fiction addresses romantic conventions, most often the importance of looking at these works as part of the romance genre is ignored. Typical is Hamer's contention that "what distinguishes Bannon stories from conventional romance (apart from the gender of her characters) is the fact that here, the nature of desire, restless and insatiable, works against this compulsory closure [the happy ending]" (69). Surprising, in my view, is this apparent insistence that desire has no relation to romance; the tendency in the criticism of the pulps is to set and reinforce the definition of romance as the expression of sexual desire, and while the importance of the sexual component cannot be dismissed, to limit romantic desire only to sex diminishes its complexity. Although she contexts her analysis of desire within a history of psychoanalytic theory, Lynne Pearce does acknowledge that desire encompasses more than the physical: "Working with the assumption that romantic love is experienced by the subject as a *complex interaction of psychic drives, cultural discourses and social constraints*, we must acknowledge that even if psychoanalysis goes a long way to explaining why we desire who we do, when we do and how we do, this will still not account for the full complexity of the experience" (19, emphasis added). What the lovers desire is, indeed, the physical connection that marks the realization of compatibility, but they also desire a recognition of each other as individuals, as possessing a complete sense of self as well as a sense of one's position within a specific community. This recognition represents the culmination of the process of engagement that the romance novel describes. What makes lesbian pulps true romances, in my opinion, is that the narratives, whatever the outcome, stress the importance of this movement.

The typical lesbian pulp romance begins with a young woman, generally in her late adolescence or early twenties, at a point of transition: she is starting college (Laura Landon in *Odd Girl Out*, Susan Mitchell in *Spring Fire*) or beginning a new life in a large urban center (Barby in *The Girls* in 3-B). The character's sense of dissatisfaction with her personal situation may also instigate this process of self-discovery; usually her sense of discomfort centers on feelings of not fitting into the world of heterosexual expectations (Beth in *Journey to a Woman* or Beebo in *Beebo Brinker*). The main character of the novel is not the only woman — or man for that matter — who expresses this sense of not fitting in. Much of the discussion between characters frequently centers on their awareness of this difference from the mainstream. A representative scene for Bannon's *I am a Woman* conveys this repeated stress throughout many of the pulps:

> "How would you like to be in here some night," [Jack] said slowly, "with Marcie beside you? And sit alone together at that little table over there? And tell her you love her?" Laura took another gulp of the drink and almost finished it. "And hear her say the same thing?"
>
> Laura put the glass down with trembling hands. "Oh, Jack, you bastard," she said, her insides aflame. "Cut it out."
>
> "You want it so badly," he said, "that it's tearing your guts out. And it's never going to happen. So open your eyes. Look around. There are some beautiful women here tonight" [65].

Jack, who acts as mentor to Laura, Beth, and Beebo throughout Bannon's series, offers each woman advice on how to manage, not only her romantic affairs, but also helps her accept her lesbian identity. Jack's experience allows him to help the others bridge the gap in their self-knowledge and understanding: "Look at me, Laura," he said and lifted her face. "We can't think straight because we always think gay," he said. "We don't know anything about a love that lasts or a life that means something. We spend all our time on our knees singing hosannas to the queers. Trying to make ourselves look good. Trying to forget we aren't wholesome and healthy like other people" (*Women in the Shadows* 91). While Jack's statement could be read as latent homophobia, his views reflect the psychological position of homosexuals as diseased that was common during the post-war decades. Importantly, even though many characters in the pulps espouse the same ideas, within the confines of New York and Greenwich Village — where many of these works are set — they also accept their difference willingly and find positive outcomes. In order for the characters to reach their ending, they must first progress through a series of interactions and introductions to their new environments.

The young woman enters the narrative often placed in unfamiliar surroundings, usually literally in a place far from her home and people she knows, whether it's a college sorority house or New York City. If the character does not leave her home, she is introduced to a different area of her community — Lorraine Harris in Della Martin's *Twilight Girl* is first initiated into the lesbian bar scene by Violet and then introduced to the world of upper class lesbians who must maintain a double life. Often this character has felt out of place in the larger world for a number of years, although she is unable to identify what the source of such feelings is. Following the standard notions of the time period, many of these women are motherless and/or fatherless; fathers, sometimes have been physically, emotionally, or sexually abusive. Once situated in her new surroundings, the young woman attempts to fit into the life of the place, and as she tries to become part of this community, she finds herself developing unrecognizable feelings for another woman: "But now, in Leda's presence, the casualness fell away, and Mitch found the old inhibitions again. She found that it was hard to talk to Leda, too, because she wanted to so badly. She wanted to remember the glib, natural responses that came so readily with others, but she could not" (*Spring Fire* 14). Usually, this character cannot initiate the desired romance; Mitch, Lorraine and Laura, all wait and long for some recognition from the object of their longings. They are usually portrayed as socially and emotionally awkward; since they have no point of reference for their feelings, they cannot convey them or make the other women understanding of the intensity of their desire.

The other woman — Beth, Violet, or Leda — is usually older than the main character and more experienced sexually. Most of these characters' past sexual experiences have been with men, and as they begin to realize that the newcomers are attracted to them, they often flaunt their heterosexuality. The pull of desire, however, is pictured as too strong to resist. Over the course of the novel these women will begin to respond to the passion expressed by their admirers and, at the turning point, will reciprocate:

> She parted the hair that hid Beth's neck and drew her fingers lightly over the white nape.... With a swift thrill of necessity she bent down and kissed the white neck for a long moment. She clasped her hand across her mouth and stared in terror at Beth, wondering how she could have let herself do it. Beth lay perfectly still with a faint smile on her lips.
> "Beth," said Laura...."Are you mad at me?"
> Beth whispered softly, "No" [*Odd Girl Out* 71].

Once this mutual acknowledgement of shared feelings occurs, the novels trace the outcomes of that moment of acceptance and pleasure. At this point, the pulps concede to the mores of the time and have the couple begin to doubt and fear their growing interest in one another. Others start to notice and comment on the exclusivity of the couple; rumors about the nature of their closeness begin to circulate; ultimately, steps are taken to prevent the couple from achieving any kind of positive outcome. These measures can be imposed from without—the dean of the college has an interview with Mitch after a letter she had written to Leda is discovered (*Spring Fire*)—or one of the couple withdraws from the relationship, fearing social repercussions—Beth refuses to board the train with Laura, instead choosing to marry Charlie (*Odd Girl Out*). Until these pressures force the couple apart, both women enjoy their intimacy and come to accept their feelings for one another.

Not all romances in the pulps end tragically, although the couples' chances of success are generally limited. At the conclusion of *Journey to a Woman* Beth, Laura's first romantic focus, after leaving her marriage to look for Laura and rekindle their relationship, is "rescued" by Beebo Brinker, and the novel ends with Beth and Beebo "walk[ing] out of the lobby together, hand in hand" (252). Although the promise of a lasting relationship is left open, the implication is that both women have found some comfort and resolution.[11] However, at this point in Bannon's series, the reader knows that Beebo's relationships do not last more than a couple of years, and Beth's attraction to Beebo may reflect more of a desire for safety than love. During the time when the couple continues to explore their attraction, they also acknowledge that what they are doing is dangerous and that they are at risk not only of discovery, but also of heartache. One common thread in the pulps emphasizes the sterility of these relationships. In the final pages of *I am a Woman*, Laura comes to Jack to understand the constant failures in her attempts to find true love. Jack's assertions reinforce that for homosexuals the chances of a lasting relationship are rare:

> "You loved Beth," he said, more gently. "You loved love. It showed in all you said to me, when we first met. You needed love and you went looking for it. You went looking for another Beth. You were bound to her. You found her in every female face that appealed to you."
>
> "Laura," Jack said slowly. "Marcie doesn't look like Beth. Neither does Beebo. Nobody looks like Beth but Beth. And Beth is gone. She Isn't yours anymore. She belongs to a man."

Laura attempts to defend Beth's behavior by saying, "She never hurt me." Jack explodes and forces Laura to realize the truth:

> "Oh, balls!" Jack said. "Never hurt you, hell! She left you, didn't she! She slept with a guy and married him. What do you want, Mother, a silk-lined accident-proof guaranteed romance? Good for six months with lotsa kicks and no pain? Or your money back? They don't come that way. Ask anybody. Ask me. Ask Terry" [228–29].

In spite of the pain that seems intrinsic to romantic relationships as portrayed in the pulps, however, the characters continue the search for intimacy and connection.

The constant searching for love, whether successful or not, dominates the movements of the pulp novels' characters. Even Jack, the most cynical of Bannon's characters, maintains the temporary belief in passion and is always devastated when his current lover abandons him. What drives the search centers on the characters longing to express their desires — physical and emotional — a quality that typifies the romance novel. For example, Paula Christian's *Edge of Twilight* concludes with a scenario more common to genre romance: Toni and Val, after a number of incidents, meet and reconcile their passion for one another. The novel ends with the two getting ready to make love. It is this awareness and expression of passion between women that separates the pulps from the earlier proto-romances. Stephen Gordon's love is always viewed as debilitating, a mark of her deviance and painful to articulate; Leo and Helen rarely express any clear indication of desire for one another over the course of their narrative. Throughout the pages of the pulps the characters continually identify what they feel for each other as love, and, more importantly, they are willing to declare these feelings for one another openly. Even when this articulation of desire of one woman for another results in rejection, the declaration often provides the main character with a new understanding of her identity: "Beth, you're meant for a man. Like Charlie. I'm not. I'm not afraid to go, I'm not sorry. It hurts, and I love you—" (*Odd Girl Out* 212).

Diane Hamer asserts that the pulps, particularly Bannon's, "defy" the designation of romance because they do not, cannot, provide the closure of the happy ending due to the fact that "the nature of desire, restless and insatiable, works against this compulsory closure. Instead of the perhaps more comforting endings conventional romance offers its readers, Bannon has captured accurately the contradictory experience of sexuality and desire in her recognition that sexual desire (heterosexual *or* lesbian) often works against the stability of monogamous coupling. The resolution that such coupling promises is only ever partial, and exists primarily in fantasy" (69, emphasis in text). However, one of the essential components of any romance novel is its framing of the narrative to create this fantasy, and while some critics object to what they see as the dangers inherent in the false hopes promised by such a scenario, the point of the happy ending is to present the potential for fulfillment. This stress on possibility, which is directed to the reader of the romance, helps explain why romance narratives end at the point they do — with the couple beginning a new life together. However, most pulp novels suggest that finding love is possible, even if not permanent, and that the chance is worth the taking.

Some pulps do end tragically: Lorraine Harris confesses to the killing of Sassy to protect Mavis, her romantic interest, from prison (*Twilight Girl*) and Leda ends up institutionalized after trying to kill herself by crashing her car (*Spring Fire*), and given the legal sanctions against homosexuality and its pathologizing by the medical professions during the heyday of the pulps, the expected happy ending for lesbian couples rarely appeared in print. However, positive endings were not unheard of; Patricia Highsmith's *The Price of Salt*, written under the pseudonym Claire Morgan in 1952, famously ends with Carol and Therese not only acknowledging their love, but implies its continuation:

> Carol raised her hand slowly and brushed her hair back, once on either side, and Therese smiled because the gesture was Carol, and it was Carol she loved and would always love. Oh, in a different way now, because she was a different person, and it was like meeting Carol all over again, but it was still Carol and no one else. It would be Carol, in a thousand cities, a thousand houses, in foreign lands where they would go together, in heaven and in hell. Therese waited. Then as she was about to go to her, Carol saw her, seemed to stare at her incredulously a moment while Therese watched the slow smile growing, before her arm lifted suddenly, her hand waved a quick, eager greeting that Therese had never seen before. Therese walked toward her [276].

Other novels ended more ambiguously, but they allowed the reader to imagine more positive outcomes.[12] Several of the pulp authors, themselves, looking back on their work, stress the benefits their readers found. Highsmith, in the "Afterword" to the 1983 reprint of her novel, stated, "I am happy to think that it gave several thousand lonely and frightened people something to hang onto" (n. p.); Ann Bannon, in a 2002 interview with Katherine Forrest, asserted, "We were exploring a corner of the human spirit that few others were writing about, or ever had.... And I take heart: if we got it wrong sometimes, we got it right a lot too" (9). Whatever the negative impacts the pulps had in terms of their representations of lesbians and their relationships, these novels serve as a transitional moment in the development of a specifically lesbian genre romance.

By the middle of the 1960s changing reader tastes and publishing strategies signaled the waning of the pulps as the dominant form for portraying lesbian life. Writers who focused their narratives on the lives of lesbian characters, although limited in number, found other publishing outlets for their work, some produced by large corporate houses. For example, Jane Rule's *Desert of the Heart* was originally published by Macmillan and Rita Mae Brown's *Rubyfruit Jungle* by Bantam. Changing ideas of and responses to homosexuality also contributed to a limited willingness for wider access to lesbian relationships appearing in print. The impact of the feminist political and literary movements of the late 1960s and early 1970s provided contexts for the discovery and exploration of previously marginalized texts and history. In fact, the reclaiming of women's history offered new representations of romantic connections between women; in 1970 Elizabeth Mavor presented a biography of Eleanor Butler and Sarah Ponsonby, the Ladies of Llangollen, a couple whose relationship lasted more than fifty years. Mavor's work presents these women's lives as positive and ultimately un-extraordinary; she chronicles their meeting, eloping, and eventual establishing of a household that became a destination for many notables of late eighteenth and early nineteenth century Britain. Mavor, however, refuses to label their relationship lesbian, preferring the term "romantic friendship" to describe it (xvii).[13] History also gave Isabel Miller the lives of Mary Ann Wilson and Miss Brundidge which she turned into the romance of *Patience and Sarah*.

Miller's novel portrays the lives of the main characters not only as a romance, but as a distinctly lesbian romance. Both women fall outside the traditional expectations of proper behavior: Patience wants to be a painter, and Sarah looks and acts more like a man than woman. After their first meeting, Patience finds that "I couldn't get Sarah Dowling off my mind, *or even try very hard to*" (19, emphasis added). This intense interest quickly turns into a more recognizable desire — physical and emotional — for Sarah; she decides to join Sarah on her journey west to establish her own home and to become, in essence, her partner: "I was going with Sarah to feed her and hold her head against me when she was sad and knead her shoulder when it ached" (26). Sarah reciprocates Patience's feelings, telling her how she has also thought of Patience since their first meetings. The immediacy and mutuality of the women's affection is a hallmark of the typical romance; the instant recognition of the perfect partner must occur if the plot is to develop along its expected trajectory. Without this sense of connection, the trials and obstacles that the couple experiences could easily overwhelm them, destroying any chance for the hoped for happy ending. The assurance that whatever negative responses from others and society can be overcome provides the couple the strength to continue the nurturing of the romance. Janice Radway indicates that "to qualify as a romance, the story must chronicle not merely the events of a courtship but *what it feels like* to be the *object* of one" (64, emphasis in text). Both women enjoy giving and receiving the attention of the other, and both take turns in pursuing and being pursued. Miller often presents Patience as the chief instigator, although the first physical contact of the couple is Sarah's kiss. Patience, however, is quick to respond and reciprocate. As the novel continues, Sarah and Patience continue to explore the meaning of their relationship. They will deal with public and private tensions as they travel from Connecticut to New York, from objections of family to the move and their moving together, from various neighbors and tradespeople who do not understand or condone their relationship, from their own doubts about their abilities to provide for one another. In spite of all the stresses on the couple, Sarah and Patience's love survives; the happy ending has been achieved:

> It has so often been that way, our hearts cool at times when heat would have been ceremonially correct and then flaming up when we couldn't really spare the time and strength. We have thought about that strangeness a lot and talked about it together. We needed words for it. I used to say, "It is as though love holds us, not we it." I used to say, "See how our blessing suits not our convenience but its own."
> It was Sarah who finally found the words.
> She said, "You can't tell a gift how to come" [190].

Miller is able to explore the development of the love story fully by placing it within a historical framework, which allows the distance of time to "soften" the rather intense descriptions of physical passion between the characters: "It was time for our feast, to have all we wanted, to be wild and careless and noisy and free. I would shout my triumph when Sarah groaned. I would groan for her. We would make the bed gallop. The floor would ring like a drum" (188). Their intimacy provides the necessary sanctuary from the pressures of the outside world, cushioning them from the potential hostility of a society that does not approve. Interestingly, though, many of the other characters in the novel come to accept the couple as a couple, Patience's sister-in-law Martha, who initially disapproves, becomes Patience's ally in obtaining her portion of her parents' estate from her brother. Others position the couple within understandable parameters; Mr. More, who sells Patience and Sarah the house and land where they will settle, refers to Sarah as Patience's sister.

Suzanne Juhasz identifies "the innocence around which the author constructs her plot. Society has no words for their feelings ... But their feelings, because they are natural, happen anyway. Acting on them is a way to create a reality that may be outside of cultural paradigms but is nonetheless true" (217). For the duration of the narrative, the couple triumphs in their desire to identify and maintain their passionate connections, even in the face of social pressures that condemn them. This optimism also explains the power of the romance for its readers; since "narrative is the way we give meaning to life, the way we order the chaos of events," stories that offer a temporary respite from the homophobia of the dominant society allow the reader to imagine other possibilities (Farwell 19). For communities that face the constant assertion that they are abnormal, that their emotional and physical desires are perverse, the portrayal of successful relationships, while a fantasy, gives readers the courage to imagine a chance for love. It is not only lesbian readers who anticipate this positive potential in the romance novel's insistence on the attainment of a successful relationship:

> Popular romances dwell on overcoming, on winners rather than losers, because that is what their consumers want to read about, even though they are well aware that not every woman overcomes the problems she faces in real life.... And it is as such that we need to try to understand the forms of popular culture which are so much a part of the world we live in, reflecting how and what we are thinking about, even as they help shape the way we live with — and love — each other [Thurston 218].

Patience and Sarah can be seen as illustrating the final step away from the pathology and ambiguity typical of the proto-romances.

Although published five years earlier than Miller's novel, Jane Rule's *Desert of the Heart* also represents a re-visioning of the romance as a form capable of describing lesbian life. As a Canadian, Rule's exposure to pulp fiction cannot be ascertained. Marilyn Schuster's study of Rule's fiction, *Passionate Communities*, provides extensive details on the author's biography and literary influences and efforts, but does not indicate that Rule was personally familiar with these works. However, given the novel's publication date, Rule's book references attitudes and ideas about homosexuality common to the period, and, when first published, was thought to be another version of "paper books of a certain sort" (146). Same-sex attraction is viewed from the lens of psycho-pathology; Ann's attraction to older women is initially presented as stemming from the loss of her mother and search for a replacement. Women who have sexual relations with other women are merely passing time until they find their proper sexual mate: "If you want a woman," says Silver, Ann's friend and occasional sexual partner, "have a woman, but remember you're a woman. You need some man-handling" (136). However, Rule takes these cultural positions for what they are and allows her main characters to work their way beyond them. Although the ending of *Desert of the Heart* does not promise Ann and Evelyn's relationship permanence, it does suggest their resolution to attempt it:

> Evelyn looked up at the clear, immense, and empty sky. Then she turned to Ann and saw in her eyes the darker color of the day.
> "It's a terrible risk, Ann."
> "And the world's full of mirrors. You can get caught in your own reflection."
> "And destroyed?"
> "Or saved."
> "And I'm afraid of the one, and you're afraid of the other. We're a cryptic cartoon, my darling. It should be one of you best."
> "I'll only draw it if I can live it."
> "In a house by the river with me and your five photographs of children?"
> "Anywhere."
> "For the while then," Evelyn said. "*For an indefinite period of time*" [221–22, emphasis added].

Evelyn's shifting of the time she sees them together signals the belief in a future together. This sense of more extensive romantic connection marks a distinct difference with the pulps; the women in Bannon's works, for example, may come together at the conclusion of the story, but because of the constant reiteration that lesbians cannot create long-standing relationships, the expectation of the current pairing lasting no more than a few months at best is established.

While Rule's intentions for the novel ranged beyond the mere telling of a love story, she does state that "the relationship which develops between the two women could be said to be the plot of the novel" (qtd. in Schuster, 140). Rule uses the attraction between Evelyn and Ann to explore the decisions individuals make and the responsibilities attached to them, since her main intent is to explore the moral landscape that the desert setting reflects. Images of heat, blinding light, dust, all suggest the impossibility of relationships being able to survive. And that Evelyn enters the story seeking a divorce suggests that romantic relationships cannot survive the stresses placed on them. At first distressed at her attraction to Ann, even going as far as denying it, Evelyn ultimately admits her feelings: "Nothing else I've ever known has been as right and as natural as loving you. And there isn't anything I wouldn't risk ... except you" (214). Evelyn discovers this desire over the course of the novel as her growing attraction to Ann forces her to reevaluate her sense of self and the way she has crafted that self to survive in the world. Ann also awakens Evelyn to her own femininity and sexual need: "She had grown almost vain about her body, and she had begun to discover, underneath the strict discipline she had imposed upon her mind, an inventiveness. She could talk whimsically, sometimes even wittily to call up in Ann not admiration so much as delight. Evelyn wanted to be charming, provocative, desirable, attributes she had never aspired to before..." (159–60). Love, here, serves the traditional romantic function of transformation. Like the typical romantic heroine, Evelyn uncovers new possibilities in herself; she fantasizes acting out of character. In the last chapters of the novel, Evelyn, in fact, behaves uncharacteristically, gambling at the casino where Ann works (and winning), going to meet her in pubic.

The influence of mainstream society's concepts of lesbians, however, remains strong enough that Evelyn asserts her rejection of this emotion and Ann, believing her sacrifice is for the best. While sacrifice of or by one member of a couple typifies a more tragic or dark type of romance, most popular romantic fantasies use the narrative to thwart such an outcome. "Love," says Scott McCracken, "is the utopian state in which both lovers transgress the restrictive boundaries of their 'lawful' gender identities and enter into a relationship that supplies mutual, total satisfaction, the abolitions of lack" (92). McCracken's couple is heterosexual, but when applied to lesbian romantic fantasy, his notion of transgression resonates beyond his concept that the idealized expression and embodiment of love offers the fictional couple and the reader a belief, however temporary, that passion trumps social norms. So, when Evelyn, accompanied by Ann as her witness, goes to the courthouse to finalize her divorce, she comes to acknowledge that she, in fact, does not love her husband and that there is no chance of a reconciliation. This recognition sets up for the conversation between Ann and Evelyn quoted above; the break with her past allows Evelyn to imagine a future with Ann.

Rita Mae Brown's *Rubyfruit Jungle* in many ways does not fit into the definition of a romance. As Bonnie Zimmerman attests, Molly Bolt's escapades place her in the company of other *picaro* figures, adolescents or young adults whose adventures replicate the journey to maturity (37–38). Molly's quest centers on discovering who she is and what her place is since she is socially illegitimate, both by birth and sexual orientation. Molly's efforts are all directed toward discovering how to deal with the various societal and personal conflicts that aim to prevent her success, but the novel does not show Molly succeeding in her quest. Molly faces the blatant sexism and condescension from the film industry as she tries to find a job, although she has graduated from college a "*summa cum laude* and Phi Beta Kappa" (245). However, as the development of the novel illustrates, being lesbian is not the sole reason for Molly's difficulties; Imelda Whelehan suggests that class and gender also preclude Molly from enjoying the benefits of belonging (123). As Molly moves from place to place, her understanding of human expectations and behaviors expand, offering her an increasing insight into the social mechanisms that influence and control a person's existence.

A sense of humor and the ability to direct that at the world around her and at herself enables Molly to maintain her desire to succeed and her belief in her ability to achieve that success. Her humor often works to deflect more serious emotional responses to the sexual and relational situations she becomes involved in. At one point Molly has become involved with Polina, an older, married woman; Polina, nervous about the affair, introduces Molly to her daughter Alice, who wants Molly to sleep with her. At a theatrical performance Molly sits between both women, each of whom is fondling her; the outcome of such a situation can either be tragic or comic. Brown opts for the pragmatic solution that emphasizes Molly's sense of the ridiculous. The mother and daughter fight, and Polina threatens to cut off Alice's financial support. Molly "gracefully exited to 17th Street where the hounds of hell gnawed at my ankles and the waterbugs organized a safari through my kitchen" (211). Generally Molly's sexual adventures involve pleasure and satisfaction for both parties, and while sometimes the affairs end abruptly, Molly readily moves on to another conquest. After each encounter Molly becomes more determined to achieve the specific goals she has set for herself, and, more importantly, she develops a pragmatic understanding of what such achievement requires. The novel ends with the suggestion of a positive outcome, but it is not one that promises romantic fulfillment. The novel's final scene that deals with Molly's sexual life — a visit to Leota, Molly's first lesbian sexual partner — highlights the precarious nature of acting on one's sexual instinct. Molly wants Leota to remember their innocence and openness when they made love, but Leota, now married and a mother, rejects any attempt to be linked with lesbianism. She calls Molly "perverted, sick" and claims that "they put people like you away" (219–20). Even though Molly proudly asserts her lesbian identity, she also asserts that she will never "marry a man and I'll never marry a woman either" (220).

Molly Bolt is not a romantic; her desires center on fulfilling her physical needs rather than emotional ones. Like other picaresque heroes, Molly enters and leaves the novel separated from any particular individual lover or community. Instead, she enters into a relationship knowing that it is only temporary, and if she feels her independence is being threatened, she will cut off the connection: "Goddammit! No matter what happens to me

I'll still have the knowledge inside my head and nobody can take that away from me. And someday, even if you can't see it coming, I'm going to make use of that knowledge and make my movies" (174). The focus of the novel centers more on Molly's articulation of a sense of self in the world than it does on her development of sense of self in personal relationship. The only deep emotional connections are shown between Molly and her adoptive mother and friends from childhood. So why, then, have I included *Rubyfruit Jungle* as part of the history of lesbian romance when even the pulps provide a more recognizable portrait of passion between women? Brown offers in the character of Molly Bolt one of the most psychologically unencumbered lesbians discussed here; while Molly does lack a secure family history, she rises above the potentially debilitating effect of such a loss. Beebo Brinker, like Molly, swaggers her way into the hearts of many women, but where Beebo is constantly tormented by her inability to reconcile her desire for women and her desire to act the man, Molly feels no hesitation or confusion. She is, simply, a lesbian. Molly Bolt is also a contemporary character, whose ideas, expectations, and actions are firmly rooted in a modern sensibility and world view. For example, Molly is aware of the growing feminist movement (the novel was originally published in 1973), although she also knows that as a lesbian she would not be welcome. Molly's daily routines and environments replicate the New York scene of the period as well. Molly is also a willing participant in that world, making no attempts to hide her sexuality or to restrict her movements to one geographic area; she moves freely and for her own reasons.

These qualities become standard components of the majority of contemporary lesbian romances. Characters rarely exhibit the self-loathing of Stephen Gordon or the women who populate pulp fiction; desire for another woman is something to be looked for and, when found, explored and enjoyed. Obstacles to a successful romance, while sometimes many and intense, are overcome, and the resolution of the story promises a long-lasting relationship for the couple. The fear of exposure is frequently omitted from these narratives as the lovers are able to situate themselves within a diverse community that accepts their commitment. Perhaps, most tellingly, modern lesbian romances allow their characters to speak openly, to frame their desires explicitly and passionately. These characters are given words and are encouraged to find the meanings that will support their relationships. Modern lesbian romances reflect and refract the content of these earlier stories and adapt them to a new audience whose experiences arise from strikingly different circumstances, although this is not to suggest that being lesbian, even in the twenty-first century is free from prejudice and limitation. Lesbian romance today allows its readers to frame their desires in a variety of ways and to create fantasies that amplify their impact. Like all readers of romance, the lesbian reader enters the world of the novel to escape and to dream, but in the end, she must close the cover and return to the everyday. Suzanne Juhasz describes this relationship best:

> The world of reading exists in a dynamic relationship with everyday life, each of them composed of yearning, disappointment, satisfaction. A yearning from everyday life may be disappointed or it may be satisfied in reading. A disappointment from reading may be subsequently satisfied in everyday life. The romance novel, as it tells the story of true love to its characters, its readers, its writer, evolves out of a dance of desire in which need and fantasy are irrevocably linked. Reading we participate in the story — as nurturing, enabling, and incomplete as it may be [*Reading from the Heart* 252].

Chapter Two

SPEAKING THE UNSPEAKABLE

The meaningful expression of desire depends on the existence of codes which are quotable, iterable. For example, the sexual desire of a man for a woman is conveyed through a range of semiotic practices.... These actions are not likely to be regarded as random or meaningless by any linguistically and culturally aware person. Why? Precisely because they are iterable signs that continually get recirculated in social life (and in media representations of it). The iterability of particular codes signifying desire is what allows us to recognize desire *as* desire.

(Cameron and Kulick, *Language and Sexuality*, 127)

Lane whispered, "I love you. I love you so much. I wanted to tell you so many times.... It was all I could do not to tell you. I couldn't tell you. I came so close, so close the last night when you talked to me and I made love to you ... when we talked on the phone I almost told you..."

(Katherine Forrest, *Curious Wine*, 159, first ellipsis added)

Language, goes the cliché, is what separates humans from animals; we are able to communicate through speech and action how we feel, what we think, and why we act.[1] Words, whether written or spoken, are the mechanism for the articulation of private concepts and the vehicle for public communication. In an ideal world no gap exists between the conception and the voicing of opinions or responses; meanings are clearly expressed and readily understood. In the real world, of course, the rift between intention and comprehension is sometimes huge. Misspeaking or misunderstanding are more likely to occur when two or more people talk together, resulting in comic or tragic confusion. Language is simultaneously a set of linguistic and grammatical patterns and social constructions as well as a reflection of an individual's specific usages and meanings based on those shared concepts. The essential characteristics of language reflect the need and ability to describe thought, to ascribe meaning to abstract and concrete ideas in a way that is comprehensible. Effective communication relies on the assumption by speakers and listeners of a shared set of terms and meanings of those terms. Speech, though, embodies not only the voicing of ideas in a recognizable medium, but also the framing of one's sense of the world and self: "The world is not simply the way it is, but what we make of it through language" (Romaine 20).

Much of contemporary language theory emphasizes the concept of construction as it connects to the ways in which an individual creates and responds to the particular environments that form her lived experience. Language becomes the bridge that links behavior and expression, and the movement from one position to the other results from a person's linguistic and speech choices. These choices reflect not only the content of one's speech, but the circumstances that surround it as well as the sense of self that the individual wishes to portray through the speech. While what one has to say and how one articulates that material are important for the individual to consider, what seems more important for the person to incorporate in the communication is what aspect of one's identity is also conveyed through the language chosen. One's speech and the self portrayed by that speech, after all, are not monolithic. The individual will consciously shape the material and the method of presentation to fit the particular circumstances that have called for it, and the self that is projected, while reflecting some aspect of the individual's personality, will also be manipulated to fit the situation: "The question of which selves are present in interaction depends on at least three overlapping elements: (1) what constitutes a culturally approved self; (2) the degree to which that self is acceptable to participants, including the speaker and the addressee; and (3) the relative power of each participant within and outside the interaction" (Liang 293). Besides the speaker's awareness of the reason for communication, Liang's list emphasizes the roles the specifically addressed listener plays in this oral transaction, as well as the wider social contexts that both participants move in. Talking requires an audience — however small or large, and both parties need common ground if the communication is to succeed.

As soon as one's speech is transmitted to a listener, the dilemma confronting both centers on accurate interpretation. What one hears may not be what the other said; what was said, not heard. The confusion of meaning may stem from a number of reasons. Some are basic errors: the speaker uses the wrong term for the topic; the listener may not be paying full attention; the language is not appropriate for the situation. In other cases, the misunderstanding may result from deliberate choices made by either party in the verbal exchange. Nuances of tone or gesture may contradict the stated topic; one participant willfully plays at not comprehending. Of course, the game of misunderstanding could be deliberately undertaken by both. The situation in which these individuals are speaking also influences understanding, since what is spoken must be transacted according to social/communal expectations: "Much of language is ambiguous and depends on context for its interpretation..."(Romaine 5). While the conversation is intended to be limited to the two parties, social settings may influence the shaping of the content as well as the meanings attached to that content: are the two people shapers of the situation or merely participants; is their speech a necessary component of or incidental to events; will their conversation shape outcomes or merely respond? This scenario, of course, assumes that the two individuals' talk is restricted to themselves. Wider social communication clearly alters the dynamics of speech and interpretation by multiplying the mechanisms that instigate speech, organize its progress, and determine its meanings.

What is talked about, perhaps, has the most influence on the negotiation of meaning, none more complex than those exchanges that deal with the identification, development, maintenance, or disintegration of some type of a relationship. And the relationships requiring the most attention to the language that embodies them, as well as the tone by which the words are chosen and the other components of communication, are those that express personal connections: "Interpersonal relationships are made of talk and related actions. By the way people speak to each other they show who counts as a friend, a stranger, or a loved one. We speak differently to loved ones than to casual friends, and most often we do not speak to strangers at all. Our interaction patterns constitute and indicate the states of our interpersonal relationships" (Hopper 31). Such communications between individuals involves an element of risk; each participant in the communication must, first, expose the particular self that the speaker has created; second, present that self through speech that may be inadvertently or deliberately misunderstood; and, third, use that speech to articulate one's desires — usually the longing to establish a relationship that supplies intimacy and fulfillment. When the situation in which such communication is positioned is factored into the act of interpretation, the risk involved can easily increase, since where the conversation takes place and who else might be part of it may influence not only how the language is framed, but what meanings will be derived from it.

Perhaps no other type of communication act is as prone to these concerns and potential difficulties as is the speaking of love. The key dilemmas rest on the difficulties of articulation and understanding; a person must first be clear about what she desires from the potential romantic relationship. Framing one's expectations, of course, combine social and personal categories of suitable behavior, presentation, and speech. The assumption is of a communal set of meanings that remains constant, so that whoever is speaking and listening to the romantic declaration will always understand what is intended. However, the hope for instant recognition seldom results; romantic speech carries both historic and situational burdens regarding what can be spoken, by whom, and to whom. Romantic speech also conflates abstract and concrete notions of what is the appropriate subject matter for speaker and listener. In addition, the couple assumes that romantic communication remains private, when often such talk operates within wider social settings that may or may not be recognized or acknowledged. To declare one's desire, even when that person has managed to identify and express it, involves great risk on the part of the speaker. One may be misunderstood, but, more painfully, one's overtures may be rejected by the intended object of that desire. Paradoxically, though, many narratives emphasize this experience of pain as the epitome of the romantic relationship.[2] Yet, the inability to communicate one's feelings also underlies many romantic comedies as the potential lovers must overcome the misspeaking that blocks the desired outcome, usually achieved when the couple finally comes to understand what the other meant. Being understood, then, becomes the touchstone for the instigation and development of one's romance.

What impels an individual to seek the desired object is usually placed with a psychoanalytic context: many critics of the romance particularly reference Freud and Lacan, and their concepts of lack, separation, or incompleteness. The individual searches for what is missing, for something to fill the gap in his or her sense of self. The object of this search is often an idealized construction that ultimately remains unattainable, therefore requiring a continual repetition of the naming of what is desired and its pursuit.[3] Many feminist critics of the romance add the ideas of feminist psychologists, particularly the work of Nancy Chodorow, Carol Gilligan, and Dorothy Dinnerstein, as it applies to the development of the heroine's sense of self and her expressions of autonomy. The end result of such expressed desire and actively sought, according to the psychological position, is sexual connection and satisfaction. Such fulfillment, however, has other dimensions beyond the physical; desire and its narratives also "attempt to impose causality, temporality and coherence on an emotional event which has none of those things" (Pearce 19). The formulas of romantic narrative offer a framework in which the person's desires can be made concrete and ordered.

This shaping of a romantic plot allows the reader to believe in the logic of the progression of the romance: after all, narrative imposes a sequence of initiation, development, and outcome that provides a sense of hope that the relationship described in the text can be replicated. This is not to suggest, however, that the reader willingly accepts the fictional world of the text as reality; Jayne Ann Krentz, in the Introduction to *Dangerous Men and Adventurous Women,* stresses that "readers know the difference between real life and fantasy and that they do not expect one to imitate the other" (2). When approaching the romance narrative, the reader engages in what Scott McCracken calls "the quest for meaning [which] gives the reader the opportunity to confront the opportunity of new and exciting selves and the threat that they may dissolve as quickly as they appear" (11). Throughout literary history this plotline has organized the details of the romantic relationship, whether tragic or comic, and gives its readers points of reference for comparison and evaluation.[4] The action of the romance narrative is only one of the essential requirements; the descriptions of settings and characters' behavior establish the criteria from which the reader may select aspects of the self she wishes to try on. As Janice Radway notes in Chapter Six of *Reading the Romance*, the descriptive detail typical of the romance novel aims to create a recognizable world while at the same time distancing the action enough to maintain the balance of fantasy and reality. This helps explain the often extensive and meticulous historical detail, for example, in a Georgette Heyer Regency or the excessive naming of designer clothes and jewelry and celebrity locations in many contemporary romance novels. However, setting and action are insufficient to carry out the romantic situation presented in the novel. The romance cannot begin — or be maintained — without the necessary speech between lovers. The essential component of any romance, whether lesbian or heterosexual, is the explicit articulation of attraction and desire by the lovers; without this declaration, and the subsequent variations in the delineation of their emotional and physical connections, there is no romance.

What drives the need for romantic speech is not only one person's recognition of desire for another, and the first difficulty becomes determining what is meant by desire, but also of the ability to articulate that desire. Typically, desire signifies a need, a longing for something; for the potential lover, this need is situated in another person, someone who, typically, embodies qualities and behaviors perceived as positive and/or beneficial to that person and the one who seeks the connection as well. Of course, the particular time and place impacts the nature of what constitutes desire, but, regardless of one's sexuality, certain shared characteristics can be identified. The first, as noted above, resides within the individual who feels some lack and yearns for that gap to be filled, usually through connection with another person. The type of connection stretches from the physical to the emotional to the spiritual. In terms of romantic desire the person attempts to combine these three areas into one all-consuming, passionate relationship. This notion of passion, for many critics of the romance novel, remains the centerpiece of desire; a person not only longs for the connection to another, but that longing is deeply felt and intensely expressed: "Popular versions of romantic love in the West over the last nine centuries have rendered the phenomenon not only visible but visibly *spectacular*: spectacular in its joys, spectacular in its grief, spectacular in its challenges and ordeals, spectacular in its transformative effect (on both the amorous subject *and* his/her world)" (Pearce 2, emphasis in text). Pearce's emphasis on the spectacular obviously references the larger than life quality of the lovers and their situations—after all, they must be more attractive and more talented than ordinary people, and they must function within exotic and dangerous environments most people cannot experience. But, the words that lovers speak must also invoke such a sense of display at the moments of their expression.

The language of love must reflect the intensity of the desire felt by each person, and because the emotions are usually presented at fever pitch, the words must replicate that dramatic emphasis. As many writers of genre romance have commented, they are often criticized for the ornate and exaggerated dialogue that accompanies the narrative. Yet, as Barlow and Krentz indicate, "Because the language of romance is more lushly symbolic and metaphorical than ordinary discourse, the reader is stimulated not only to feel, but also to analyze, interpret, and understand" ("Beneath the Surface," 22). What critics of the romance see as repetitive, clichéd, and overwrought, romance writers and readers accept as necessary for the important purpose of such language—to convey the truth of the lovers' emotions and commitment.[5] The descriptions of setting and the relating of the story comprise only one part of this presentation; essential to any romance is the interaction between the main characters. From *Pride and Prejudice* to Jayne Ann Krentz's 2006 *All Night Long* the verbal exchanges become the centerpiece for tracking the relationship of the couple as they come to discover their compatibility as lovers. It is not enough to speak openly or to speak clearly in order to be understood; the lovers must be able to converse numerous times during the course of the story. Without continual conversation, at whatever point in the development of their attraction, their desires will not be made known, acted upon, or resolved:

> If you do not have good dialogue, you do not have good romance. Dialogue is "where the action is" as far as the romantic chemistry is concerned. Dialogue is the verbal sculpture of the characters, and their dialogic interactions sculpt their chemistry. If what the characters are saying is not interesting and if their dialogic interactions are not interesting, then I do not care how beautiful and sexy they are, their love relationship will not interest me [Andresen, "Postmodern Identity (Crisis)," 180].

Romantic speech, then, involves not only what is said, but how it is said, to whom it is said, and how often it is said.

Of course, dialogue clearly requires a speaker and a listener and the willingness of both parties to exchange these roles. Part of the tension within the typical romance narrative is the exchange of power that the relinquishing of control of the conversation represents. Controlling who talks and when and what the subject of the conversation will be becomes a measure of the realignment of the relationship. As both hero and heroine become comfortable with the ability to vocalize desire, they become more open to the possibility of achieving an idealized level of communication. The hero cannot just declare his intention to overwhelm the heroine physically, sexually, and emotionally; he must also "prove his commitment to the relationship" and acknowledge his desire for permanence in the relationship (Barlow and Krentz 20). Contemporary romance novels frequently present a hero who engages in extensive conversations not only about his personal feelings, but his attraction for and interactions with the heroine. The stereotype of the strong, silent male is becoming less common in genre romance. While the heroine is typically viewed as the initiator of these conversations, this is not always the case. In Krentz's *All Night Long* Luke Danner, the novel's hero, is more likely to open up the dialogue with Irene Stentson, the focus of his sexual and romantic desires. In much romance fiction the heroine frequently exhibits reticence in her interactions with others, and she often must develop the ability and the courage to declare her affections and intentions regarding the romance. Frequently, the romantic heroine enters the narrative diminished in some way, either by her economic situation, her lack of self-knowledge, or her being controlled by others. As the story continues, she learns to become assertive, able to articulate her personal desires, and active in the pursuit of them:

> The heroine of the romance novel, then, undergoes two great liberations. She overcomes the barrier and is freed from all encumbrances to her union

with the hero. She cheats ritual death, symbolically or actually, and is freed to live.... Her choice to marry the hero is just one manifestation of her freedom[6] [Regis 15].

One important sign of the romance's happy ending is the sharing of speech and the willingness to listen by both members of the couple.

The essential moment in the typical romantic narrative remains the explicit declaration of love. In fact, these two components of the declaration — explicitness, saying exactly what one means by desire, and verbalization, the formal, spoken acknowledgement and declaration of that desire — mark the completion of the lovers' search for connection, and many romances, in fact, end with this moment of explicit speech. The quality of the lovers' commitment to one another and the relationship can be open to question without such a vocal statement; the conscious and deliberate assertion of emotion from the couple establishes, in a sense, a set of obligations between them. Even if no other person hears the declaration, the lovers must be able to announce that they have created a relationship and will be bound to maintaining it. Think of how many romance stories have one lover demand that the other say, "I love you." The lovers reveal their true natures at this moment of declaration, exploring the process of discovery, discussing the meaning of their words, beginning to imagine a new life together. Once the declaration has been made, the romance novel follows one of two traditional plot movements: either ending at the point of promise with the implication that the couple has attained completion or using the assertions of commitment as the impetus to guarantee a successful outcome. In this second situation, the declaration marks the beginning of a series of trials — usually separation of the couple — that must be overcome in order to achieve the happy resolution.

What happens to the articulation of desire, however, when the lovers are lesbians, members of that community whose love "dare not speak it name"? Does the lesbian have the same ability to incorporate the conventions of romantic speech into her identification and articulation of desire as her heterosexual counterparts: Are these standards even transferable when the pursuer and pursued are both women? Given the dependence of the romance on clichéd sentiments, can the lesbian lovers have their declarations carry the same meaning? Clearly, although the words used remain the same whether spoken by lesbians or straight women, the implications of this language are radically altered by one woman openly declaring her desire for another woman. And, just as mainstream readers of romances discover possible linguistic models in a variety of popular media, lesbian readers also discover examples of speech suitable for initiating romantic connections. The role of literature, especially popular genres, in the creations of models of behavior is particularly important for those communities who do not share in the privileges of mainstream culture. As Kevin Kopelson iterates,

> "Literature," for better or worse, has been a privileged site of cultural expression for so long that many modern subjects are predisposed to turn to it for what seems like self-articulation, self-validation, and self-explication. This is especially true of lesbians and gay subjects, who often find themselves represented unsympathetically — if, indeed, they find themselves represented at all — in non-literary cultural forms [*Love's Litany: The Writing of Modern Homoerotics* 10].

By appropriating the narrative, speech, and character forms of the mainstream romance novel, lesbian authors provide frameworks within which the lesbian reader can position her romantic (emotional) and erotic (sexual) desires.

Katherine Forrest's *Curious Wine*, considered a classic of modern lesbian romance, references many standard narrative practices of mainstream genre romance; at the same time, Forrest manipulates these conventions to foreground the progression of Diana Holland's initial confusion over her attraction to Lane Christianson, their growing intimacy, temporary separation, and eventual emotional and erotic reunion. Other lesbian romance novelists not only adapt the conventional formulations of the mainstream romance, but replicate Forrest's template as well as adapt its representations of lesbian desire and romantic behavior, although they will reconfigure physical descriptions, settings, and experiences to more closely reflect changing times and attitudes. Just as heterosexual romance writers continue to adjust the requirements of the genre to changing ideas of appropriate social behavior and expectations, lesbian novelists also incorporate the shifting experience and expression of lesbian life, providing for their readers a continual updating of the popular signifiers of what being lesbian means. Just as popular romances offer readers models of romantic possibility, lesbian romances represent "some idea of the behavior and courtship and all of the other patterns of our community" (Brandt, interview with Katherine Forrest, *Happy Endings*, 88).

Forrest's novel presents crucial differences from the standard romantic narrative trajectory as described by Janice Radway and Pamela Regis. Both critics share the positioning of the romance within a specifically defined social setting, with its expectations about the appropriateness of the eventual romance; the assumption of the couple being comprised of a hero and heroine; an initial antagonism between the characters that will eventually be reconciled; the disruption of a smooth courtship due to a number of external and/or internal situations; and the final restoration of the couple and acceptance of their union.[7] Each of these characteristics depends on the heroine and hero being able to convey their ideas about the relationship through speech that embodies their private desires in an acceptable way. During the course of the story, these characters must come to the recognition that they are meant to form a relationship that will, ultimately, reconcile the perceived differences between them. What is seen and interpreted as physical dominance or sexual manipulation must be reread as the expression of desire; what is viewed as emotional distance or lack of response must be understood as based on previous failure to communicate that desire effectively, and only through speaking at the right moment, with the necessary words, will this new understanding be achieved.[8]

The most obvious, but still essential, difference between Forrest's romance and the heterosexual novel is the make-up of the couple. The traditional male/female paradigm is broken as *Curious Wine* traces the developing attraction of two women for one another. With this redefining of the romantic couple comes the realignment of the concepts of hero and heroine and of the way each woman will articulate her understanding of the attraction that is pulling them together. Typically, the hero assumes the dominant position in the story, although it is the heroine whose desires tend to drive the plot development. In fact, there is an on-going debate among the critics and the writers regarding who really is the central character: many of the essays in *Dangerous Men and Adventurous Women*, as well as the statements on the All about Romance website, illustrate the shifting narrative prominence of both. The story either traces the reclamation and/or reformation of a psychically wounded man whose description usually includes terms such as aloof, arrogant, domineering, decisive, brooding, and sensual, or follows the emotional growth of the heroine who becomes more self-assured and confident in articulating her wants. His coming to realize and accept his attraction and need for the heroine is seen as the crucial moment in the development of their romance, and this is usually signified not necessarily through his actions, but at the moment when he speaks fully and openly about his feelings: "One of the most significant victories the heroine achieves at the close of the novel is that the hero is able to express his love for her *not only physically but also verbally*. Don't just show me, tell me, is one of the prime messages that every romance hero must learn" (Barlow and Krentz, "Beneath the Surface," emphasis in text, 23). Her discovery of her autonomy yet willingness to cede that for a relationship marks the happy ending so necessary to a successful romance. Many traditional romances also depend on stereotypical gendered behaviors in the creation of the characters; both hero and heroine represent conventional notions of appropriate masculine and feminine looks, beliefs, and behavior, although these qualities tend to be exaggerated. Romance heroines and heroes are more attractive, more intelligent or intuitive, more socially well-connected, and more verbally adroit. While there are variations to this basic rubric, these characters remain stridently heterosexual in how they frame their desires and work to attain them.

Both women are attractive; Lane, as viewed by Diana, particularly so: "Leaping firelight reflected gold highlights in her hair, which was shades of blonde and silk-textured, reaching just below the nape of her neck, framing her face and falling over her forehead.... In the firelight, the warm tones of her skin suggested the topaz she would become under a summer sun" (2). Even at such an early point in the story Diana's attention becomes riveted on Lane as indicated by the extended description and highly metaphoric language; this passage contains a comparison of Lane's hair to "autumn trees" whose leaves are like "sunlight coins" (2). Such descriptive language will appear throughout the book, and as Diana's attraction and desire for Lane become stronger, her attempts to articulate these feelings depend more and more on words that reflect this intensity because, although the initial attraction rests on physical beauty, the courtship must be played out through speech. And only when they can enunciate their need will Lane and Diana achieve physical fulfillment. However, Diana cannot lay sole claim to this need for emphatic speech; Lane must also express her fears and wants in language that reflects the growing intensity of her passion. Their attempts to find the right words, though, remain separate from their interactions with the rest of the women; in their public engagements Diana and Lane keep their conversations general, especially since they are both newcomers to the group. They do not dominate either the physical or emotional space of the story when they interact with the other characters; in fact, they share the same reticence in being noticed by the other house guests or becoming the center of attention. The plot centers on a long weekend party of a group of women friends and the increasing emotional tensions that develop over their stay. One of the major events proposed as entertainment is a series of games that are meant to give insight into each woman's personality. The focus of the games is on trust and on devising images and descriptions that are supposed to reveal one's true nature. However, given that several of these women have shared histories, the intent of the exercises quickly deteriorates into criticisms and recriminations that have long histories. Among the revelations and apologies, Lane and Diana will fall in love, and, not surprisingly, the instigation for their romance springs from their intuitive understanding of the descriptions each offers to the group where the others do not.

Neither Diana nor Lane can be identified with the standardized image of the romantic hero. Throughout the course of the novel, the women's interactions show none of the conventional imbalance in the progression of their attraction. Lane is a lawyer, but she does not discuss her cases or their outcomes during the weekend. She is clearly successful in her profession since she buys Diana an expensive pendant as a gift and flies from San Francisco at a moment's notice to spend one night with Diana, but she never imposes her reputation into the interactions over the weekend. However, Diana's career — she holds a managerial position in the company she works for — is also marked by financial success. Both women, then, enter the story as equals, at least in the public realm. Interestingly, it is the other women who are intimidated by Lane's beauty, forceful personality, and success. When the group gets together much of their conversation directed towards Lane comes across as hostile, charged with innuendo and outright anger: "Liz [the weekend's host] stared at Lane. 'Tell me, dear. Honestly now. Do blondes really have more fun? Do you really have more and better orgasms than the rest of us?' (50). At their introduction Lane and Diana do not engage in much talk; both, as newcomers to the group, are more content to remain in the background, answering questions, but offering little. However, from the beginning they seem to share an intuitive understanding of one another's moods; having to share the loft bedroom allows the women to reveal the selves they have kept from the others. They discover similar tastes in music and for the poems of Emily Dickinson, which enables them to express aspects of themselves that would strike the others as odd. The loft, in fact, becomes an intimate space that encourages intimate talk and revelations, and things spoken here as dreams become realities at the conclusion of the novel. Diana and Lane do share the conventional position of the hero coming into the story with previously damaged, romantic relationships. Surprisingly, though, these previous experiences have been heterosexual: Lane has lost her early lover to the Vietnam War and Diana's current relationship has fallen apart because of his infidelity.

As the novel continues, the reader learns that Lane has previously experienced an attraction for another woman, but she runs away from the revelation:

None of the boys I'd been with, and I wasn't a virgin then either, none of them had made me feel even remotely like that. Nothing happened between us — I was too terrified. I put on my clothes and fled. I wouldn't see her again. She finally gave up trying. I knew how badly I was hurting her, but I knew if I saw her again it would happen again, and I knew I wouldn't be able to stop it again [98].

At this point, Lane and Diana have made love for the first time; Lane's previous sexual overtures — and in this way Lane does resemble the heterosexual hero in her initiations of physical intimacy — have been rebuffed. Lane's admission of her earlier fear of becoming involved with another woman replicates Diana's own confusion and anxiety. As their post-coital conversation continues, they explore the reasons for their retreat and examine the implications of what their actions mean. In fact, Lane clearly tells Diana that she must take control of and responsibility for her decisions: "I had no right to do anything. I've had the same fear of this as you. I've run from it for years. You had to make your own decision about it" (99). Diana, on the other hand, comes to an understanding of her attraction to and complete desire for Lane after a number of private evaluations of her romantic life. She has agreed to join the weekend party in an effort to sort out her feelings for Jack, her current lover. In these first scenes, she, like the traditional romantic heroine, believes the breakdown to be her fault: "Angry at his hurt, she had refused to listen, turned away repelled when he tried to touch her.... There was more evidence: You never wanted children, she accused herself.... Living with him unmarried had given her the excuse to avoid discussion or admission that she did not want children — that there was a cold and unloving core in her, that there was something wrong with her" (11).

In an effort to reassure herself that she is not a lesbian, Diana agrees to a quick sexual encounter with a stranger at the casino. This turns into a disaster as the man's sexual behavior is compared to Lane's; his hands are large and coarse, his kisses rough, his touches become brutal; the sex quickly transforms, for Diana, into rape. Even more demeaning is his expressed view of women as either sexual teases or controlling bitches who "think they know better than I do how I should use my balls" (87). He also verbally links such women with lesbians, reinforcing the dominant social view of forceful women as unnatural. Only Diana's desperate plea that she has no birth control brings the encounter to an abrupt end. Even in the face of her fear the man still sees their time together as positive, and he even offers Diana the opportunity to stay with him for the rest of the evening. Diana's assertion that "she thinks she'd rather become a feminist lesbo" signals the beginning of her sense of autonomy (88). Said as a way to deflect his continued come-on, these words mark an important moment in Diana's recognition of her true identity and desire. This moment is also emphasized by her taking a shower to, literally, wash away any traces of him and, it can be said, heterosexuality.

At the end of the novel, when the women have come to the point of the final and most emphatic declaration of their love, Diana explicitly rejects the idea that Lane should be the man: Lane has just expressed her fear that she cannot "take care of you ... be enough for you in all the ways you'll need" (158, ellipsis in text). On hearing this Diana forcefully rejects what she sees as Lane's assumption of masculine prerogatives, going as far as accusing Lane of the worst kind of male control: "You don't care about me at all. You want to be a man for me? You *are* like a man, and the worst kind. I'm just a woman's body to you" (158, emphasis in text). Only after Lane's shocked response that she has misunderstood her desires does Diana realize the real quality of Lane's feeling. Instead of Lane responding as the typical male hero would do — demanding that Diana understand his need to dominate — she expresses her own fear of rejection, of being hurt emotionally. This recognition of Lane's vulnerability calls up Diana's own desire to protect Lane from all harm, the very position that she rejected just moments earlier. What distinguishes this moment from the heterosexual romance is the mutuality of care and protection; in straight romance the heroine cedes her power to the hero, including her power to nurture, even as she succeeds in bringing about essential changes in his ideas and behavior.[9] During the developing of their attraction, Lane can be seen as the aggressor, particularly in Diana's initiation into sexual intimacy, again a standard male hero's prerogative. However, Diana is a willing pupil once she has realized it is exactly this kind of physical and emotional connection that she has felt lacking in all of her previous romantic encounters. As she waits for the time of their self-imposed separation to end, Diana has a final confrontation with Jack to bring their unsatisfying relationship to an end. Even though Jack presents a positive relationship — shared pleasures of travel, friends, and sex — Diana repeats, "It isn't enough" (141). What seems to be the source of her rejoinder may be Jack's constant use of we and us, suggesting a merging of her identity into his, making the couple more than the two individuals. Although she does not reveal the gender of the person she admits to loving in place of Jack, Diana at this point in the novel has fully accepted being lesbian; in fact, her coming out becomes an essential part of the narrative movement. Many lesbian romances include such a scene and position it at key moments in the story.

Of course, there are variations to the coming out component, but its appearance in so many novels emphasizes its importance.

For many lesbian novelists, the romance embodies two distinct but related articulations of desire: the first is finding a partner who will fulfill all of one's fantasies, whether they are sexual, emotional, or social. The second may perhaps be called the romance of the self; acknowledging and accepting one's attraction to and desire for another woman demands an intense reevaluation of her private sense of self as well as the public expressions of that self: "Coming out is the rite of passage through which a lesbian establishes and affirms herself.... Coming out is an expression of activity, implying movement from one state of being to another.... But the first movement is always a personal and interior one, the claiming or discovering of the lesbian within one's self" (Zimmerman 34). As Diana becomes more assured in taking on a lesbian identity, Lane cautions her not to jump into their romance blindly; Lane asks that Diana take a month to examine her feelings and behavior to make sure she is comfortable and sure of pursuing their relationship. Diana's confrontation with Jack represents one outcome of this reevaluation of her identity, and as the chapter details the passage of that month, the reader sees Diana experience a full range of emotions — doubt, fear, anger — that indicate the intensity of her coming out process. At one point she tells a close friend, "I'll be better soon. I just need to be by myself for now.... Things will be ... will change, I promise" (146, second ellipsis in text). Diana visits her father near the end of the month and during the conversation she finally frames her new sense of herself as lesbian. Surprisingly, her father's reaction reveals his loving concern rather than a rejection of who she is; his questions focus on her happiness, his confusion about her choice, his willingness to accept. The most important moment in this meeting occurs when he asks, "'Diana, what if this doesn't work out? What then?' She understood what he was asking, and *she deliberated for some time over her answer*, 'I would look for it again'" (150, emphasis added). In that moment of deliberation Diana has made the conscious choice to accept being lesbian, and in openly speaking that choice, she lays the foundation for the reunion with Lane that follows and which provides the happy ending required of all romances.

Explicit speech, of course, dominates the identification and development of any romance, lesbian or straight. However, most romances also include other methods for the potential lovers to signal their attraction, the look, the touch, the written word.[10] Just as speech is open to misinterpretation, gestures can also be misread; such misunderstanding can have devastating consequences for the hero and heroine. Usually these situations create a — temporary — break in the development of the couple's intimacy which requires them to take every action, sanctioned or not, to resolve the situation. The heroine is particularly susceptible to being misread or misreading: her interactions with other male characters may be viewed as flirting, challenging the hero's proprietary interest; she may become jealous of the hero's interactions with other women, although she fears more a collapse of their connection rather than a loss of control. Diana experiences just this jealousy during the imposed separation: "Thoughts of Carol [Lane's first lesbian attraction] haunted her. Jealousy was a new emotion, and it savaged her.... Did Lane still care for her even after the interval of years? Would she seek her, released from the inhibitions that had prevented a relationship she had desired so much? Diana thought of Carol incessantly..."(147).

Emily Dickinson's poetry, a device Forrest uses at key scenes in the developing relationship, becomes a communicative bridge that allows both women to express their hope and fears that what the weekend has revealed will not be a transitory experience. At the beginning of the novel, once Lane and Diana have discovered their shared pleasure in Dickinson, the poet has the ability to express what the women cannot yet articulate. The first night Dickinson's poems allow the women to connect through the descriptions of nature's beauty and power to attract; by sharing their appreciation for the aesthetic and emotional qualities of the poetry, Lane and Diana open themselves to a refocusing from the subject of the poem to one another. During the trust games played by the group on the first evening, Lane quotes the lines "We talked with each other about each other / Though neither of us spoke"; however the others clearly do not understand the words and quickly move to new topics. When Lane asks for the month-long separation, she again uses Dickinson not only to verbalize the intensity of feeling, but to reassure Diana that the waiting will help them discover if the weekend is merely an aberration or the beginning of a permanent connection. The novel ends with the quoting of Dickinson's famous lines "The Soul selects her own Society —/ Then — shuts the Door" as the indication of the completion of the couple's romantic journey.

Curious Wine differs from its historical precursors by establishing a set of new romantic conventions for a specifically lesbian audience. Unlike Hall, Renault, and others, Forrest's lovers are presented not only as self-identified lesbians, but fully satisfied and confident with that identity. The ambiguity of the texts discussed in Chapter One disappears because both women have discovered a sense of their true selves and the conviction that these selves are sufficient to a sense of completeness regardless of the opinion of the wider world: Diana cannot contain her emotions as Lane steps off the plane and greets her with a kiss that quickly turns passionate and extends beyond acceptable social expectations. Heterosexuality is no longer accepted as the avenue through which Lane and Diana will define themselves and their relationship; they are complete when the door is figuratively shut on mainstream concepts of love and suitable partners. The happy ending reflects Bonnie Zimmerman's notion of the "green world," that is "both a place of refuge for the lovers and a limitless zone outside time and space where they soar and merge" (82). The lesbian romance's happy ending, like its heterosexual counterpart's, indulges in the reader's fantasy of total immersion of one person into an appropriate other; the romance's outcome both establishes and reinforces idealized definitions of courtship while at the same time reinforcing traditional cultural values. Here, the value of the lesbian romance increases. Ultimately, in the earlier romantic texts, the weight of the larger society diminished or destroyed any chance of lesbian love succeeding. Stephen Gordon surrenders Mary to a conventional heterosexual marriage; Leo willingly leaves Helen for Joe. The pulps portray lesbian desire and fulfillment as something either to be prevented, through death or institutionalization, or lesbian relationships as being incapable of providing any sense of stability or permanence. To be lesbian is to be tortured with self-doubt and self-loathing. Even *Patience and Sarah*, although offering a portrait of a successful lesbian relationship, positions the narrative in another time, and while in their home they know the real nature of their relationship, in the world outside, Patience and Sarah are misread as sisters or simply as friends. Forrest's novel, originally published in 1983, places its action in a contemporary setting, perhaps a few years earlier than its publication date, and the impact of social shifts, particularly second wave feminism, can be seen in the characters' career choices, economic security, and sexual freedom. Interestingly, Forrest does not interject Lane's and Diana's developing attraction into the group; the others seem remarkably unaware that Diana and Lane have become lovers. Being lesbian, then, still carries a greater social stigma, and, since the novel's main narrative focus is on the couple, Forrest allows the fantasy of the lovers' complete enthrallment to suspend this lack of awareness by the rest of the group. As Lane and Diana plan for a life together, they both acknowledge having to confront challenges but, as the romance novel must assure its readers, know that their commitment to one another will make that possible.

In "Lesbian Romance Fiction and the Plotting of Desire" Suzanne Juhasz pinpoints an essential component of genre romance stories for its readers. After briefly summarizing Terri Castle's notion of the ghosted lesbian figure in literary texts, Juhasz states,

> Yet this very necessity for metaphor and suggestion points to a counter need: for literalness. Not to have to "read between the lines" but to encounter lines which lesbians are there: *out* rather than *between*. When lesbians' stories are plotted before our very eyes, romances in which girl goes out and gets girl, we may be reading fantasy, but we are engaged in a real way with a story which we desire for ourselves.... These plots validate the sense of identity that readers have or seek and also show us something about what might constitute that identity [68, emphasis in text].

Lesbian romance novels rely on the same repetitions as conventional straight romances; readers, in fact, look forward to the highly patterned plotlines, characters, and speech. As the quotation from Cameron and Kulick which opens this chapter suggests, the very fact that desire can be continually re-articulated is essential to its understanding. Romance provides, through its clichés, the assurance of recognition as well as the enjoyment of seeing the patterns and their acceptable variations work themselves out. The romance novel receives much criticism for what is seen as its reliance on language that is overwrought, dependent on exaggerated descriptions and explanations, clichéd dialogue, and a deliberately abstract and limited vocabulary. However, Barlow and Krentz defend these linguistic usages as essential to the romance's success; they argue that the excesses of language found in these novels allow the reader to immerse herself quickly into the physical and emotional worlds of the narrative ("Beneath the Surface" 28–29). Readers expect to find this type of language because it encourages them to create the fantasy of romantic fulfillment, but at the same time, letting them know that the fantasy is a temporary one:

> The romance's peculiar narrative strategy seems to encourage the reader in her desire to have it both ways. She can read the story as a realistic novel about what might plausibly occur in an individual woman's life without having to face the usual threat of the unknown. This is possible because all contingency is erased by the narrative's continuing reassurance that it reveals nothing that is not previously anticipated [Radway 207].

Most lesbian romance novels incorporate these repetitive narrative and language tactics to represent an imagined reality for their readers; of course, there will be adaptations in how characters talk and what they talk about as the stories reflect the changing experience of lesbian lives.

The model of lesbian attraction and satisfaction of desire offered by Forrest in *Curious Wine* appears consistently in the lesbian genre romance.

Many of the narratives utilize the plot device of introducing one of the women into a new environment where she must accustom herself to the particular communal and social expectations. Janet McClellan's *Winter Garden*, Claire McNab's *Under the Southern Cross*, and Shelley Smith's *Horizon of the Heart* are just three of many examples. Not all of these narratives, however, introduce the exact same configuration of the main characters and the development of the romance; like Diana, some of these women have previously experienced heterosexual relationships in the past that have either been broken through death of a spouse (McClellan) or divorce (Smith) or they have had sexual experiences with men which may have been satisfying or not (McNab). They assume, however, that any sexual encounter will be framed as straight. Other main characters are presented as asexual; they have closed themselves off from even the smallest articulation of desire, usually due to past violence with a male partner — an abusive husband in Diana Simmonds' *Heart on Fire* or parental sexual abuse in McNab's *Silent Heart*. Having the women who will become the focus of the story both be lesbian is also common in lesbian romances, and these characters represent a range of emotional and sexual histories. In Ann O'Leary's *The Other Woman* Joanna Kingston and Fiona Maddison, both highly successful and out lesbians, are strangers at the beginning of the novel; other patterns include lovers whose relationship is in doubt or who have lost their long-term partner, often through death, and believe they will never find love again.

The trajectory of the narrative also reveals variations in the positioning of the interactions of the couple. Diana and Lane are both strangers not only to one another but to the group, thus having a point of reference that helps establish their connection. More often one of the women clearly controls the environment — Sally Windrow owns the farm and hires Nicole Jaeger as temporary help; Grace Davanzo's family runs the truckstop in the Australian outback where Jody Johnson's tour bus has broken down. In these novels the object of desire comes into the home space, either intentionally or serendipitously. Interestingly, though, the newcomer to the scene becomes the focus of the other woman's attention, and unlike Forrest's couple, the women have no commonalities that would seem to support any kind of relationship developing. However, when the attraction does come, it seems almost automatic; some unknowable connection, compulsion, begins the process that will end with the declaration of their need for each other and the eventual consummation of that need. Often, as in the typical straight genre romance, this attraction is a response to physical beauty: "Her attention was continually drawn to a woman fielding close to Cathie. Unlike everyone else, she was wearing shorts — as short as panties. Her legs were superb — long and strong-looking. Her shoulders were square and broad, her hips narrow. Agile but graceful, she had a perfect athletic body" (Simmonds 19). In some cases the intruder seems arrogant or unsuitable for the environment which initially creates an impasse between them; in *Winter Garden*, during Sally's interviews with potential farm hands, Nicole appears to take control of the hiring from Sally by noting how most of the individuals already questioned do not bring the necessary skills and interest to the position. Sally's comment, "You're very sure of yourself," is answered with "The Army never paid me to be a shrinking violet" (45). Yet, two responses arise simultaneously as Sally worries whether Nicole will fit into the farm's rhythms but also feels herself attracted to Nicole's air of command and assurance. Another common scenario has one woman responding, not only to the other's looks, but more to a perceived emotional need unacknowledged by the other. In *Horizon of the Heart* at the very first meeting between Jenny Winthrop and Danni Marlowe, Jenny's reactions shifts: "The woman standing before her was tall, blonde, cool; her eyes were chips of cold blue ice. Her stance was haughty, arrogant, yet there was a completing sensuousness about her. When she smiled, as she did now, Jenny saw the expression of a shy child on her face" (4).

What differentiates these narrative gambits from their heterosexual counterparts centers on the impact changing the gender of one of the romantic couple has. In straight romances the control of the progression of the relationship generally belongs to the hero, and while the heroine does have the right of refusal, that position is quickly overturned as he uses words and actions to court her affection. His responses, whether gesture or verbal, provide the foundation for the heroine's desires and the impetus for her behavior. Even in the most contemporary romances the heroine still relinquishes final autonomy to him:

> A heroine who is true to herself, whatever her self may be — jet pilot or bashful spinster — is enough to make her part in the mechanics of a romance workable, if not a work of art. I am *not* proposing that authors shouldn't bother to create convincing heroines; indeed we should, and must. What I am saying is that in the rank order of reader interest and identification, the heroine always falls second to the hero... [Kinsale, "The Androgynous Reader," 41, emphasis in text].

This acquiescence is typically signified by some explicit verbal statement that signifies her approval of the newly defined relationship; after all, there must be no ambiguity about her acceptance. The entire purpose of any romance, it can be argued, is to bring the hero and heroine to this moment of declaration. While the outcome in lesbian romance stories remains the same, with the creation of the new entity, the couple, the balance of power is reconfigured. One partner in the relationship may be offered a dominant position, but generally she does not accept it; Diana, in *Curious Wine*, says, "You make love with the person, not to them, when it's equal" (159). Grace, after realizing that she does love Jody and has traveled to Sydney to tell her, "I want us to be happy. I want you to be happy and I want me to be happy — whatever that takes. I know your life is complicated and demanding ... I have no idea how to cope with all that. But if you can, I will" (Simmonds 165). This establishment of shared control in defining the relationship may arise from so many of the characters leaving previous situations, lesbian or heterosexual, where they were not treated as equals.

Because the forms that the language of desire take reflect a particular cultural time and place, and because that language tends to be situated first within a heterosexual context, two women speaking the tropes of passion automatically call into question the implications of what is said and meant: "Intimacies are poignant examples of how desires may feel private, but are unavoidably shaped through public structures and in public interactions" (Cameron and Kulick 115). The appropriation not only of the words, but their generally accepted meanings transforms lesbian love talk into a transgressive act.[11] Saying I love you, then, in a lesbian romance, becomes a radical act even though the narrative framework remains very conservative, and many of the characters in these novels seem to recognize that their declaration will alter how the rest of their community will respond to them. *Horizon of the Heart* ends with Jenny and Danni reunited after a series of emotional confrontations that have challenged Danni to recognize her attraction and need for Jenny. After their declaration in the small town's grocery story, Danni and Jenny start to ride home on a bicycle — Danni is pedaling, Jenny the passenger — and "as they stopped for the traffic light at the corner of Spring and Main Street, Jenny turned and kissed Danni on the lips" (170). However, the happy ending that is essential to the romance erases the public censure for such visible displays of affection. This outcome is especially important in novels that have one of the women moving from the security of heterosexual identity to accepting a lesbian one; this woman discovers that the claiming (or reclaiming) of real love overcomes confusion, even hostility of family and friends: "I know your mother loves you; she's even managed to talk to me lately without looking like an oncoming storm cloud. I know your daughter loves you, but you know that, too. You certainly shouldn't be confused as to how I feel about you. I understand, too, that there's a lot of work to do, but even with that, I can't remember ever being happier" (*Winter Garden* 180).

Since the words of passion have already been defined by the dominant culture, lesbian lovers have no option but to use them; however, they can make such language their own by reimagining the circumstances that establish the boundaries of the romantic situation. In essence, the lesbian romance lays out a blueprint that illustrates the passing of lesbian desire; the heterosexual notions of correct romantic pairings, courtship, and consummation become the palimpsest for the lesbian couple who draw their explicit desire over them. This re-coding of meaning can be seen when lovers appropriate the social institution of marriage and especially the emotional notions of passion and desire that are attached to it; in the romantic fantasy *First Lady*, the first woman president of the United States marries the reporter who was originally sent to do a campaign biography. One of the subplots follows the wedding plans, and the reader watches the dilemma of fittings, balancing politics and love, integrating a newcomer into a family. In *Contractor for Hire* it is Melissa Wright's mother who reminds her that love crosses socially restrictive boundaries: "If it's love you don't have to think it's right. You already know it is" (116). *Rebecca's Cove*, a comic romance, ends with the wedding of the main characters. In each of these novels not only are the lovers accepted by the heterosexual community, but their relationship and union is actively encouraged. Many lesbian romances end with the lovers remaining in a predominantly straight social environment and maintaining friendships and business relationships with straight people. This may appear to contradict Bonnie Zimmerman's identification of the retreat of the lovers to the "green world" mentioned earlier, but even the characters, like Diana and Lane, whose story ends with the literal closing of the door on the rest of the world, cannot completely ignore the presence of mainstream society. By actively reshaping the models of romantic behavior, lesbian romances may be seen as assuaging the fears of a straight audience while at the same time encouraging the lesbian reader to feel secure enough to lay claim to these rituals:

> Thus the central issue seems to me to be not so much whether language or even subjectivity is "free" from culture or constructed by it, as whether that culture, the situation in which language users are embedded, includes the experience and vision of alterity and difference. People do imagine something other that the status quo, and they struggle in various ways to attain and to validate that difference. Practice as well as theory embodies that struggle [Juhasz, "Lesbian Romance Fiction and the Plotting of Desire," 80].

These two views of how the language of desire operates in lesbian romance novels, on the surface, contradict each other. If speaking the words of passion for a lesbian represents a radical defamiliarizing of socially normal speech, how can it also assert and support the underlying conservative notions of love embodied in such speech? The point of reconciliation can be found within the conventions of the romance itself which is, as most critics of the genre note, a highly conservative form. Since, as Scott McCracken asserts, "The only clear element that unites all romance narratives is their concern with desire and the prospect of its satisfaction," every technique at the author's disposal is directed toward achieving that outcome. Every romance novelist who contributed to *Dangerous Men and Adventurous Women* continually stresses not only the importance of providing their readers with the happy ending but also of not varying the formula beyond reasonable or acceptable limits. The reader's demand for the constant repetition of the formulas and clichés becomes the initiating force for her continued consumption; this demand for sameness is also the foundation for most of the negative criticism. Although she does not develop her idea fully, Kathleen Gilles Seidel notes that "reading romances is not the only thing human beings do repetitively" ("Judge Me by the Joy I Bring" 176). Her statement implies that some degree of engagement is always made between the reader and the text in spite of its utilization of seemingly worn out techniques. The reader experiences the comfort of recognizable characters, settings, and conflicts which may help encourage the fantasy of connection and satisfaction. Already knowing much of the story enables the reader to concentrate on the emotional relationships and anticipate their consummation: "Reading popular fictions is not a mindless and submissive process. On the contrary, it requires the constant exercise of one's interpretive powers.... The pleasure from and active involvement in this literature derives from its ability to stimulate and exercise our powers of observation, inference, and interpretation" (Swirski 70).

Just as the narrative and other technical codes of romance must be repeatable, the codes of romantic language must also share this characteristic. Without a shared sense of meaning any attempt at communication will be thwarted, and the communication of one's most intimate desires is, perhaps, the most important moment when the individual wishes to be understood: "When desire is expressed or represented in language ... it is intelligible because it draws on codes of signification that circulate within the wider society.... Individuals cannot choose *not* to have their desires understood in terms of prevailing social norms..."(Cameron and Kulick, emphasis in text, 132). Therefore, the words lesbians utter acknowledge their own passion ("*The same Karen that could make you laugh during your low points ... the same Karen that you miss if you don't speak to on a regular basis*"); claim the fulfillment of their desire ("Oh, God, darling. I love you desperately. All I want is to be able to be with you — all the time"); accept the implications of commitment ("In my whole life I never thought I'd ever be able to make anyone that happy ... and I promise that I'll try never to do anything to mess that up"); and imagine the permanence of their relationship ("You don't work here. You belong here, make no mistake about that. We own this together now. I wouldn't want to do it without you").[12] Any lover, lesbian or straight, would recognize both the language and the intent that impels the speech. Any reader, lesbian or straight, would, perhaps, sigh with pleasure as she recognizes that such words signal a happy resolution to the tensions and potentials dangers that the couple faced. This shared identity of the characters as lovers first, regardless of sexuality, represents the promise and limitations of the romance, by holding out the fantasy of complete acceptance and integration, but only within the pages of the fictional text. Yet, the power of the text, through its reiteration of the fantasy, encourages continued exposure to and pleasure in the narrative.

Chapter Three

CODING THE EROTIC

> Perhaps what confuses feminist film theorists is the irrevocable association in the twentieth-century Euro-American cultural lexicon between lesbian visibility and a certain set of stylistic markers generally associated with masculinity — short hair; austere, tailored clothing; accessories like neckties, men's hats, leather jackets, and sensible shoes; and such gestural traits as a purposeful stride and robust handshake. Certainly, every woman who fits this description is not a lesbian, but it remains difficult to imagine how a lesbian could be visible without at least several of these accoutrements or mannerisms.
>
> (Martha Gever, *Entertaining Lesbians: Celebrity, Sexuality, and Self-Invention*, 31)

> Lily regarded herself in the full-length mirror: her plain black vintage dress with its tattoo-concealing sleeves, her black stockings, and the black Mary Janes with chunky high heels, which were the closest thing to a respectable-looking pair of shoes she owned. She had pulled her white-girl dreadlocks into a messy bun so her hair didn't look too wild, and she had replaced the silver hoop in her nose with a tiny silver stud. She had considered removing her body jewelry altogether, but she couldn't bear to. Her multiple piercings were the only thing that prevented her from looking like someone's grandmother from the Old Country.
>
> (Julia Watts, *Wedding Bell Blues*, 3)

Speech may be the dominant way that desire between two people is made known, but before one person speaks to another, other cues must be read and interpreted. The role and importance of the visual in the initiation and development of attraction often helps determine the success or failure of the relationship. Like speech, the meanings of gesture, dress, and setting rest within particular social and cultural environments, and potential lovers must negotiate these meanings as they seek to satisfy their personal desires. Two levels of negotiation must be played out as the couple enters into their relationship: first is the representation of the self, which combines the individual's own interpretation of those categories with public versions; second is the individual's engaging with another person's understanding of acceptable and appropriate gesture.[1] In addition to the creation of the public image a person wishes to present to the world, and a possible romantic partner, is the matter of properly interpreting the image that is offered to another's view. Just as speech can be misheard and misunderstood, the outward signs of one's character that are displayed open the individual to misreading. Of course, the person may also deliberately present a false picture to the world or another individual with the intent of manipulating those responses.

Most theories that examine the positioning, utilization, and outcomes of appearance and gesture frame their discussions around visual media — art, television, and especially film. Many of these analyses concentrate on the role of the viewer in the making of meaning within the frameworks and conventions of the particular medium, paying particular attention to the concept of the spectator and the act of watching. (A favorite critical term that appears in this criticism is the gaze, applied both to the viewer and the creator of the film.) Typical of such a critical approach is Andrea Weiss' use of the ideas of Mary Ann Doane, a film theorist, in Weiss's study of the representations of lesbians in film, *Vampires & Violets*:

> Doane defines the position assigned to the female spectator by the cinema as a "certain over-presence of the image — she is the image".... To simplify a complex argument, Doane finds that the theoretical female spectator's pleasure in the cinema can take the form of masochism in over-identification with the image, or of narcissism in becoming one's own object of desire, or it may be possible, by re-inserting the necessary distance, for the woman's gaze to master the image [39].

The emphasis here centers on the relationship initiated between the viewer of the film and the images projected on the screen and on how the viewer responds to those projected pictures. Much of the theory concentrates on the ways that identity — the incorporation of the social expectations portrayed on the screen or their rejection — is organized. However, this interaction is a complex one, combining these private and public constructions of identity and behavior with the personal interpretations of the director. The film-goer is invited to respond to the range of visual representations offered and may choose to accept or reject them. The female viewer's participation in the act of watching especially receives a great deal of critical attention as her position as observer becomes the nexus of a variety of theoretical frameworks. Doane's approach, for instance, clearly relies heavily on a psychoanalytically based reading of the woman's response to how she may see herself portrayed on the screen.[2]

In addition to criticism of the moving image, the creation of identity through static representations of appearance and gesture has been the subject of numerous critical commentaries. Such studies range from describing the rise of consumption (William Leach's *Land of Desire: Merchants, Power, and the Rise of a New American Culture*), the history of taste (Russell Lynes' *The Tastemakers*), the impact of advertising (Ellen Gruber Garvey's *The Adman in the Parlor: Magazines and the Gendering of Consumer Culture, 1880s to 1910s*) and the meaning of clothes (Anne Hollander's *Sex and Suits: The Evolution of Modern Dress*). Here much of the discussion considers the intersection of public expectations and representations and private desire and choice; for example, Hollander in describing fashion notes that

> all social facts about the wearer can theoretically be masked except for personal taste, and even that may be suppressed at will for politic ends. Nevertheless people uneasily realize that the unconscious sources of personal taste in modern fashion can make it convey a whole spectrum of social and personal information much like what is straightforwardly offered in traditional dress, only unconsciously instead of on purpose [20].

As with film studies, this criticism examines the interactions between the reader and the picture and how conceptions of identity and suitable public and private behavior is articulated and interpreted. Here, too, women's engagement with such portraiture receives the majority of the critic's attention; she may be seen as a passive consumer or active participant in this relationship. Not surprisingly, feminist critics emphasize the connection between a negative body image for women, particularly young girls, and standards of beauty presented in commercial advertising as well as how the redrawing of the markers of class access impact social relationships; as Joanne Hollows puts it, "If our sense of who we are increasingly comes from what and how we consume, then this, it has been claimed, makes people aware that our identities are not fixed but something we can *play* with, construct and reconstruct through our use of commodities ... [and] the freedom to play with lifestyles often neglects very basic questions about access to opportunities to consume" (132–133, emphasis in text).

Lesbian cultural and literary critics are especially concerned with this relationship between media representations — whether in film or in print — and their implications for the lesbian viewer/reader and mainstream society. One of the key questions centers on who exactly is creating the images, therefore defining what a lesbian is and how she should be seen and, even, judged: "Descriptions or pictures of lesbians in the popular media can work to assure heterosexual women that lesbians are just like heterosexuals, an assumption that might offer lesbians more status in the dominant society but that can also negate the differences that make up their cultural identity" (Inness 74). In her analysis of the ways in which lesbians were portrayed in popular women's magazines during the 1980s and 1990s, Sherrie Inness stresses how the primary goal of these journals centered on framing a picture of the lesbian that would not only be familiar but safe by placing her within recognizable contexts. The common feature stressed in these magazines is that lesbians look just as normal — read feminine — as the typical heterosexual reader; such a view downplays the potential disruption of gender norms particularly those embodied in the butch: "A group of man-hating lesbians dressing as men might be a potential threat to heterosexual harmony, but an isolated few lesbians, attractive and well dressed, seem to pose little danger and do not remind readers of the many other real lesbians who might not be so polite and decorous" (68). This possible blurring of the assumed clear lines that define gendered look and therefore gendered behavior signals the point at which mainstream popular culture retreats from treating the lesbian as a full member of society.

In "Girls Who Kiss Girls and Who Cares?" Sue O'Sullivan traces the shifts in popular heterosexual culture's portrayal of the lesbian and asks what motivated this shift from once seeing the lesbian as different, in terms of gender appearance and behavior, to showing her as recognizable, if only in a sexually framed way. For O' Sullivan, the new image of lesbian as media darling stresses her sexual otherness at the expense of her full social reality: "In these articles the focus is completely on 'naming' and transgression and no one ever mentions that people who live out their lives 'transgressively' may have trouble in the world — trouble with jobs, family or trouble with violence" (87).[3] For mainstream society, then, the modern lesbian must be separated from any radical environment, whether it be the political, ethical, or relational, in order to become acceptable; at the same time, though, she must remain exotically other so that she can be prevented from achieving full integration into mainstream social norms. Critics like O' Sullivan, Sherrie Innes, and others continually note that the lesbians offered for view in these magazines replicate the standards of beauty designated as heterosexually feminine — the tall, thin body, long hair, up-to-date fashion, and make-up. That lesbian romance novels of the 1980s and early 1990 would incorporate characters who reflected these standards is not surprising. (See Shelley Smith's *Horizon of the Heart*,

Katherine Forrest's *Curious Wine* or Claire McNab's *Under the Southern Cross*, for example.) Of course, it is not only how a lesbian looks, but where she lives, what she does, what she surrounds herself with, and who she associates with that are also co-opted by the mainstream heterosexual media. Usually, the lesbian as portrayed in mainstream popular journals resides in middle or upper-middle class neighborhoods, furnishes her home or apartment in an up-to-date style, works in either a cutting edge career or socially valued profession, and enjoys her free time participating in the current venues. The accumulation of these details establishes an image of the lesbian that while satisfying mainstream curiosity and calming heterosexual anxiety not only restricts the representation of a fully constructed lesbian life but prevents her successful integration into the dominant culture.

The above representations, of course, are dictated by the dominant, heterosexual conception of what a lesbian is — her looks, behaviors, relationships. The essential question becomes what changes when lesbians take control of the medium and the message. How invested are lesbian portrayals of themselves with mainstream views, and, more importantly, where and why do lesbian reenact such images to reflect a self-determined projection to the wider society? In her article "Pussy Galore: Lesbian Images and Lesbian Desire in the Popular Cinema," Yvonne Tasker underscores the importance of placing specific lesbian texts within "the contemporary lesbian culture that produced it" (182).[4] The delineation of any lesbian culture must be recognized, as is all culture, as limited; it cannot be applied to every lesbian in every situation. The specific categories of lesbian representation that form the basis of this analysis are grounded in the period between the mid 1980s and the present, marking a time period when homosexuality has moved, if not completely into the mainstream, at least further from the margins.

Once mainstream media accepted the lesbian by including her within its pages and on its screens, lesbians themselves began to engage with them. These strategies have taken the form of re-reading the context in which the lesbian appears; for example, often the gal pal of a straight heroine, as reconceived by the lesbian this character moves to the foreground and redirects the heroine's romantic interest towards herself. This basic scenario (with adaptations) appears in movies such as *Kissing Jessica Stein* and in many lesbian romance novel plots. See, for example, *Forty Love* by Diana Simmonds or *An Emergence of Green* by Katherine Forrest. Such re-visionings are possible because taking control of the construction of the image allows the lesbian to usurp the power of determining meaning:

> In every sector of modern consumer culture ... normative definitions of sexuality, gender, and class are routinely mobilized and reinforced. At the same time, the devices used to arouse and satisfy audiences' desires establish an imaginary, but also material, foundation for lesbian passion: activities coded as feminine, where the pleasures of women's company may be taken for granted; opportunities for voyeuristic delight in the display of female bodies: enactments of fiery relationships among women, even if overtly asexual; and depictions of forceful, not always typically feminine women. All such common features of popular culture can be plausibly described as potential lesbian occasions [Gever 76–77].

Essentially, a lesbian-authored text not only gives the lesbian reader permission to look, but to look as a lesbian looks, and since the situations and characters available to the lesbian reader aim for a wide audience, the variety of lesbian experience presented in these works provides a greater possibility for reader recognition.

Popular fiction, of course, "expresses and reflects the aesthetic and social values of its readers," including the material constructs that embody those values (Swirski 6). The concrete representation of these values appears in genre fiction through the author's use of a variety of techniques, including the physical descriptions of characters — reflecting a particular culture's concepts of beauty; the kinds of behaviors available for the characters to engage in — usually offering them some degree of freedom, particularly in sexual matters, but retaining a connection to social standards; and placing them within recognizable settings — giving characters, as well, the ability to fill these places with material goods that reflect a particular culture's notions of what is suitable. While all three components help establish the reality of the novel's world, the impact of setting, perhaps, becomes the most prominent shaper of the reader's response. The importance of setting to the creation of the text's narrative and thematic purposes need not be reviewed here, but its role in the reader's connection to and pleasure in the text should not be forgotten. Although he is discussing the role of setting in relation to nineteenth-century texts, Philip Fisher's concept of "privileged settings" offers a framework to consider the meanings of setting to a modern genre text. These settings, according to Fisher,

> are ideal and simplified vanishing points toward which lines of sight and projects of every kind converge. From these vanishing points, the many, approximate or bungled, actual states of affairs draw order and position. Whatever actually appears within a society can be interpreted as some variant, some anticipation or displacement or ruin, of one of these privileged settings [9].

In other words, the descriptions of physical environments and character behavior and appearance entice the reader to enter the world of the text. Accuracy of descriptive details encourages the reader to participate in the fantasy being offered through the particular genre's story and characters; the ability of the writer to create readily identifiable and relatable situations allows the reader to determine how she will respond to what is presented. Representations of time, place, dress, and behavior, therefore, establish points of comparison between the reader's experience and the characters.⁴ Fisher, of course, applies this concept to his larger thesis of how such settings and the repetitive exposure of the reader to them helps in the familiarization process that transforms the unimaginable into the ordinary, and while the purposes of this process vary, genre fiction also relies on the power of extended and repeated detail to make the readers comfortable with the sometimes exotic narrative situations offered for their enjoyment.

In the romance novel these social codes are woven into the narrative in a variety of ways and provide a background against which the couple will develop their relationship. These physical details may be explicitly introduced into the story as part of the descriptive fabric of the text, or they are more subtly woven into the construction of the narrative, adding verisimilitude without intruding into the dominant courtship plot. For example, in *Scruples*, a bestselling romance from the 1980s, Judith Krantz deliberately references the specific as a way of presenting not only the setting, but personalities as well; it's not just a suit, but an Armani, not just a crystal glass, but Baccarat, not just the summer home, but the one in the Hamptons. Cataloguing like this, however, may also interrupt the progression of the courtship, especially when such details are simply piled up and serve no other function than branding.[5] More often, though, an author assumes the reader's familiarity if not with the actual product or environment, at least with the cachet such labels carry. In this novel, the constant naming of expensive goods and society locations establishes the value in obvious economic terms, but also in moral ones, of the major characters; the heroine and hero belong in such places, have earned the right to obtain such goods. The major plot of this romance, in fact, centers on the main female character's efforts to become part of the world of fashion; Scruples becomes the name of the high-end department store she establishes. The physical environment also reflects the characters' discernment, although often the heroine will misread the outward appearance as an accurate representation of another's real personality. She comes to learn, through a variety of trials, that the surfaces do not always indicate an individual's real self. This frequently happens during the development of the romance itself, when the hero is described as physically scarred or viewed as not fitting into the particular social milieu of the novel; the heroine must learn to re-read the details and reconstruct the final image of the hero if the desired outcome of romantic union is to be achieved.

Writers of historical romances are particularly aware of the importance of incorporating accurate architectural, decorative, and fashion description into the narrative. Georgette Heyer, considered a master of the Regency romance, "took immense pains with her historical detail, never obtruding it, but weaving it into the background so that one dates the books from some casually mentioned fact.... If she names the brand of polish that a valet uses for his master's Hessian boots one can be sure she has got it right" (Avery, "The very pink of propriety," 408). Such specificity helps create the requisite fantasy element essential to the romance. With historical fiction the texture of the setting presents not only a sense of unfamiliarity — the reader is literally introduced to a time and place with which she has no connection — but also, due to this building up of physical detail, allows the reader to feel connected to the personalities of the hero and heroine. This ability for the reader to develop sympathy with the heroine depends on the ability of the author to maneuver the setting so that it directs the reader to see her similarity with the heroine's desires and actions despite the separation of time and place. As Pamela Regis notes in discussing Heyer's novels, she "does not write historically accurate heroines. Instead, they have unusual notions about how to behave (as the conventional-minded characters surrounding them are constantly pointing out), and those notions are distinctly twentieth-century. Her heroes are similarly ahistorical" (127). Unless the reader and heroine can break through the reality of an historical romance, the necessary identification of shared desire cannot occur.

Like their mainstream counterparts, lesbian romances set their narratives within conventional settings. Perhaps the most common backdrop for the love story, especially in novels set in the present, is the city. The prominence of this environment reflects its importance in the history of gays and lesbians: the city has always been seen as providing the gay man or lesbian a surrounding in which the individual is able to express non-traditional sexual desire more openly. The city offers anonymity at the same time it facilitates the creation of a shared community. Lillian Faderman in *Odd Girls and Twilight Lovers: A History of Lesbian Life in Twentieth-Century America* stresses the role of large urban centers like San Francisco in the development of lesbian identity (126–127). This preferred setting appears even in the pre-romances of Hall (London and Paris) and Renault (London). For the lesbians portrayed in the pulps, the city, usually New York, becomes their mecca, offering them acceptance and the ability to survive. Urban settings still dominate modern lesbian romances, although the geography has broadened; narratives are situated in Boston, Chicago, Atlanta, Philadelphia, Sydney, Melbourne, as well as London, New York, or San Francisco. Not surprisingly, as lesbians have moved beyond the borders of specifically identified gay neighborhoods, the characters in these novels have also taken up residence in every corner of the city.

However, the lifestyles enjoyed by the characters in lesbian romances tend to reflect a middle to upper-middle class status. Very few lesbian characters belong to the working class; very few are presented as living economically distressed lives. Those characters who work in blue-collar professions tend to be self-employed and generally successful.[6] The professions for most of the characters in these romances range from lawyers to advertising executives, to vineyard owners, to doctors, to entrepreneurs; if the profession is less common, the character tends to be very successful. This monetary affluence is reflected in the characters' living spaces:

> The colossal refrigerator sported light oak panels on the front, matching the rest of the kitchen's décor. A state of the art cook's island sat just off the middle of the room and was complete with a stovetop and sink as well as a garbage hole and built in cutting board. Above their heads was a wrought iron rack holding the brilliantly finished copper pots and pans [Miller, *Accidental Love*, 70].

The portrayal of lesbians as economically successful is constantly reinforced in these books and may be seen as contributing to one aspect of the romance novel's creation of fantasy, not of romantic passion but of material comfort. The association of financial security with a lesbian identity attempts to bridge the gap between perceived deviance (lesbian) and socially approved status (wealth); the one condition assumes acceptance of the other. Another component of this fantasy, whether mainstream or lesbian, requires that the main characters exist in a larger than life world; such exaggerated images of the characters' appearance and their environments offers the escape from the ordinary that is essential to the reader's engagement with the text: "The primary task of the romance writer is to create for her readers a vision of an alternative world and to give mythical dimension to its landscape and characters. Piling on the detail by means of a generous use of the romance codes is an effective way to achieve this goal" (Barlow and Krentz 24). The high economic and/or class status often held by one of the characters in the romance must not be seen as an impediment to the eventual union of the couple, but as the mechanism by which one of the couple — typically the hero in heterosexual narratives — is able to provide to the heroine the missing nurture and support.

Many lesbian romances, in fact, utilize the contrast in the class status of the couple as either a complication that must be resolved if the happy ending is to be achieved or as a marker of suitability. B. L. Miller's *Accidental Love* constructs the romance around the first plot situation; Veronica Cartwright, the eldest daughter of a wealthy family and manager of its many businesses, has struck Rose, a younger woman running away from a mugger, with her car. Veronica uses her influence to cover up the accident and, on discovering that Rose has no financial resources, arranges to cover the medical expenses. The required plot complications have Rose moving into Veronica's mansion, and their developing attraction and passion is chronicled. However, Rose eventually discovers Veronica's complicity in the accident and sees all of her behavior as an attempt to buy Rose's silence: "*That's why you wanted to help me so much. It was all a lie to protect yourself*" (312, emphasis in text). Only after Susan, Veronica's sister, shows Rose that while Veronica's actions may have begun as self-interest, real love has replaced such feelings. Rose, of course, acknowledges the truth of Susan's explanation and reaffirms her own desire, and the novel closes with the giving of a ring and the acceptance of its implications.

Rose is not to be read as a gold-digger; from the beginning of the novel she is determined to make her own way. Even though Veronica offers her the stereotypic life of luxury, Rose successfully argues for her independence and teaches herself the skills needed to become Veronica's assistant. Whatever salary Rose would make must be seen as incidental to the imperative of her maintaining a sense of agency; by refusing to be ultimately seduced by Veronica's economic power, Rose retains her integrity. The material goods that are showered on her over the course of the novel, in a sense, are the reward for her assertion of her own value. Not surprisingly, Rose's actions have a beneficial influence on Veronica as she comes to understand that value must be calculated in terms beyond the monetary. Through Rose's explicit and implicit influence Veronica reconciles with members of her family who resent her control of the family fortune and who cannot accept her lesbianism. At the beginning of the novel, Veronica is already pictured as dissatisfied with much of the responsibilities that accompany her position; in order to smooth the political snags to obtain a zoning variance for one of the family business, she has had to leave her "fine home in the middle of one of the worst blizzards to hit Albany" (8). Miller paints Veronica's relation to her wealth in a, perhaps, conventional way, but does strike a balance between the arrogance of power and a real understanding and appreciation of the responsibility of that power. Veronica lives in the family home and works hard to maintain its physical and emotional value. Rose's support for bringing the family together for Christmas, a tradition that has not been upheld for several years, illustrates the increasing connection between the two women.

Without the luxury that Veronica's wealth provides, the progress of the romance would be thwarted. Because she is taken care of, in every possible way, Rose has the freedom to become aware of her feelings for Veronica; she also has the time to understand not only the emotional aspects of her attraction, but the physical expression of those feelings. At one point during her convalescence, Rose discovers Veronica's stash of lesbian romance novels and erotic videos. Veronica's wealth also allows her to protect Rose from the blackmail of the woman who raised her after the death of Rose's parents. Rose does not ask for any of the expensive goods Veronica showers on her, but this constant offering of money has become the typical pattern in the Cartwright family for showing affection or buying cooperation. Until the accident Veronica's generosity is often forced rather than freely given; for Rose, money becomes the image of what she lacks in terms of material and emotional support. As their relationship develops, Rose and Veronica discover that giving need not be tied to obligation. By the end of the novel the exchange of expensive presents signifies the resolution of all the attempts to prevent the happy ending.

When both women in the lesbian romance share class or economic status, the role played by the descriptions of setting replicate standard genre values. These women embody a set of conventionally constructed and approved looks and behaviors; the opening gala event in *Course of Action*, presents the two main characters dressed in haut couture: one wears an "ice blue Ungaro evening dress," the other "an elegant black dress decorated with a cascade of rhinestones stretching from her left shoulder down around her waist and onto the form-fitting skirt" (13–14). Even when casually dressed, these women's clothing rarely comes off the rack. The homes such characters live in, of course, echo this rarified taste, architect designed and furnished and offering stunning views of the city or a natural setting. Like their mainstream counterparts, these characters participate in a varied social life, although the venues will often be specifically lesbian or lesbian friendly. Not all novels position their characters in the upper echelons however; they will reside comfortably within the middle class and share educational, professional, and romantic values. A particular sub-set of lesbian romance novels began to appear in the mid–1990s that brought together a group of women who work together (Elizabeth Dean's *It's in Her Kiss* and R. J. Stevens' *The Best of Friends*), live in the same neighborhood (Diane Salvatore's *Paxton Court*), or enjoy and rely on long-standing friendships (Paula Martinac's *Chicken*). One of the prominent features of these group romances — because while they could be classified as comedies of manners like their mainstream counterparts, finding suitable, long-term partners is the narratives' starting point — is the shared environment in which the characters reside. Not surprisingly, these novels do not replicate the traditional romantic plot; the narrative tends to center on one of the group, tracing the ups and downs of her searches for romantic relationships. The circle of friends provides a full range of support, criticism, and blind dates. In fact, in these novels, keeping one's friends becomes more important than individual passion. The ending of *Between Girlfriends* typifies this camaraderie: "*On New Year's Eve, The Girls will celebrate their first anniversary as friends. We're still arguing about what we'll do for the evening. But I'm sure that we'll eventually find common ground. We always do*" (234, emphasis in text). In fact, Gracy Maynard, the character whose view about this group controls the narrative, uses the various permutations of their relationships as the source for her columns on contemporary lesbian life.

Of course, the images of the lesbians portrayed in these novels reflect a rather limited set of experiences that, as Dana Heller's article on the television series *The L Word* notes, is "consistent with [an] emphasis on conventional femininity and its portrayal of women as non-threatening (read non-butch) objects to be visually enjoyed by some imagined mainstream (read non-queer) cable audience" (57). While the reader of these books will most likely be a lesbian, the homogeneity in characters, their backgrounds, expectations, and behaviors, cannot be overlooked. Differences appear in what can be called the superficial attributes of the characters — career, fashion, hobbies, and the like; however, with romantic desire, these differences evaporate. Each member of the group wants to find true love, establish a permanent relationship, and maintain that connection. This constant emphasis on a shared goal — intimacy — becomes the focal point of the narrative, and so the novels concentrate on the ways that these women work to develop these connections. While the patterns of becoming involved and breaking up are easily identified, usually one of the couple has cheated or let work or social obligations interfere with the relationship, the intention to break the pattern dominates the storyline:

> I thought about walking through the door to my house and being greeted by Maria. She'd throw her arms around my shoulders and pull me close to her. I'd breathe in her spicy, sweet scent and bury my nose in her hair.
> I thought about holding Katrina in my arms and breathing in her soft baby scent, the watching her fall asleep in her crib.
> I thought about the "sweet November" Maria and I would soon be sharing together [Dean, *It's in Her Kiss*, 293].

Romance remains the driving force in such novels and, in spite of the sameness the characters share, their desire makes them unique.

The comic tone of these novels represents another distinguishing factor for more traditional romances. The stories concentrate on the characters' idiosyncrasies and the impact such behaviors and outlooks have on the intertwined relationships traced throughout the novels. The potential for a tragic outcome is generally overturned by the recognition of the silliness of the potential crisis. In *Chicken* Lynn Woods, the central character, is back in the dating game and attempts to juggle seeing more than one woman at once; instead of intense introspection on the morality of the situation, Lynn deals with the logistics of balancing the two lovers (85–87). In *All the Bold Days of My Restless Life*, Bailey Connors must negotiate dating after being dumped and over the course of the novel is set up with a series of totally inappropriate women — an Internet sex show host, a New York police officer, a woman with six children. With the help of her friends this character maneuvers through the potential disasters and, ultimately, discovers the partner who will satisfy her needs.[7] Love is taken seriously in these novels, but is positioned within a narrative structure that asks its participants to recognize the importance of a sense of humor in the building of a relationship. Most mainstream romances, as well as many lesbian texts, treat the romantic couple and the progress of the romance as very serious, the dominant and driving force that controls their entire sense of self and purpose:

> "You and no other" is a cry that reverberates through the centuries as one of the most passionately held "first principles" of romantic love.... The *literature* of romance ... prefers (as in popular fiction) to limit its narrative to the moment of (first) consummation or to have its lovers die (spectacularly) before their vow can be put to the test. No common-sense prognosis will, however, prevent lovers feeling — and believing in — the exclusivity and non-repeatability of their love when they first succumb to it [Pearce 9, emphasis in text].

The happy ending marks the resolution of the turmoil experienced by the couple, and while it does signify a regaining of private and public equilibrium and the return of social stability, the ending provides the couple a deep-seated satisfaction rather than a light-hearted conclusion.

Whatever the backdrop against which the romance is played out, the characters must dominate the narrative; without a compelling couple for the reader to focus her own desires on, the fantasy of true love, between the right partners cannot achieve its outcome. Before the couple exists, though, each eventual partner in the dominant pairing must be presented, and before a reader can judge the suitability of the couple, she must believe that each woman is worthy of the other. The main purpose of the romance, after all, remains tracking the progress of the search for intimacy and union, and if the main characters are found not to be matched, then the fantasy of total satisfaction cannot be reached: "A novel that ends with the hero and heroine not in love, not betrothed, is simply not a romance novel" (Regis 114). The heterosexual hero and heroine usually enter their story as diametric opposites, in class, mobility, and power. Typically, the hero enjoys not only the privileges of his gender, but the constant expression of them; he is, to use Jayne Ann Krentz's term, the "alpha male" who dominates all of the other characters in the book, but most importantly the heroine ("Trying to Tame the Romance" 107). His physical appearance signifies this masterful personality: he is typically taller and more muscular than average; his features are generally described as rugged, reflecting an idealized masculine attractiveness; his coloring is usually imaged as swarthy or tanned. Blond hair, lighter skin tones, and smaller builds are not attributes given to the hero; such figures become false heroes, temporarily misdirecting the heroine's desires in malicious or accidental ways, or they are subordinates to the hero. Think of the difference between Rhett Butler and Ashley Wilkes. Depending on the sub-genre in which he appears, the hero is the successful entrepreneur, the swashbuckling privateer, the crusading politician, or the aristocratic gentleman. At the beginning of many romances, the hero appears in disguise, sometimes a literal masking, but more commonly, hiding his sensitive qualities since maintaining his public position requires presenting him in command of himself and his world. Of course, only the heroine is able to see through the surface, and her main role in the romance, as well as romantic goal, centers on her ability to reveal this hidden personality.

In recent mainstream romances, the hero has become the center of the novel's plot and reader attention. He exhibits a personality that balances contradictory expectations: "The heroes in romances are a bit larger than life, but they also possess the very real qualities that women look for in a life-mate.... A romance hero is able to be gentle and tender, while at the same time remaining strong and masculine.... The romance hero is exciting and dangerous, and erotic because of it" (Williamson "By Honor Bound," 126–127). Whatever nurturing qualities he brings to the relationship with the heroine, he still dominates the progression of the romantic narrative; it is his decisions, his responses, which direct and determine the heroine's reactions. Although he may be "tamed" by the heroine's love at the novel's conclusion, his dominance is never questioned. Even as the modern hero is more willing to reveal his emotional vulnerability or to express his feelings openly, he still represents and supports the traditional ideas of society, and usually the heroine acquiesces to them. In Jayne Ann Krentz's romance *All Night Long* this accommodation of social norms is underscored in the party that ends the novel: the mystery at the center of the novel has been solved, the emotional damage of both Irene — the heroine — and Luke — the hero — has been understood and healed and now the family is celebrating upcoming marriages and births. The last words are given to Luke and Irene as they contemplate their future:

> Joy, bright and full of promise, flooded through Irene. Luke tugged her closer, his arm around her waist.
> "What are you thinking?" he asked.
> "I'm thinking that this is how it feels to have a family. That with a love like ours and a family like this one, we can handle whatever comes along in the future."
> He smiled, looking *satisfied and certain*, "Talk about your astonishing coincidences. I was just thinking the very same thing" [320–321, emphasis added].

The narrative movement of lesbian romances replicates the traditional progression towards the creation of the couple and the consummation of the relationship. Just as in mainstream novels, the plot concentrates on tracing the paths of two main characters as they seek out and eventually find the desired romantic consummation. As in heterosexual romances, lesbian novels establish these characters with complementary personalities and abilities; however, the configuration of the lesbian couple does not fully replicate the model found in mainstream romance. This is, perhaps, the essential difference between the two genres: without a definite hero and heroine, the traditional romance cannot work: "In a romance novel, the relationship between the hero and the heroine *is* the plot. It is the primary focus of the story..." (Krentz "Trying to Tame the Romance," 108, emphasis in text). He must be aloof; she must be able to connect. He must acknowledge his emotional need; she must accept the responsibility of nurturing those feelings. He must take and retain control; she must be willing to cede power. Even if the ending presents some awareness by the couple that both are responsible for maintaining the relationship, the conservative framework within which the romance works requires the recognition that male desire still directs it. This dynamic will be found in the pages of lesbian romance, but with important differences, particularly in the ways the shifting of engagement between the couple is achieved, the balance of power in determining the progress of the relationship is determined, and emphasis on mutual erotic and emotional happiness is required. The obvious sources of these distinctions spring first from the realignment of the major characters: there is no hero, in the traditional genre sense of the term, in a lesbian romance. This is not meant to suggest, however, that one of the potential lovers does not enjoy a prominent position. Veronica Cartwright of *Accidental Love* discussed above does embody many of the qualities listed; yet, the novel's reiteration of her desire for connection from the beginning, of her constant questioning of her involvement with Rose, and of her recognition of Rose's agency represent a marked realignment of the hero's character.

The personalities of such women are powerful; since many have positions of authority, both in professional and social situations, their mannerisms are forceful and confident. Typically, this woman becomes the center of attention when she enters the scene. Her looks may be the first attraction, but her intellect, decisive action, ability to evaluate people and events quickly redirect others' first impression. In addition to Veronica Cartwright, Kennedy Nocona, Laura Kasdan, Alex Margulies, and many other characters fall into this category. However, it would be a mistake to see these women simply as the romantic hero in drag. The physical qualities of these women, of course, adhere to the romantic tradition and expectation of beauty beyond the average; these characters tend to be tall (anything over 5'10" is typical), have a thin but muscular (how developed often depending on their career), and embody an androgynous look (although they retain a strong feminine quality). The following description of Katherine Kyle, from Lynn Ames' *Price of Fame*, is representative of this figure's look:

> Katherine Ann Kyle was singular. It wasn't just the fact that she was classically beautiful, with long raven hair, piercing blue eyes, high, chiseled cheekbones, clear, lightly tanned skin, and a lithe but muscular body on a six-foot frame. It was more the unconscious way that she carried herself: strong, assured, and completely unaware of her attractiveness. She had an intangible quality that made her at once compelling and yet somehow unattainable [11].

Tall, dark, and handsome, but not masculine, this woman will never be mistaken for a man, so although she may appropriate the privileges of the masculine gender, she cannot look the part. This avoidance of giving this character a distinct butch identity marks the lesbian romance novel's clear separation from the reality of lesbian experience.

The butch represents both a look and a behavior.[8] From the moment lesbianism was formally identified and categorized, the sexologists attempted to position same-sex attraction between women within dominant social norms, leading to such identifications like the mannish lesbian, as well as the delineation of such a relationship along traditional heterosexual lines, a man and woman. One of the couple, whether she was a man trapped in a woman's body or a woman aping the look and status of the male, was automatically presumed to take on various male roles — the breadwinner, the physically aggressive partner, the protector, and the like. To be butch, therefore, required a partner who embodied the opposite characteristics — the femme. Set apart because of her appropriation of the masculine image, the butch constructed an attitude that duplicated conventional notions a male behavior. The basic facets of the butch personality demanded stoicism; it was not that the butch could not have emotions, but that she would not reveal them, especially in public. Like the stereotypical male, the butch remained cool until pushed to the breaking point; then she responded either with physical or verbal force. The butch's conversations centered on the superficial and routine — work, entertainment, gossip. Discussions of the personal would not take place, even with a lover. Intimacy, even in sexual situations, was seen as inappropriate. Once these perimeters of lesbian identity were established, the woman's connection to them became fixed; the butch could not renegotiate her social status.[9]

The butch readily became a prominent character in literature, both straight and lesbian, often included as a stock figure in mysteries, social comedies, as well as serious novels. In the proto-romance discussed in Chapter One, the butch figure has acquired an easily recognizable appearance and set of behaviors: Stephen Gordon, Molly Bolt, Bebo Brinker, all replicate a particular masculine look — short hair, men's clothing, usually in dark colors, cologne rather than perfume, no make-up or jewelry, unless a man's watch or ring — common to the time in which the novel is set. Interestingly, the butch look imitated a young male appearance, especially in the mid-twentieth century: she wore jeans and tee shirts (with cigarette pack rolled in the sleeve); she appropriated the leather jacket and motorcycle of the beatnik; she spoke with the cadence and slang of blue-collar workers. The dandyism of the sophisticated mannish lesbian of the early twentieth century became less common. Besides presenting a particular image to the public, the butch acted in accordance to accepted male models, and here, the options available to the butch fall into restrictive class categories. Traditionally, the butch moved within the working class; she preferred, or could only find, jobs that required manual labor and lived in marginal neighborhoods. Such choices not only reflected but reinforced the butch's outsider status. If she were not working class, the butch lived and moved within the upper echelons of her society; Stephen Gordon's background is landed aristocracy, which provides her the economic freedom to pursue her personal desires. While not all butch lesbians come from the upper classes, they often reflect the attitudes of that class, particularly if they pursue artistic careers. Leo in Mary Renault's *The Friendly Young Ladies* is an author and associates with other creative individuals whose positions on people and events can be called bohemian. Leo and Helen, for example, live in a Thames River houseboat and pursue their careers when necessary, presenting a sometimes cavalier attitude towards traditional social expectations. Whatever social or career position the butch represents, she is still limited in how she can express her identity by the equation of butch and male.

As Sherrie Innes notes, however, "masculinity, in short, is a set of signs that connote maleness within a given cultural moments, and masculinity is as fluid and changing as the society defining it. No one universal presentation of masculinity exists in our contemporary culture" (185). In addition, recent gender criticism emphasizes that the rigid assigning of identity categories like butch or femme has diminished as many lesbians deliberately play with the visual signs of gender, switching identity affiliation at will.[10] Manipulating gendered markers of identity represents a new method of establishing one's position within a series of social and personal environments; the individual determines how she will perform a specific set of gender behaviors depending on the impact she wishes to make. Clear lines between butch and femme become moot, since the person has taken charge of the image and its components; in fact, a woman assuming the look and prerogatives of masculinity is no longer seen as perverse or transgressive. Women in positions of authority have become as normal as women in pants. This fluidity in the representation of gendered images, however, does not readily cross over into the lesbian romance novel; even in the most recent romances, the portrait of the dominant female retains its traditional appearance, like the description of Katherine Kyle above. Such a reliance on a particular look has been seen by some critics as a caving into the demand that lesbians, if they are to be accepted in mainstream media, embody a heterosexist conception of the female body. The lesbian cannot threaten the dominance of a vision and version of beauty:

> What this emphasis on beauty does is leave in place stereotypical notions about what is attractive in women.... Nonfeminine images must be deleted or hidden, because what the magazines do not wish to convey is that other standards of beauty exist, ... Creating a stereotype of lesbian attractiveness conveys a false impression not only to heterosexual women but also to homosexual ones, who are led to believe that they, just like their heterosexual sisters, should strive to achieve the images that the magazines tout [Innes 66].

However, other critics applaud the variety in the representation of lesbians, especially given the prominent, and negative, view of all lesbians as butch.

A third possibility for the reliance on a limited range of descriptions for this figure links with the dependence of the success of the romance on the ability of the reader to see these characters as models for fantasy. The potential must exist for the reader to find some point of connection, some recognizable quality, in the portraits drawn by the author. If the characters in the story are too far removed from credibility, the reader's suspension of disbelief is nullified. These characters must be more compelling, physically as well as emotionally; after all, they represent an ideal that offers the reader an escape from the ordinary. As Krentz and Barlow in "Beneath the Surface: The Hidden Codes of Romance," assert,

> The reader trusts the writer to create and recreate for her a vision of a fictional world that is free of moral ambiguity, a larger-than-life domain in which such ideals as courage, justice, honor, loyalty, and love are challenged and upheld. It is an active, dynamic realm ... the romance writer gives form and substance to this vision by locking it in language, and the romance reader yields herself to this alternative world in the act of reading. Allowing the narrative to engage her mind and her emotions and to provide her with a certain intensity of experience [16].

So for the lesbian who typically enters the narrative at its beginning, the character who enjoys a high social and economic position, but whose emotional life is diminished, must adhere to the romantic requirement of heightened attractiveness; otherwise, the reader has no desire to follow the progress of her romantic awakening. The character's physical beauty, however, must always be subordinate to the development of her need for connection; while stunning looks may by instigate attraction, without the acknowledgement and active pursuit of intimacy, she will never attain her real desire. Many lesbian romances open with such women engaging in dramatic situations that illustrate their ability to separate the private need from public reputation, from performing life-saving emergency surgery (Lynne Norris' Alex Margulies) to rescuing a person from a burning building (Trish Shields' Andrea Khalkousa) to running the newsroom of a major television station (Maggie Ryan's Laura Kasdan).

Unlike the typical romance hero, these women, since they must operate within the dominant society, are required to negotiate their relationships in both worlds; in spite of the successes and approbation she enjoys, the lesbian is never fully accepted by her heterosexual associates. Male heroes are rarely presented worrying how others view them or wondering if their positions are valid. The male hero's dominance of his environment or the heroine may be challenged, but he does not question his right to assert such authority. Most often the pressures of maintaining her public position intrude into the private realm, interfering with the developing romance. The lesbian romance's dominant character often becomes conscious of the detriment that such a view of her social or personal value has. To counter the biases of mainstream society, she will develop a public personality that allows her to determine how she will engage with others; usually such interactions are carefully orchestrated to protect the character from being hurt. Feeling in total control, however, prevents this character from obtaining the intimacy and connection to others that she actually craves. This is a key difference between the straight hero and this lesbian, because to call her the hero misrepresents her movement from isolated figure to fully engaged lover. Traditionally, a male hero, while acknowledging that he has been separated from real emotional relationships, must be coerced, explicitly or implicitly, by the heroine's responses and behaviors towards him. In the lesbian romance, this dominant character, from the beginning of the story, is already aware of her emotional needs: "Losing Nicole in itself wasn't what was causing this pain that grew stronger as the room darkened with the setting sun. Rather, it was knowing that she had lost her battle with the inexplicable emptiness she had tried so long and hard to overcome. But living with Nicole had only provided a shallow and temporary distraction from the hollow aching feeling that now left her sobbing in the dusky shadows of her empty home" (Carrerra, *Inside Out*, 1). The cause may be the recent break-up of a relationship, the death of a partner of many years, or the belief that a permanent connection is impossible, but whatever the source for such emotional distance, this character first appears in the text maintaining a clearly defined distance. Once she becomes aware that her isolation need not continue, she actively participates in the process of her emotional recuperation. She cannot achieve this integration into an intimate relationship or into a larger community of friends without the help of the woman who will become her romantic equal.

The woman who will become the lover of the dominant character in lesbian romance cannot be identified as the traditional romantic heroine. The traditional romance heroine embodies fairly conservative social ideas about a woman's behavior and expectations; she believes that she will find the perfect romantic partner who will provide her not only with material support, but emotional and sexual fulfillment as well. She actively works for the establishment of, and commitment to, a monogamous relationship with the hero, even if a wedding does not mark that decision. She willingly cedes or reduces her autonomy for the sake of the couple. Even though contemporary heroines exhibit personalities and behaviors that seem to undermine this description, these core attributes remain. The heroine may enjoy a higher social status, pursue a successful career, be able to match the hero's intellect or verbal skill, and even retain a degree of control over the progress of the courtship than earlier heroines, but she still must acknowledge that her ultimate goal is attaining the love of the hero: this remains the heroine's ultimate desire. Without this validation of her efforts, the heroine cannot be considered complete. Obviously, this conclusion reinforces a heterosexist vision of romantic and erotic possibility.

Unlike her heterosexual counterpart, the other woman of the eventual lesbian couple engages in the development of the romance from a different position of personal awareness. That is, she generally must confront one of two dominant situations: as she discovers her attraction for the other woman, she discovers her own, true, sexual nature. Many lesbian romances incorporate this character's coming out as an intrinsic part of the romance narrative; in fact, the romance cannot succeed without this recognition and acknowledgement by the character. From *Curious Wine* to *Heart on Fire* to *Horizon of the Heart* to *Turning the Page*, this new awareness often marks the moment at which the couple is created. This moment also marks the dividing line between this woman's past — her heterosexual identity — and the acceptance of a future — her lesbian identity. Of course, most lesbian romance novels represent this awareness as positive and permanent, since is enables the character to accept and give her total commitment to another woman. The coming out is typically presented as an epiphany, the sudden coming to consciousness and articulation of a completely new self. Danni Marlowe's moment of recognition in Shelley Smith's *Horizon of the Heart* is typical:

> Dani sat on the second floor sunporch. The word lesbian came into her mind. She allowed herself to think about it, running the syllables repeatedly over her tongue.
> Les-bi-an: lover of women. Lover.
> I love a woman, she thought.
> I love Jenny.
> *I love.*
> Feeling the power of those words for the first time in her life, she cried. Tears flowed freely down her cheeks and in the darkness she felt not sorrow, but peace [167, emphasis in text].

An interesting adaptation in the coming out storyline in lesbian romance presents the dominant woman experiencing this awareness. Laura Kasdan of *The Deal* and Anna Kaklis of *Shaken* illustrate this variation in the coming out story; both of these women fit the description of the more dominant character, assuming prominent public positions, succeeding in demanding careers, although at the expense of a personal life, and possessing the standard exceptional physical attractiveness. Surprisingly for these women is the lack of any sexual component in their lives; unlike Dani Marlowe and others like her, women who have had previous heterosexual experiences, these women seem to have denied sex any place in their lives. Any hints of a sexual history are relegated to the character's past and usually viewed as something no longer necessary to her well-being. Despite their sexual appeal, to both men and women in the novel, these women seem more asexual, so the coming out opens them to intense emotional turmoil that will be eased with the acceptance not only of the identity but the intimacy that is its essential component. Therefore, unlike the traditional romantic heroine whose narrative and emotional purpose is to bring the hero to the recognition of his own emotional lack, the lesbian romance will split this movement between the couple. Laura Kasdan, for example, is shown to be surprisingly naïve with any suggestion of intimacy and panics at the thought of losing control: in her pursuit of Laura, Christine Hanson must become teacher as well as lover, showing her that such fears are harmful to Laura and their relationship. However, when Christine's career (she is a reporter for a television station who is moving to an anchor position) becomes the focus of the novel, Laura's expertise will benefit Christine's newcomer status. As the two plot lines merge, both women become more assured in their knowledge and abilities. The novel ends, not with a rapturous consummation, but with a promise to work for their mutual happiness:

> Chris reached for Laura's hand and laced their fingers together. "This is as much of a public display of affection that we can indulge in here, but I can

tell you that I love you. I can say that a million times a day and it won't even come close to expressing how much I feel the actual fact ... pardon the newspeak..."

"I want us to have a life, and I don't know how. This is one thing I can't plan for." [Laura says.]...

"We can make this work, but no secrets, no re-thinking — and no running away." [Chris responds.] [268–269].

All the typical hero must do is accept the heroine's offer.

If the other woman in the lesbian romance is already aware of and secure in her sense of self as lesbian, she will often be portrayed as the pursuer, whether the object of her desire is out or not. This presents another major realignment of the heterosexual romance; in these novels the hero generally pursues the heroine, and although the modern romantic heroine engages in the romantic quest more deliberately and actively than earlier characters, she ultimately drops her own pursuit to accommodate the hero's. Several romance writers in Krentz's essay collection *Dangerous Men and Adventurous Women* assert that the quest for the happy outcome can only be achieved when both heroine and hero ultimately share the same goal; They are complementary figures, whose conflicts actually mask their true connection: "Very early in the novel, the heroine both senses and triggers the need for love that lies within the hero. She also senses that success — mutual love — is possible.... Yet, even with insight into the hero's potential for love, love is not an easy thing to achieve.... It will take an unusual heroine to get past [the hero's] defenses long enough to show him that love strengthens rather than weakens a man" (Lowell, "Love Conquers All," 93–94). While it can be argued that the pattern of pursuit and retreat appears in straight romances as well as in lesbian novels, the key difference between the two centers on the establishment and maintenance of a balance of power between the lovers in the lesbian text. As noted above, both Laura and Christine negotiate whose desires take precedence during the development of their romance. Other couples display similar maneuvering as they work to define the nature, expression, and outcome of the courtship. Throughout *Shaken* Anna Kaklis and Lily Stewart must revise their understanding of their passion for one another as they deal with a series of challenges to their relationship, some of which, Lily's acknowledgement of her alcoholism, the taking in and eventual adoption of Lily's nephew, or Anna taking on full responsibility for the family's business, pose serious threats. What marks another difference between straight romances and lesbian ones is this attention paid to the continuation and maturing of the relationship after the initial period when passion dominates the couple's interactions. Many romances typically end with the literal and figurative consummation of the hero and heroine's desire; like most fairy tale endings, the romance does not usually follow the couple into the mundane worlds of work or home. To do so would spoil the necessary fantasy element that is essential to the romantic narrative; larger than life characters should not be re-imagined confined by the demands of the ordinary. While early lesbian romances do adhere to this more standard ending, novels from 2000 on give as much, if not more, narrative time to detailing the women's life after the emotional highs of first love. This is not meant to suggest that physical desire or erotic fulfillment disappears from their relationship since that would also break the fantasy element required of any romance.

Like the dominant partner in the lesbian romance, the other woman, whether pursued or pursuer, embodies certain physical and behavioral characteristics. She tends to be smaller in stature and presents a more typically feminine shape than her eventual partner. She is also very attractive, although her coloring usually contrasts with her lover's; blonde typically contrasts brunette. She will tend to be younger than the dominant figure, although extreme age differences are rare. Such physical characteristics obviously link this character with the typical romantic heroine, who will always be overshadowed by the hero's sheer physical presence. The heterosexual romance heroine's behavior also tends to reflect her physical limitations. In earlier straight romances, the heroine's appearance — young, blonde, buxom, the epitome of femininity — indicated her innocence and naivety; she was not only sexually inexperienced, but lacked any understanding of the world outside her limited range of relationships. These characteristics explain this particular heroine's behavior in the story, her passivity, her fear of the hero, her inability to make decisions. In fact, one of the duties of the hero in such narratives is to educate the heroine, to bring her to emotional and sexual maturity, making her a fit companion for him. More contemporary romances no longer rely solely on this version of the heroine; more often the reader encounters an already mature character: she tends to be older, already established in a career or social position, and sexually experienced. Despite the standard heroine's new assertiveness, these qualities simply add to the hero's interest and desire; attracting such a woman requires the hero's complete attention and effort, making the reward of her love that much more satisfying. The woman who becomes the romantic foil to the dominant character in the lesbian romance does present the conventional physical attractiveness necessary to spark the lover's interest. In many ways she can be said to represent a figure commonly identified as reflecting a component of the lesbian community—the femme.

The importance of the femme figure has gained in prominence in recent gender criticism.[11] This individual assumes the appearances and behaviors generally accepted as traditionally and heterosexually feminine; she looks just like any other "normal" woman; much popular media, according to Sherrie Innes, reinforces the perception "that [w]hat this emphasis on beauty does is leave in place stereotypical notions about what is attractive in women" (66). In the pulps, for instance, femmes tend to be passive, waiting for their butches to act for them. If the femme works, her choice is limited to secretary, salesgirl, and other lower level professions. Just as straight women did, the femme waited for a butch to provide her with financial and material support. Surprisingly, the one area where the femme took control in the relationship was in the bedroom; she was often the initiator of sex and determined its progression. In all other situations, however, the femme's desires were centered on supplying the butch with emotional support. However, the femme's position within the lesbian community is not restricted to being part of a couple. Even in the 1950s, many lesbians who identified as femme saw themselves as rebels, enjoying a sexual freedom not available to heterosexual women. Lillian Faderman states that while "most young lesbians went along with [accepted notions of femme roles], they actually had little intrinsic meaning for many of them. The roles might be merely the rules of the game that you followed if you wanted to be one of the players..." (*Odd Girls and Twilight Lovers*, 171). This notion of a self-consciousness in creating one's public image has become more prominent in recent gender theory, especially the idea of gender as play or performance. The key aspect of performativity is found in the deliberateness of the individual construction of a specific public representation, usually manipulating "feminine stereotypes—the little girl, the bitch, the queen, the sexpot—and making those images into your sexual language" (Faderman, *Odd Girls and Twilight Lovers*, 265–266). The femme's ability to pass as straight has also become the center of the critic's discussion of the social anxiety such a figure represents since, unlike the butch, one cannot readily determine her sexual orientation. This establishes a different kind of ambiguity in the femme's relationship with the wider society. Like the butch, her "real" identity, and the conventional associations made based on those assumptions, remains fluid; she looks like every man's romantic or erotic dream, yet she prefers the love of women. She behaves and responds in ways that reinforce traditional notions of femininity but, at the same time, pushes these boundaries by exerting unexpected dominance and control in the most intimate situations.

In the pages of the lesbian romance, the second woman of the eventual couple displays some femme characteristics — her appearance, her strongly feminine personality, and her ability to move more comfortably in straight society; in one area, however, she deviates from the femme. This woman does not manipulate an identity; the self she constructs reflects a deeply held set of beliefs and behaviors that represent an important component of the person she offers to the other woman and which becomes part of the necessary foundation for a successful courtship and eventual relationship. Frequently, this character continues the romantic pattern of complementariness found between heroine and hero; she brings skills, knowledge, and experiences that balance the other woman's abilities. However, each woman also works to maintain her individuality so that they do not become totally dependent on one another whether in material or emotional terms. In situations where the more dominant woman could easily overwhelm this character, she takes care to assert the importance of her own agency and role in the relationship. Although these efforts may appear to mimic the ceding of the traditional romantic heroine's power to the hero, this character's efforts are intended to strengthen their union: "A thousand times in the hospital she felt the strength of the bond that drew them together. Not just as lovers, but as friends. Together they had seen each other through the darkest times in their lives, survived the worst and come out stronger in spite of it all" (Norris, *Second Chances*, 423). As a result of her determination not to be overwhelmed by the dominant's woman's personality or passion, this character cannot be called the lesbian romance's heroine.

The individual qualities of heroine and hero, of course, instigate the reader's interest in and response to the romantic narrative. Also at work in romantic fiction is the maneuvering from the isolated look and response of one potential lover for the other to a shared perspective on the new configuration — the couple — and how they will project themselves to a wider community. The heterosexual couple enjoys the reader's complete support for their union since they need not fear a total rejection of how they embody the social definitions of appropriate romantic gesture; while the suitability of the hero or heroine is often seen as an initial barrier to the desired outcome, as their courtship develops what has been initially seen as potentially dangerous to one or both characters is revealed to have little influence on the outcome, since the turmoil of the story proves that these two belong together. The objections tend to fall into conventional categories: class, which often has the heroine labeled as a golddigger or opportunist; the hero may also face similar criticism; family, either hero or heroine may lack the proper social status, may have lost one or both parents, or may be illegitimate; reputation, the hero is more likely to have some mystery or scandal in his background, often connected with his professional behavior or his sexual history. The heroine's sexual past, when she is presented as a more experienced woman, may interfere with the initial stage of the romance, but usually this behavior is often shown as misinterpreted. Only the hero can enjoy the reputation of profligate as it enhances his position in the courtship and in the particular settings in which the narrative takes place. By the end of the novel, however, these barriers have been overcome. Love, after all, must been shown to embrace the seemingly irreconcilable:

> In the case of many contemporary romances that have an internal barrier that hinges on the emotional lives of the characters, the declaration of a character to herself that she loves the hero (or to himself that he loves the heroine) is as much a recognition as it is a declaration. It is part of the new information that will help fell the barrier, and in modern books, the key piece of information, the knowledge without which the book cannot go forward is "This is *love*" [Regis 44, emphasis in text].

The lesbian couples' negotiations must also account for whether mainstream society will approve or disapprove of their participation in these social codes; unlike the heterosexual couple, however, these women cannot assume a wider approval or acceptance of their relationship. The very fact that two women have determined to pursue a passionate relationship contravenes traditional social norms and expectations, and often the pressures of society will force the couple apart. This, in fact, occurs in those earlier romances discussed in Chapter One. In each case, with the exception of Rule's *Desert of the Heart* and Miller's *Patience and Sarah*, the demands that the lovers adhere to society's conceptions of proper female looks and behavior destroys or limits not only their relationships but their very lives. Although the circumstances are different, Stephen Gordon and Helen give up all claims to Mary and Leo, a decision that signals the renunciation of their relationships. Throughout the pulps the recognition that a woman's desires for another woman are called deviant challenges her very sense of self, and the institutionalization, the deaths, and the emotional and social isolation that are offered as the only possible outcome for expressing such desire indicates the terrible price for transgressing social norms. Even Molly Bolt in *Rubyfruit Jungle* is pictured alone at the end of the novel with no suggestion of finding a romantic connection. What the lesbian romance provides is the opportunity for the reader to imagine, in addition to the story of how two women can express desire for one another, the possibility of a wider recognition of their relationship. The marginalized couple becomes part of a larger and accepting community.

This clash between the social expectations of relationships and genre requirements of romance novels illustrates the ways through which popular forms effectively draw attention to such tensions. Although Thomas Wartenberg's description of the unlikely couple is based on his analysis of film, his discussion helps explain the power of continued popular literary representation to critique and challenge to assumption of the dominant social view:

> Because these films question the extent to which hierarchic social relationships are legitimate, they inevitably raise important questions about a wide range of philosophic issues: What role can romantic love play in the lives of human beings? How can individuals transform their lives to bring them more fully into accord with their sense of what is an appropriate life to live?... What is the nature of human desire? What assumptions about gender structure our sexuality? [5].

The unlikely couple represents a union of two people who should not be accorded the privilege; social pressures founded on class, race, ability, and sexuality become the social stumbling blocks for the couple's achieving success. Wartenberg identifies two points of view that work against each other as the narrative develops: the "social perspective," which identifies the couple as "inappropriate because its composition violates a social norm regulating romance," and a "romantic perspective," which places "the love the two partners share above the conventions it violates" (2). Because the genre text must achieve its expected resolution — for romance the happy ending — the potential for tragedy in this confrontation must be reconciled. This reconciliation results from the couple, despite their seeming inappropriateness, behaving in the traditional ways of lovers. Even though the lovers are both women, they speak a recognizable language that allows them to declare their passionate longing; they face public and personal challenges as they move towards a declaration of desire; they acknowledge the overarching demand that love and connection are the most important aspects of their lives. Since the majority of romance novels deal with the reconciliation of opposites and the (re)establishment of personal and communal harmony, the lesbian couple is granted the same possibility for happiness.

In September 1995 lesbians were introduced to two characters who dramatically altered the physical look, behavior, and emotional development of the romantic couple in the novel. Where previously the women would reflect a more varied range of physical types, the impact of these new models set up, surprisingly, some descriptive limitations. The following examples illustrate this: the one is a corporate lawyer who uses her success to take on pro bono cases; she is the head of the emergency trauma unit at a major hospital; she is the youngest, most productive news director for the network; she is the captain of a charter yacht. She stands taller than most women and many men, athletic yet sensual, aggressive but tender. She has jet-black hair and piercing blue eyes that can attract or repel. The other is a paralegal unwillingly involved in her firm's insurance fraud; she is an intern doing her ER rotation; she is the local station's up and coming reporter/anchor; she is a literary agent, involved in an unraveling relationship, taking a vacation. She is small but athletic, often combining an artistic ability with her career. She has golden hair and either sea or emerald green eyes that can seduce or challenge. These physical characteristics immediately cue readers to a series of situations and relationships that will develop between these characters. The prototypes for these figures are, of course, Xena and Gabrielle from the fantasy adventure series *Xena, Warrior Princess*.

From its first broadcast, *Xena, Warrior Princess* teased its audience with suggestions of more than just a friendship between its two main characters. Often deliberately, the stories would imply, even flirt, with intimate and erotic undercurrents developing between the two women. However, the show's position in mainstream television and popularity kept such behavior strictly on the level of campy innuendo.[12] While Xena and Gabrielle could play at being more than just friends, the requirements for keeping a mainstream audience prevented the relationship from crossing the boundary from play to actual romantic connection. Yet, it is this consummation that recent lesbian romance novels play out again and again. Having the two women not only openly declare their love, but initiate a physically intimate relationship can be seen as just the wish fulfillment of avid lesbian Xena fans. What is striking in the majority of recent lesbian romances, however, is the authors' insistence on incorporating what can now be seen as iconic images and characterizations, especially since the show went off the air in 2000. In fact, the frequency of Xena- and Gabrielle-based characters is so common that some texts have begun to acknowledge the references; in the 2003 *Heart's Passage*, the cell phone of one character plays the theme song from the series. "Hey, I'm a fan, all right?" (120), and it should not surprise the reader that it is the character based on Xena who states this. Like her model Jo Madison is tall with dark hair and blue eyes; she also carries herself and directs the boat's crew with assurance and skill. When difficulties arise, whether conflicts with the passengers or sudden bad weather, Jo's cool head and nerve carries the day. Cadie Jones, the Gabrielle figure in this novel, surprisingly, does not project the more active qualities of her reference; she tends to be more passive, more emotionally vulnerable as she is caught up in the political intrigue that surrounds her current lover — the first openly lesbian United States senator. Other characters modeled after Gabrielle engage more emphatically in the storylines detailed in the novels.

The first question the Xena/Gabrielle pairing raises is what is the attraction involved with this specific set of physical characteristics: There seems to be some deliberate manipulation of the butch (Xena)/femme (Gabrielle) dichotomy so familiar in much lesbian representation: tall/short, dark/blond, physically strong/verbally adept, aggressive (masculine)/ reserved (feminine). Yet, over the television series, viewers saw a transformation in Gabrielle from a passive observer and reluctant combatant to a more formidable opponent and often the dominant participant in various engagements. In the first year Gabrielle wore a long skirt and typical peasant dress; her hair was long and worn down. By the last year she was baring a well-defined body, easily seen in a costume that consisted of a much shorter skirt and "sports bra"-like top. Her hair was shorter. In addition Gabrielle's ability with weapons vastly improved. Xena's basic physical characteristics and abilities did not as radically change, but her personality became "feminized" as the series developed. Since her moral redemption was an instigating component of her travels, Xena had to learn more typical female traits, like humility, forgiveness, compromise. But Xena was never stereotypically butch either. Her frame was voluptuous; her hair was luxurious and long. The viewer always knew she was looking at a woman. By embodying contradictory physical features and emotional responses, these characters present the lesbian romance reader a stretching of standard romantic conventions.

The first adaptation is, of course, the transformation of the clearly defined roles of hero and heroine; instead of giving all — or most — of the control of the story to the male, the trajectory of the plot, dramatic and romantic, is shared between these two women. In *The Deal*, for example, much of the initiative for the eventual romance belongs to Christine Hanson, the Gabrielle-based character. She sees Laura Kasdan, finds her attractive, and determines to pursue a relationship; however, her aggressiveness is tempered when she recognizes Laura's surprising lack of intimate experience. Especially when Laura acknowledges her own attraction, Christine becomes both teacher and lover. Laura has not yielded total control of the courtship to Christine; as she becomes more comfortable and confident in her feelings, Laura is able to balance the constraints their shared profession places on them — Laura is the general manager for the news division, Christine a employee — with her growing passion. In fact, Christine must accept that Laura's greater experience in this area will protect both of them. When Carson Garret, in *The Bluest Eyes in Texas*, agrees to become the plant needed to reveal the insurance fraud in the law firm at which she works, Kennedy Nocona, the more powerful Xena figure, must give way, especially because at this point in the novel, the two have declared their shared passion and have become lovers. After the situation is resolved, Kennedy is able to assure Carson's legal and financial security with the chief partner of Garret's law firm. These revisions of the conventional romantic couple illustrate that the control of the relationship cannot belong to only one person; the power to frame the relationship and determine its progression must be shared if a truly happy outcome is to be achieved.

The second area of the romance that has been impacted by the revamping of the Xena/Gabrielle duo focuses on the personal qualities of the couple. Instead of the responsibility for the couple's private lives being placed solely in the hands of the heroine, both come to understand that the success of the relationship depends on their valuing their emotional connection. Unlike the typical romance which ends with the declaration of mutual love, the lesbian romance continues to explore the implications of that assertion beyond this ecstatic moment. Once the couple has accepted their attraction and expressed this acceptance by making love, their story is not complete. Particularly in more recent novels, the women must confront a variety of challenges that must be faced together, whether they come from work (*The Deal* or *The Bluest Eyes in Texas*), from family (*Second Chances*), from past relationships (*Heart's Passage*), or from their own emotional conflicts. In the television series Gabrielle and Xena also had to learn to accommodate one another's weaknesses, balancing their physical and emotional gaps with the other's strengths and abilities, and often a particular episode concentrated on portraying such growth at the expense of the adventure. The lesbian romance that replicates the series' character and plot configurations gives the majority of the narrative to tracing a similar movement; questions of trust, depth of feeling, willingness to adapt, and other aspects needed for building a complete relationship become the central concern of the story.

What Xena and Gabrielle give to the lesbian romance reader is a couple who, through their own passion and energy, surmount the obstacles that would thwart their success. Like their mythic counterparts, the lesbian romantic couple actively engages with the world in which they live. They must confront self-doubt and public ridicule about their developing passion; they must consciously decide to pursue private happiness at the expense of social approval; they must refuse to compromise their new identities to external pressures. In the pages of the lesbian romance novel these efforts are rewarded with the couple being able to create a relationship that promises satisfaction on the material and emotional levels; the lovers are also able to establish an environment in which they will be able to communicate their affection not only between themselves, but to a wider supportive community. Although this couple will utilize the language and gesture of mainstream society to represent the romance's outcome, this appropriation can be seen as conditional. Since there is no other language for lesbians to use to articulate their passion or its fulfillment, they must reinterpret the generally accepted meanings and implications. However, by their constant incorporation of conventional speech and behavior, the lesbian romance encourages the conceptualization that what is perceived as extraordinary — two women falling in love and promising long-lasting commitment — is actually quite ordinary: "We also need stories that tell about those aspects of our lives that we share with *all other lives*— without, however, minimizing or marginalizing the particular slant that lesbianism gives to our point of view" (Zimmerman 231, emphasis added). The romance requires a happy ending, a couple.

Chapter Four

EROTIC ACHIEVEMENT

> It is this complexity in the female experience of pleasure — the interpretation of many different kinds and intensities of stimuli to the brain as erotic, and her ability to sustain pleasure over relatively long periods of time — that helps explain both the attraction and satisfaction women find in the erotic romance. It also helps explain why romantic fiction has been such a popular entertainment medium among women...
> Carol Thurston, *The Romance Revolution*, 156

> Sara pulled Chloe closer to her, wrapping a long arm around Chloe's ribcage, and then taking her other hand, she stroked across the surface of the white slip, and their eyes met in the mirror as Sara's had dipped into the neckline, so deliberately and softly, trailing a roughened thumb and forefinger across a hardening nipple. She pinched it lightly, and then lightly again, as she watched Chloe's reflection in front of her. Chloe moaned, and Sara saw the eyes of the younger woman flutter at her touch, so she repeated it, this time just a little harder. Then all was lost...
> L. A. Tucker, *The Light Fantastic*, 438

To separate sex from romance, in the final analysis, is rather like trying to separate the oxygen and hydrogen while attempting to drink water. The definition of sex does not typically include any reference to the emotional characteristics, but romance without this physical component for many readers is unthinkable. The meaning of romance, with its emphasis on intimacy, generally assumes that the couple will share a physical as well as an emotional connection. While sex may not always be immediately anticipated within the romantic relationship, to ignore its importance to the couple's ultimate success seems impossible. Since the end goal of the romantic story is the fulfillment of the couple's desires, they must overcome any hesitancy to their total commitment to one another. Sex, then, becomes the prelude for both partners' acceptance of the responsibilities of the relationship. The willingness to engage in physical connection signifies the literal and figurative closing of the distance between the lovers. However, without the acknowledgement that sex represents only one aspect of the couple's feelings, the outcome of the story will be diminished because sex for its own sake remains ultimately a selfish act. The recognition and acceptance of the couple as a new paradigm guarantees the happy ending: "The woman can enjoy abandoned and passionate sex freely without losing anything of herself, because the act itself is elevated by the depth, power, and above all the *exclusiveness* of the couple's mutual love.... The sex act [also] leads to a rebirth for the hero. A man meets a woman, a strong, courageous, honorable woman, a heroic woman, and through the act of loving her, he is uplifted, enhanced, made complete" (Williamson. "By Honor Bound," 130–131, emphasis in text).

Surprisingly, however, most early romance novels managed to divorce the two levels of intimacy from their pages. A number of publishing and cultural factors influenced the means through which explicit sexual behavior was allowable in the pages of the novel — the perception of what the readers would tolerate, the particular moral standards that could lead to censorship, and the willingness of authors to include such material — among them. What these restrictions led to was the utilization by romance novelists of a variety of technical stratagems which allowed them to incorporate the needed sexual contact; these codes, to use Barlow and Krentz's identifier, rely heavily on a limited descriptive language that utilizes repetition, abstraction, and exaggeration. What these codes establish for the reader is a sense of familiarity; the reader, having come in contact with this language in previous novels, already knows what to expect and how to respond to the characters and their situation:

> Romantic readers have a keyed-in response to certain words and phrases (the sardonic lift of the eyebrows, the thundering of the heart, the penetrating glance, the low murmur or sigh). Because of their past reading experiences, readers associate certain emotions — anger, fear, passion, sorrow — with such languages and expect to feel the same responses each time they come upon such phrases [21, emphasis in text].

In addition to allowing the reader to identify the emotional content, this consistency also enables the reader to decode the sometimes disguised sexual subtext. Taken out of context, the sexualized language of romance seems absurd. Terms like piercing, throbbing, gripping, are connected with the hero's developing passion and represent the physical manifestation of his sexual longing; the heroine melts, swoons, and gasps, the words capturing her orgasmic release. Placed within the genre's reliance on such conventional linguistic techniques, this description provides the reader with a sense not only of familiarity, but security in that the text replicates a reading experience that keeps the reader continually seeking a re-engagement with the basic narrative fantasy of fulfilled desire.[1]

For most readers, however, the sexual content and its expression must adhere to certain social expectations about the role of sex within a relationship. Radway's analysis of the romance, which originally appeared in 1984, does emphasize the importance the Smithton readers placed on a fairly conservative and traditional concept that sexual activity only belonged in a committed relationship; it is not the sexual expression that these readers object to; it is the context in which it is expressed. They approve and applaud the creation of heroines who reveal "the open expression of sexual desire [but] *only* if it is understood as the sign or symptom of a previously existing love" (170, emphasis in text). According to Radway, these particular readers still felt that the hero must be the initiator of all sexual activity and frequently expressed their disapproval of heroines who behaved in ways they felt indicated a promiscuous personality. The date of Radway's research and analysis becomes important in considering the reader's acceptance of the presence of explicit sexual behavior and her response to it. In the three years between the publication of Radway's *Reading the Romance* and Carol Thurston's *The Romance Revolution* noticeable changes in women's ideas of and reactions to the overt sexual activity of the romance's hero and heroine appeared. Thurston notes that by the early 1980s the erotic romance novel began to appear on bookstore shelves with greater frequency and "portray[ed] a female sexuality that was no longer repressed or made obtuse and mysterious through psychoanalytic symbolism and innuendo, forbidden to the heroine by the double standard" (140). This new acceptance of explicit sexual situations is seen in language that combines the innuendo of more reticent novelistic representation as well as the descriptions of erotic situations that take a prominent position within the narrative.[2] In addition, the heroine was now permitted to initiate the sexual activity without being seen as promiscuous.

This increasingly common incorporation of a more intense and, sometimes, graphic sexual content opens up the traditional heterosexual romance to questions of the implications this activity has for the narrative itself. Is sex an absolutely necessary attribute to the courtship's success? What does the willingness of the couple to engage in sex as well as their expectations of their performance indicate about their compatibility? Is the sex a signifier of mutuality, an important attribute of the couple for many critics, or is it still an indicator of the couple's uneven power relationship?[3] The actual depiction of sex varies in the pages of the typical romance novel; often the couple's passions are presented escalating as their desire for union begins to dominate all of their thoughts and actions. However, because of publisher requirements the final bedroom scene is left to the reader's imagination, although the expectation of physical intimacy is clearly indicated. Surprisingly, the frequency of sexual behavior does not, according to Thurston, appear to have a negative influence on the perception of the characters, particularly the heroine; in fact, many contemporary romances show her as not only the instigator of sex, but as thoroughly enjoying it (103). The sex, however, remains situated within an understanding by the couple of the exclusiveness of their relationship; whatever relationships they may have participated in before their meeting, the couple assumes an acceptance and commitment to monogamy once they have become lovers: "Once the hero and heroine meet, even the thought of any relationship with another partner, no matter how brief or superficial, [is] quickly eliminated...," (Thurston 103). Before the sex occurs the couple generally declares their love for one another, thereby placing the act of sex within the traditional framework that allows both, but especially the heroine, to display sexual passion: "The ideal romance persists in maintaining on an overt level that loving commitment is the proper condition for complete sexual fulfillment" (Radway 170). No matter how sexually adept the lovers may be, they must both willingly abandon any hint of satisfying their physical needs outside of the relationship.

But, having committed to one another, the lovers are free to indulge their physical longings as long as both achieve complete satisfaction: "Sex is depicted as a healthy, rapturous communion between two adults. No one partner is supposed to get more out of it than the other. When the experience isn't shared equally, it is considered a failure, a conflict that requires resolution" (Arnold, "Women Do," 138). Fulfillment refers, of course, more to the emotional connections that are established through physical contact than having orgasms. However, the hero's prowess as a lover reflects his masculinity; he must be capable of providing her with the sense that her total happiness is his responsibility in all areas of the relationship. The heroine, after all, has risked a great deal by the offering of her sexual self; if the heroine is a virgin, the consequences of sex include the possibility of pregnancy, the potential social ostracism, but more importantly, by having sex, the heroine opens herself to the hero's rejection. She has put herself in a vulnerable position which has the real potential to destroy her. The early critics of romance often framed this threat as a conflation of the hero's acting on his desire for the heroine and rape.

The dilemma of the romance, as Radway describes it, centers on presenting the aggressive, even violent, behavior of the hero as something that the heroine ultimately realizes and accepts as necessary to her emotional and sexual maturity (141–143). Romance writers confront this concern by emphasizing the developing emotional relationship that eliminates the danger and aggression. Although she may not be able to articulate her needs, the virginal romantic heroine does instinctively realize that she has such longings and that the hero is the deserving recipient of them: "Virginity is a gift that can only be given *once*, and it is ideally bestowed on a woman's great love. This giving of virginity adds an immeasurable element of drama and power to a story. It changes the heroine, of course, but in romance novels it also changes the hero" (Malek "Loved I Not Honor More," 118).

It is the hero whose transformation becomes of major concern for writers and readers of the modern romance novel, even more so than the heroine's. Whatever the motivation for his sexual behavior towards the heroine, his response to her marks a reformation of behavior that was previously perceived as dangerous and the reawakening of his more sensitive nature. Typically he is described as emotionally distant, his forceful personality and behavior masking a fear of being hurt. Rather than allow his more sensitive nature to be seen, the hero works to prevent the heroine's discovery of this sensitivity. However, for the romance to end happily, the hero must come to accept his need to express all of his feelings; unless he is willing to learn and accept the healing power of love, the hero will never find complete satisfaction. The heroine becomes the facilitator of these changes in him through her willingness to risk her security and cede her independence to him. Of course, the paradox of the romance defines this relocation of power as a gain for the heroine and for the couple. Often, in fact, the hero's discovery of the heroine's virginity instigates his changing understanding of her value; his discovery that her protestations of innocence were not just a ploy to entrap him forces him to acknowledge the sacrifice she has made in giving herself to him (see Thurston 104–105). Her sexual awakening not only brings the hero to a new understanding of the importance of acknowledging the emotional component of the relationship, but it frees her to accept her own sexual need and encourages her to express those desires.

When the heroine is presented as a more mature woman, and one who comes into the narrative with sexual experience, she faces the dilemma of how the hero will view that awareness. Often she will be accused of using sex to trap him, putting him into a vulnerable position because of his physical desire. Despite the power given to the male, surprisingly his dominance is easily contained through the heroine's awareness of the power of sexual drives. For many modern romance novelists, the heroine's greatest strength lies in her understanding of the transformative power of sex: "The power is in the woman's hands—*she* does the choosing of her mate and *she* maintains control over him through her heroism and her irresistible sexuality, which remains forever unsullied and therefore of value no matter how many times she participates in the sex act" (Williamson 131, emphasis in text). Her passion, freely given, awakens the hero's finer self and lets him acknowledge his own deeper desires. If the heroine is not seen as a blackmailer or golddigger, she uses her sexuality as a way to protect herself from emotional vulnerability. Often a previous relationship has proven destructive to her sense of self and has made her question her abilities in both public and private behavior. The most devastating loss is her sense of trust not only in the wider world, but in her ability to articulate her own desires and her skill in achieving them. Sex with the hero restores the heroine's psychological equilibrium, enabling her to recover a sense of connection and belonging that will guarantee the couple's success.

Of course, there is a clear line drawn that separates appropriate sexual behavior from pornographic description. While readers applaud and approve a heroine who is willing and capable of taking the initiative in sexual matters, they disapprove of heroines whose "formal attachment to [the hero] at the end seems more a capitulation or a surrender to uncontrollable sexuality than a triumph effected by her ability to transform him into an emotionally expressive individual" (Radway 171). Likewise many readers show a strong distaste for heroes who use sex as a means of punishing the heroine. Some readers enjoy the ability of the heroine and hero to engage in less conservative sexual practices, like fellatio or cunnilingus, but they do not express interest in either character demanding such acts repeatedly in the story. Nor do readers appear to enjoy highly explicit sexual language, preferring the more coded descriptions; however, "euphemisms do nothing to impede readers' understanding of what is going on..." (Thurston 142–143). This paradox seems to allow the reader to enjoy the sexual freedom engaged in by the couple while at the same time maintaining a public allegiance to conservative moral ideals and cultural views of women's appropriate behavior.[4] The heroine cannot enjoy sex too much or actively seek out sexual pleasure for its own sake or her own fulfillment; the hero may use his sexual prowess to overwhelm the heroine, but he must abandon such behavior at the moment of his recognition of the heroine's true feelings for him. These points of awareness in the plot signal the containment of sex and its positioning within a secure social environment. Sex without restraint crosses the line into pornography.

Do lesbian romance novels portray the sexual component of the narrative differently from heterosexual ones? In many ways the incorporation of sexual intimacy functions in the same manner within the pages of the lesbian romance as mainstream stories. The couple desires the intensity of physical connection, since it signifies the moment of recognition of a mutual attraction and commitment between the lovers. Sexual passion and expression parallels emotional desire and articulation. Just as heterosexual romances do, lesbian novels present a range of situations: sex can become a weapon used to thwart the desire for a beneficial relationship, often becoming a way to manipulate the feelings of others; a means for one woman to separate herself from deeper emotional connections by her developing a reputation as sexually profligate; the means through which one woman will realize her lesbian identity; the representation of the couple's final and total acceptance of their relationship. Unlike its heterosexual counterpart, however, the lesbian romance must contend with a mainstream essentialist view of the lesbian: the equation of sexual identity with sexual practice. [5] The straight romantic couple need not limit their intimate behavior only to sexual practice, neither do they need to worry that the wider community with which they interact will characterize their relationship only as a sexual one. Most importantly, the couple has the ability and freedom to reframe the way they will be acknowledged and dealt with by others. Although the romance traditionally ends with the couple concentrating on their private lives, the narrative implies their eventual integration into some social setting. As stereotypically defined by heterosexual culture, the lesbian's sexual behavior becomes the sole marker of her identity, restricting her personal and private behavior to one kind of intimate expression. It is sex, and sex alone, that identifies the lesbian as a person; obviously the refusal of the wider society to recognize the full humanity of a lesbian forces her to the periphery of the dominant culture. The lesbian romance novel, recognizing this dilemma of belonging, utilizes a range of narrative situations not so much to ameliorate the gulf between the two communities, but to offer the lesbian reader another version of the fantasy that underlies the romantic quest.

The lesbian romance, as indicated above, incorporates certain standard representations of sexual intimacy between the lovers, particularly the desire of both partners to discover their compatibility with one another. Just as in the heterosexual romance, this realization comes with the discovery that in spite of seemingly insurmountable differences the lovers are truly meant for each other; they bring complementary ideas and behaviors to the new relationship that allow them to become "equal partners in every way, [who] will live out their life together" (Donald, "Mean, Moody, and Magnificent," 83). However, before the couple reaches this point, each woman must first come to terms with her lesbian sexuality; this moment of recognition will take several forms the first, and frequently incorporated into the narrative, centers on the traditional coming out epiphany where one of the women will acknowledge herself as lesbian for the first time. Coming out remains the essential marker of an individual's new awareness of her orientation; however, to claim a lesbian identity does not require a woman to have sex with women. In her study of gay and lesbian relationships Betty Berzon devotes a chapter describing the six stages that an individual moves through as she comes to identify herself as lesbian; the primary focus of the process centers on the means through which the woman becomes aware of a feeling of difference from the heterosexual mainstream; her responses to the articulation of this new identity, including moving between acceptance and rejection; and her eventual integration of a balanced view not only of herself, but the wider society (50–60). Lesbian romantic fiction cannot claim to represent such a process in an accurate clinical or theoretical manner; however, the characters who do come out because of their initial attraction to the other woman do experience a shift in their perception of attraction, belonging, and passion. They also come to understand that this new self-awareness will have sometimes serious repercussions, including rejection by family and friends, loss of social status, and potential violence. However, since these are romances, the isolation proves to be temporary as those closest to the character readily accept her newfound identity. Those who don't are quickly removed from the story so that the couple may seal their relationship.

The novels offer a number of variations of this situation, usually centered on the woman who is in the process of re-evaluating her life and her needs, although at the early stage of the narrative, she cannot explicitly articulate what those needs or desires are. Heather O'Brian, in *Class Reunion*, typifies this woman; coming to the high school reunion that sets the romance in motion, Heather intends to put to rest her memories of an unspoken attraction for Jennifer Moreland, who came to her defense when Heather was being teased by a group of boys. Over the weekend, however, her feelings become stronger, and she finally declares her unacknowledged desire for Jennifer: "This wasn't supposed to happen. You were supposed to be living happily in New York with your lover, and I was supposed to feel absolutely no attraction to you whatsoever. I wanted to be able to look you in the eye and say to myself, See, it was nothing. That crush you had all those years ago was nothing more than that" (117). Her intention to deny her earlier feelings is completely overturned with Jennifer's announcement of a similar desire; before the two can bring their romance to its happy outcome, however, they must deal with Jennifer's past sexual relationship with Shelia. After several tense confrontations, including the possible separation of the reunited couple, Heather and Jennifer reconcile, and the novel ends with the couple, still together after ten years, dealing with the ordinary issues of finding time to be together, planning for a child's college education, and deciding how to balance work and home life. In another version of this scenario Melanie Larson, in Georgia Beers' *Turning the Page*, is presented as dissatisfied with her life and, using her sister's marital problems and her company's merger as the reasons, decides to leave Chicago and take over a bookstore in Rochester, New York. There she meets Taylor Rhodes and finds herself immediately drawn to the younger woman. This attraction, of course, parallels the standard romantic convention of love at first sight between the destined couple, and Taylor also responds to Melanie's beauty and character. Unlike Heather, Melanie reveals no previous crush on or involvement with another woman; she does admit to sexual fantasies that include women, indicating if not a predilection for same-sex engagement, a curiosity. Later in the novel, Melanie questions her lack of any previous sexual experience once she realizes she is becoming attracted to Taylor. The novel implies that she has put her professional life ahead of a private one. Melanie's growing interest in Taylor, however, is complicated by Benjamin Rhodes' own attraction to Melanie. Seeing her father interested in Melanie, and believing she will reciprocate his advances over hers, Taylor at some points hesitates to show her feelings, while at others she deliberately woos Melanie as her father's rival.

As the story continues, Melanie becomes more relaxed in her interactions with the various inhabitants of the small social circles in which she moves. The harried company executive gives way to an independent bookstore owner who follows her own interests in developing the business, even if the decisions go against sound business practice. This letting down of her professional guard impacts her personal life, as she gets to know the other business owners close to her store and actively wishes to establish a relationship with Taylor. At first all Melanie looks for is friendship, but Taylor's focused wooing infiltrates Melanie's subconscious awareness. At the key moment,

> She was unaware that Taylor was only inches behind her and when she turned, they ran right into one another. Their faces were barely two inches apart, their eyes level since Melanie was standing on a step. They stood frozen.
>
> Taylor dropped her gaze to Melanie's full lips and when the older woman wet the bottom one nervously with the tip of her tongue, it was all over [132].

Melanie's immediate reaction surprises her: "I kissed Taylor and enjoyed every second of it.... And I want to do it again" (137). Melanie must deal with the implications of her discovery over the course of the novel including how to deal with Benjamin's feelings, as well as what her own family will do. Throughout this process of coming to understand these new emotions and desires, Melanie is surrounded by a supportive community of other women, many of them lesbians, who help her interpret her feelings. Her lack of specific sexual experience does not hinder she and Taylor building a successful relationship; in fact, even though she is younger than Melanie, Taylor, an out lesbian, is able to provide a secure environment in which Melanie can become sexual.

The inclusion of some previous same-sex attraction that one of the characters has experienced, which ranges from an intense crush on another woman or some level of physical intimacy, is more typical in lesbian romances However far removed that initial desire was for the character, she retains some memory of a passionate longing for connection to another woman. If the woman has not experienced actual emotional longings, she is described as never having found any kind of fulfillment, whether emotional or sexual, from a male lover: "Intuitively, she had never expected so much from the men she dated.... It seemed only possible from another woman. She had found bits and pieces and interludes, some with her mother and some with her sister and her college friends.... Now for the first time in years she felt compelled to try again" (Martin *Love in the Balance*, 20). Connie Bradford has just met Kasey Hollander, a new client, and realizes a hope for some relationship, although at this point in the narrative she has no exact name for it. The reference to this character's earlier sense of needing or of having had a connection to another woman to feel complete suggests that lesbian romance novelists may be countering the stereotype of the innocent heterosexual woman pursued by a predatory lesbian. This image appeared in many of the pulp novels of the 1950s, reflecting the dominant social view of the lesbian as not only perverse, but dangerous, and generally this figure had to be destroyed — literally as well as figuratively — in the narrative: the institutionalization of Leda Taylor in *Spring Fire* or Lorraine Harris' acceptance of her arrest for the murder of Sassy Gregg in *Twilight Girl*. Characters in contemporary lesbian romances have already abandoned their ties to heterosexuality, often before the particular story begins. She may resist her attraction and initially reject the desire of the other woman, but this character ultimately achieves two desires: the discovery of love and, perhaps more importantly, the recovery of her true self. In many of these romances, the declaration that "she was in love with Samantha"; that "I'm in love with Jenny and I know she loves me"; that "you actually make me feel a bit brave and crazy ... [and] it means I love you and I don't think we should uphold the status quo," marks the point at which this character achieves completion.[6] What drives this character to take the risk of admitting and accepting her passion for another woman is the first time they connect physically.

Once the couple has recognized the pull of desire, they actively seek to satisfy those feelings; sometimes this means an immediate move to the bedroom, although many times this degree of intimacy so quickly realized proves a setback rather than the foundation to the eventual happy ending. Frequently one of the couple acts because she has let her guard down (Hobie Allen of *Rebecca's Cove*) or she has drunk enough to act on her sexual urges (Johanna Marshall in *One Summer Night*) or she indulges in sex in order to release her frustration (Gretchen Kaiser of *Too Close to Touch*). In each case, the sex provides no positive outcome as the women generally face embarrassment or dissatisfaction afterwards. Not surprisingly, these feelings of regret or revulsion are more pronounced when the two women who have just had sex discover that they are the perfect complement each has wished for. Hobie and Johanna spend much of the narratives dealing with their anger while at the same time longing to repeat the experience. The conflict centers on these characters' awareness of the distinction between having sex and making love; the women with whom they have originally slept with — B. J. Warren and Kelly Sambino — are presented as arrogant, aggressive in their social as well as sexual interactions, and selfish by placing their own satisfaction above anyone else. Yet, these qualities are also what attract Hobie and Johanna to them; each negative characteristic represents a positive way for B. J. and Kelly to engage with the wider world by enabling them to overcome personal and public limitations on their abilities and ambitions. Like the traditional male romantic lead, such flaws entice the eventual lover to chance her emotional safety because, ultimately, these characters have the ability to help in the transformation of the other's view of sex into one that emphasizes its nurturing qualities. Dawn Heinecken identifies this understanding of the role of sex in the romance as "good" sex, which "involves love and tenderness and complete reciprocity of feeling between the hero and heroine" (170). Characters, like B. J. and Kelly, have used their sexual ability to set clear limits on their relationships; before they can be rewarded with the appropriate partner and the happy ending, they must come to realize that sex must be freely given and received.

Not all characters in the lesbian romance need to confront the basic issue of their sexual orientation; many have already acknowledged their orientation and have had previous sexual experiences and romantic relationships. Obviously, in the coming out storyline, the more experienced character will be the one to initiate the sexually naïve woman into the pleasures of sex. In this way, she duplicates the traditional romantic hero whose sexual knowledge and ability contribute to the heroine's paradoxical responses of attraction and fear. Unlike the romantic hero, who, traditionally, uses his sexual power to overwhelm the heroine's resistance and dominate her will, the more experienced lesbian in her romance will behave more as the teacher: "Taylor knew this was Melanie's first time with a woman, and therefore let her find her own way around, trying hard not to direct her in any way" (*Turning the Page*, 232). There is typically no threat to the uninitiated woman to her sense of well-being, although this character may feel threatened by her intense emotional and physical responses to the other's desire. Of course, not all novels describe the first sexual encounter in such gentle terms; often the passionate feelings of both women overwhelm them. First kisses and touches quickly lead to entwined naked bodies. The intensity of the first experience drives both women to continue to explore the relationship illustrating their desire to re-experience those initial passions. This hope provides the underpinning of the characters' efforts to overcome the various obstacles standing in the way of this shared goal. Sexual satisfaction becomes the sign of emotional fulfillment, and as the lovers discover their mutual longing for permanence, their sexual practice becomes more intense. In some lesbian romances sex scenes do become more frequent and take up more pages in the text, sometimes to the point of reducing plot development. In some romantic novels, lesbian or straight, the line between erotic description and exaggeration bordering on the pornographic becomes blurred.[7]

Not surprisingly, most descriptions of sex in the pages of lesbian romances offer the reader much more detail about what the women are doing in the bedroom. Here, lesbian texts differ noticeably from heterosexual ones. Although contemporary traditional romances will describe the sex between the hero and heroine in explicit language, these scenes tend to be brief and limited in frequency, and the emphasis is geared more to the emotional build-up and release than the physiological: "Within the act of sex itself, the emotional states of the hero and heroine are in a constant process of transformation. Sex is thus no longer a mere physical act, but is understood to be an expressive form of communication, signaling things that are outside of the physical act itself" (Heinecken 168). While the same focus on the emotional climax appears in lesbian romances, the importance of the couple having sex is highlighted through the detailed portrayals of their sexual scenes. Many novels give particular attention to the first time the women make love, lingering over images of hands and lips moving over their bodies, paying attention to every nuance of desire expressed in the lovers' passion-soaked voices. Later scenes of love-making may either continue the pattern of extended description or discretely close the door on the couple. When the women have their first sexual encounter plays an important role in the development of their romance. The moment when the couple discover and act on their mutual passion may occur early in the romance, but more commonly, the first lovemaking takes places well into the narrative, at least one-third the way through the story. This allows both women time to evaluate their personal feelings, to articulate to each other their fears and hopes, and to reconcile the views and expectations of others. Of course, passion will overcome the couple's attempts to understand and quantify their attraction; Joke Hermes, in her essay "Sexuality in Lesbian Romance Fiction," points out that heterosexual romances "recognize two kinds of knowledge: intellectual and emotional," and even though Hermes claims that lesbian romances emphasize trying to intellectually defend lesbian love at the expense of the emotional, many lesbian writers do, in fact, let feeling determine the course and outcome of the couple's relationship (60). Sometimes this scene will be delayed until the last pages of the novel, representing the literal as well as narrative climax of the relationship. If the couple's sexual passion is documented throughout the novel, the descriptions move between the explicit and the suggestive; again, many stories end with the expectation of sex, not just the immediate coupling that may signify the couple's reunion, but also conveying the promise of the relationship's maintaining of their strong sexual desire. As in heterosexual romances, the sexual drive does not fade away; even after ten years Jennifer and Heather of *Class Reunion* are still able to feel the same sexual tension and longing:

> Jen held her tightly, a soft smile hovering on her lips as she thought of the past. "Do you remember the first time we made love?"
> "Of course." Heather alternately nibbled and kissed Jen's neck. "It was right in that room." She nodded toward the open doors that led to the bedroom.

Jennifer smoothed back the hair on Heather's brow, then let her hands begin to wander. *No matter how familiar she was with her lover's body, she never tired of the feel of her smooth skin beneath her fingers* [160–161, emphasis added].

The depiction of sex for characters, like Kelly Sambino and B. J. Warren, who initially use sex as a way to enhance their reputations tends to be limited; the sex is nothing more than a way to enhance a public image that both have deliberately crafted. Sexual attractiveness and ability provide both a certain status that, as the novels take care to show, cannot satisfy their real longing for connection. Since both of these women will become part of their novel's primary romantic couple, their initial sexual behavior must eventually be seen as a false representation of their attitudes towards sex. Throughout *Rebecca's Cove* B. J. is placed in situations that challenge and overturn her sometimes inflated idea of her own importance and status. Her expectations about what will happen during her time on the island of Ana Lia are continually undermined as her urban, sophisticated notions of social relationships prove unworkable in the small, somewhat insular community. Like many mainstream romantic heroes, B. J. must reveal the gentleness and insecurity that have made her erect the domineering exterior she presents at the beginning of the novel. As she and Hobie become closer, B. J. begins to recognize depths of emotion she believed she was no longer capable of feeling: "Baylor was surprised at how natural it felt to be lying there with Hobie. There wasn't any of the usual discomfort related to sleeping in the same bed with someone for the first time. *We must be meant to be,* she though just before she drifted off to sleep again" (206, emphasis in text). Importantly, although the couple is sleeping together at this point, they do not make love; the dominant emotions are comfort and acceptance. Unlike the typical romantic hero, though, once Baylor's defenses have been breached, she abandons her earlier behaviors and welcomes the establishment of a new vision of intimacy offered by Hobie's reciprocal affection. In the chapter "The Ideal Romance" Radway explains that even though the romantic heroine is able to breach the hero's defenses, he retains his embodiment of "masculinity as total autonomy. The hero is permitted simply to graft tenderness onto his unaltered male character. The addition of the one, the romance implies, need not transform the other" (148). B. J. eagerly accepts that her previous separation from real emotional connections has damaged her ability to enjoy life. *Rebecca's Cove* ends with Hobie and B. J. settled into the relaxed rhythms of Ana Lia.

Similarly, Kelly Sambino, in *One Summer Night*, has decided to accept the public perception that she is sexually promiscuous, which becomes the main obstacle that must be overcome if her and Johanna Marshall's eventual romance is to succeed. Johanna brings her own fears into their relationship which also interferes with its development, and the novel follows their ongoing efforts to resolve these tensions. The women's emotional desires become intertwined with their sexual passions; they frequently will have sex, using physical intimacy to reflect or engage deeper feelings, at the expense of confronting those emotions, which drives them further apart. Yet, Kelly, supposedly the person who is incapable of taking any relationship seriously, is the one who recognizes the harmful influence this confusion of motive has on their efforts to create a relationship:

> "I can't believe you," Kelly whispered. "If you want to think that last night meant nothing, that it was just about sex, well, that's fine."
> She walked away from Jo, then stopped. "I guess you're right. There's not anything between us. My mistake for thinking that there could be," she said bitterly. "You've got to have trust in a relationship, any kind of a relationship, and we don't have that. I'm not so certain any more that we can even be friends, much less lovers" [118].

For most of the novel the women's sexual encounters express desperation more than consummation, especially since Johanna is unable to acknowledge that she loves Kelly. Her past rejection by a previous lover has shaped her outlook on romance and prevents her from articulating the depth of her longing for Kelly. In spite of her growing emotional attachment and desire for Kelly, Johanna seems unable to imagine them outside of a purely sexual relationship. Their interactions, however they begin, end with the couple having sex, but every outcome presents a stalemate. Even during the most intense moments of lovemaking, Johanna cannot, will not, say what she feels. To be able to speak the words, I love you, marks Johanna's point of breakthrough; until that moment, she has remained emotionally frozen. Only when their separation seems permanent can Johanna finally say out loud that she loves Kelly, and at that moment, sex is transformed.

Having sex represents the point at which the couple takes deliberate action to establish the relationship. Sex is no longer seen as a gauge of individual ability or power; instead, the couple must relinquish any claim to separate control or satisfaction. Until they reach this understanding, that passion and its expression must be mutual, the women will not achieve their ultimate goal. Controlling the movement towards having sex and the manner in which physical passion will be expressed is usually seen as the responsibility and prerogative of the hero. Even if the heroine knows her own depth of passion, she usually waits for the man to instigate their lovemaking, and by her acceptance of his right to take charge of this most important moment in the romance, the heroine guarantees her position not only within this particular and private relationship, but also within the wider community. Her acceptance of her subordinate position assures the continuation of a conservative social construct of female and male roles: this resolution, according to Radway, teaches the romance's readers "about the nature of patriarchy and its meaning for them as women, that is, as individuals who do not possess power in a society dominated by men. Not only does the romantic drama evoke the material consequences of refusal to mold oneself in the image of femininity prescribed by the culture but it also displays the remarkable benefits of conformity" (149). Krentz and the other novelists collected in *Dangerous Men and Adventurous Women* continually stress that the real power in the sexual arena belongs to the heroine through her ability to withhold sexual gratification from the hero; however, once she yields her body to his passionate demands, the heroine relinquishes her control of the outcome of that passion.

Lesbian romances rely on the understanding in both women that giving in to physical desire for its own sake may harm, even destroy, the sought for connection; simply having sex undermines the mutuality that is essential for the partnership to succeed. One woman controlling the purpose and outcome of sex indicates that she is unable or unwilling to imagine the possibility of a more substantial relationship: Joanna Holbrook-Sutherland of *Cold* and Carolyn Black of *Course of Action* represent this position. However, since the novels in which they appear center the narrative on their redemption, both of these characters will discover the damage such an attitude has done to them. When these women realize the negative impact of their behavior and actively work to correct it, they have achieved an important awareness, that their private behavior cannot be based on an immature understanding or articulation of want. Suzanne Juhasz asserts that the "story to be told in women's romance fiction is one of maturation, as much as love, for love and self-development prove to be aspects of one another. The complications and difficulties that the relationship occasions provide as well the opportunity for self-development" ("Lesbian Romance Fiction and the Plotting of Desire" 74). Once this self-awareness is achieved and, more importantly, accepted, these women are able to find ways to build a successful relationship with the women who will become their romantic conclusion. Of course, not all lesbian romances frame the storyline in this manner; more typical is the couple's increasing awareness that they must find the right balance of controlling and being controlled, of dominance and acquiescence if their relationship is to become permanent.

This merging of intention is illustrated in the novels, first, through the women developing an appreciation for one another's strengths and weaknesses of character. In novels that chart the development of the romance over an extended period, this understanding comes gradually. Throughout L. A. Tucker's *The Light Fantastic*, Chloe and Sara meet and separate and meet again, each time learning more about one another's experiences and expectations. Both women must distance themselves from preconceived ideas of what the other thinks, feels, and wants, and both must accept their own limitations and flaws before they can find the happiness each seeks in the other: "[Sara] stopped in front of [Chloe] and gave her a small smile, projecting her love through her gaze, and waited for Chloe to answer her in some way. Chloe turned away and took a step toward the house, and then stopped, and looked back at Sara, and nodded. The two of them walked their way across the green grass, heading toward the warmth that lay ahead, leaving the cold night behind them" (330). Interestingly, this scene does not occur at the end of the novel as a reader would expect. Chloe and Sara will still have to negotiate the ramifications of their courtship, especially since it occurs within a community of interested friends and neighbors who are just as concerned with Sara and Chloe's happy ending as they are. Obviously, the couple's opportunities to enjoy the physical side of their developing relationship will have to accommodate the various demands of daily life as well as the supportive and potentially harmful interruptions of others. But, since their story is a romance, Sara's and Chloe's desires will be allowed to find fulfillments.

The second way the realignment of power in the couple's relationship is presented is in the even balance of the giving and receiving of sex. Proportionally in the love scenes each woman takes the opportunity to instigate sex and to control its progress. Each is also able to cede this dominance to the other woman and allow her to direct the progress of the lovemaking without feeling imposed upon or coerced. The reciprocity of sexual performance reinforces the couple's recognition of their reliance on one another to provide the needed sense of completeness that the romantic plot has traced. The level of sexual experience each woman brings to the relationship influences how she will contribute to this aspect of the courtship. Those characters who are in the process of coming out usually reveal a surprising lack of sexual knowledge, even those who have been previously married. In such cases the sexual component of these relationships has been abusive (Grace Davanzo's marriage in *Heart on Fire*) or non-existent (Margaret Paige's in marriage of convenience in *Up, Up and Away*). In several novels, the woman in the process of coming out has had a child, clearly indicating sexual experience, although the marriage has not provided the emotional satisfaction this woman desires. Often the husband's presence is removed through death or divorce. There are a few novels, however, that bring the husband's reaction to his wife's emerging sexuality into the story; that response is usually violent, as in the marital rape that occurs in Forrest's *An Emergence of Green*. Most often, though, characters whose coming out initiates their romantic longings have not been able to develop successful or fulfilling relationships, so they enter the story unattached.

Lack of connection does not mean lack of desire for these women; in fact, as the romance develops, they reveal a clear awareness of a lack, that only by coming out can they identify:

> "But Kay, you're straight! You were married, for God's sake!"
> "Oh, Rose, I only married Billy Ray because Jackie was gone. Don't you see? I didn't know what I felt then, I couldn't put a name to it." Kay paced across her living room, trying to put words to her jumbled thoughts. "Not even when I found out Jackie was a lesbian. I never thought that label applied to me" [Hill, *Behind the Pine Curtain*, 261].

This declaration can occur at the ending of the romance, as the above example does, and traces the character's shifting emotional responses to this growing awareness. The reader follows her initial rejection of such feelings, fear of being identified as a lesbian, hesitancy in coming to understand her feelings, and finally wonder and joy at the discovery of love. The character can also come to this realization earlier in the novel, and instead of dealing with the questions and implications of her new understanding, she is able to share the coming out with the woman who has brought her to this moment. The confrontation between the two women reflects a range of emotion — from direct challenge to coercion to astonishment. Whatever expression the declaration takes, both women take responsibility for the coming out to lead to the consummation, both physical and emotional, they both desire, as the following extended scene from Maggie Ryan's *The Deal* indicates:

> Laura hopped out of the doorless Jeep and followed the reporter up to the porch of her house.... "Is this the part where I kiss you goodnight and tell you that I'll call you later?" Laura wasn't too nervous; after all, it was dark, and darkness could hide a multitude of sins. *Or clumsiness.*
> "You could do it that way, or I could just kiss you." Chris took one of Laura's hands and laced their fingers together, but didn't step any closer.
> "I think I'd like that," came the soft answer ... [Chris] reveled in the tentative softening of Laura's lips and reminded herself to go slow.
> *It's different from the last one,* Laura thought. *More needy?* She pulled away slowly and Chris looked at her, puzzled.

> "I don't know what to do with my hands," Laura whispered.
> Chris couldn't hide a smile. "Anything you want." [After a passionate kiss] Laura stepped away, her hands falling to her sides. "I'm ... going ... now." Her breath hitched and she backed up, nearly tripping down the steps before catching herself. "Tomorrow ... okay?"
> Chris watched in a stupor as Laura stumbled away to climb into her Jeep and drive off, stalling the engine twice before she reached the corner. *I've just been kissed senseless by a rank amateur* [130–131].

At this point in the novel Chris and Laura have admitted an attraction, but Laura's fears of intimacy and lack of experience have determined how Chris will work to bring about her desired outcome. Although their personalities suggest that Laura would be the aggressor in all aspects of her public and private behavior, she has deliberately avoided creating any kind of interior, emotional life. Chris, therefore, becomes the pursuer, but she also understands Laura's hesitancy and refuses to take advantage of Laura's innocence. This restraint is particularly important, since Laura is the general news director at the station where both women work, although, as in the situation of the lovers in *The Light Fantastic*, the rest of the news division actively roots for the romance's success.

Once the couple has become intimate, the novels chart the ways in which they manage desire and its physical expression. As would be expected, passion frequently overwhelms the women when they meet. Usually these feelings will first be expressed by surreptitious glances or excuses to be close to the one another; often "accidental" touches will call up extreme physical reactions, sudden intakes of breath, shivers, and racing heartbeats, all traditional signals of rising desire. Sometimes the object of one of the main character's interest is unaware of the turmoil she creates for the other, and it is only the direct comment of another character, most likely a friend of one or both of them, who brings these behaviors to her notice. However the initial recognition scene is played out, once mutual desire has been acknowledged, the couple must negotiate its impact on each woman individually, as well as on them as a couple. Since the purpose of the romance centers on the delineation of the discovery of being capable of loving and being loved, each woman needs to be both assertive and receptive in articulating what she wants from the other. This reciprocity is seen during lovemaking, as each woman takes turns being the instigator of the sex and directs how the other will achieve orgasm. The novels utilize the clichéd requests for knowing that a partner has been satisfied: "How was it for you? Did I please you? What would you want/like me to do? Can we do it again?" Since the proper pairing of lovers has been accomplished, this satisfaction is ensured as the narrative works towards its conclusion, and an important part of that satisfaction is the new-found awareness that each woman is not only an ardent lover, but one capable of giving and receiving.

Wherever the first bedroom scene appears in the novel, a key moment is reached when the women face one another, mutually undress, and engage in making love. It is interesting to note in these stories that the sex relies on physical contact between the lovers; hands, fingers, tongues, lips are the means by which pleasure is given and received. Rarely does the couple make use of any artificial methods — dildos, vibrators, or other sex toys — in their intimate moments. The use of artificial devices to mark the couple's essential moment of connection would undercut the trajectory of the romantic plot. The intensity of the couple's passion can only be fully expressed through their physical actions; literally and figuratively they cannot get enough of each other. In romances from the 1980s several sex scenes will be included, and often the descriptions become longer and more graphic. In *Curious Wine*, for example, over a three-day period Lane and Diana make love six times, a rather remarkable feat since six other women are sharing the cabin. Other novels will include only one such scene to mark the emotional as well as physical climax of the developing relationship. Of course, not all sexual encounters, even between perfectly matched partners, end with both women achieving mutually experienced orgasms. The waning of the desire for sex — lesbian bed death — the use of sex to control a partner, or interruptions in the performance of sex also occur during the novels and impact the development of the romance.

This emphatic presentation of sex in lesbian novels underscores the explicit measure of difference between lesbian and heterosexual romances. First, of course, is that two women are indulging in the physical expression of love, so the descriptions highlight the ways that women satisfy their desires. Arousal and delay are as important as sexual release, so many love scenes show the couple taking time; this appears particularly in situations where one of the couple has just acknowledged her sexuality and depends on her lover to initiate her. This responsibility, obviously, influences how the more experienced woman plays her role:

> Taylor had a very difficult time keeping herself from taking control. She wanted to flip the smaller woman onto her back and ravish her repeatedly until the only word she could muster was Taylor's name. Instead, she held herself in check, allowing Melanie to keep the lead, repeatedly surprised by how well the redhead seemed to know her and how readily she responded to Melanie's touch [*Turning the Page*, 232].

A large portion of the love scenes are given to foreplay as well, adding to the delay of satisfaction for the lovers. New lovers will spend time admiring one another's beauty and each other's ways of responding to erotic stimuli. As the newly out woman becomes more confident in her lovemaking ability, she will also become more comfortable in initiating sexual contact. Even though the other woman in the couple has previous sexual experience, she will discover in this relationship deeper passionate feelings and find herself more willing to express them. The treatment of explicit sexual expression in heterosexual romances has become the center of much critical commentary and often reflects the critic's view of the genre. Ann Snitow's important 1979 article, "Mass Market Romance: Pornography for Women Is Different," represents a common view that supporters of the romance still react to. Snitow definition of pornography stretches it beyond the purely sexual:

> Though pornography's critics are right — pornography is exploitation — it is exploitation of *everything*. Promiscuity by definition is a breakdown of barriers. Pornography is not only a reflector of social power imbalances and sexual pathologies; it is also all those imbalances run riot, run to excess, sometimes explored *as absurdum*, exploded. Misogyny is one content of pornography; another content is the universal infant desire for complete, immediate gratification, to rule the world out of the very core of passive helplessness [316, emphasis in text].

For Snitow, romance novels assert that the heroine can achieve both sexual freedom and public approval of that sexuality through marriage, while at the same time being acted upon by the hero's desires and actions. This incongruous balance of fictional expectation and realistic achievement illustrates the exploitation that marks the pornographic: "The romantic intensity of Harlequins [the particular romantic text Snitow uses to illustrate her thesis]—the waiting, fearing, speculating—are as much a part of their functioning as pornography for women as are the more overtly sexual scenes" (318). The type of heterosexual romantic text influences how much explicit sexual content is allowed, but generally the number of sex scenes in mainstream straight novels is limited. The exception would be those novels that advertise themselves as explicitly erotic. However sex appears in these works, a distinct pattern of engagement can be discerned. The heroine's sexual awakening, for example, must come from the hero; while the heroine may express a desire to become sexual, she tends to wait for the hero to take control of and direct the sexual activity. The expression of desire marks the limits of her active role in achieving this fulfillment. The hero's expression of his passion may take a number of forms, from highly aggressive to tender; the heroine responds from these cues. She may show pleasure as her passion is awakened, but her emotional focus remains centered on gratitude to the hero. Although modern romances do not require marriage as the signal of the legitimizing of sex, they still place the heroine's expectations of continued physical engagement with the hero as an exclusive one. Ultimately, what these romances do is encourage the heroine's passivity and acceptance of the hero's dominance, which Snitow also sees as pornographic.

Many of the descriptions of sex in lesbian romances are quite graphic, some even bordering on the pornographic. This raises the issues of the purpose for the inclusion of such scenes and what they might contribute to the particular romance traced in the novel and the impact on the reader in general. The arousal factor for a reader cannot be overlooked; the extended descriptions, with their combination of explicit sensual detail and intense observations of the characters' responses, invite the reader into the scene, but not in a prurient, voyeuristic way. As with straight readers of romance, the narrative of these texts positions the lesbian reader both inside the characters' perception as well as outside as the observer of the lovemaking.[8] The effect of this dual perception is to provide the reader with a paradoxical and simultaneous experience of the ecstatic newness of the moment for a character and the expertise of the other. In addition to the strictly personal response such scenes provoke in the reader, the inclusion of numerous sexual encounters offers the lesbian reader an opportunity to re-imagine the meaning of lesbian relationships. Although they are discussing the television series *The L Word*, Lorna Wheeler and Lara Raven Wheeler's assertion on one outcome of the portrayal of sex can be applied to lesbian romances: "The plot emphasises [sic] that sexual encounters between the female characters are dangerous to the social order, which serves both to affirm the straight viewer's idea of lesbians as dangerous (and therefore sexy) and to reinforce the lesbian viewer's self-image as extreme (and therefore sexy). ("Straight Up Sex in *The L Word*," 104). The appeal for a straight reader must be discounted since the audience for lesbian romances tends to be self-selected. The repeated sex scenes validate the ability of the characters to behave in an enjoyable and, more importantly, permissible way. The lesbian reader sees two women experience the most intimate of connections, sees them give and receive pleasure, and discovers that there is no guilt in such engagements. In one way, then, the sex scenes "normalize" what mainstream society would label as deviant.

Critics who take a more positive view of the romance, as well as romance writers themselves, refute the implication of Snitow's critique.

The impact of explicit sexual description on the reader varies depending on its incorporation in the narrative; the writer must balance the expectations of the reader and her willingness to accept such overt physical detail. Usually, such acceptance must be tied to the eventual marriage of the hero and heroine, which sanctions the various sexual encounters that occur between them; Janice Radway emphasizes the importance of this linking between sex and emotion throughout Chapter Five of *Reading the Romance*. Carol Thurston also highlights the integration of sexual pleasure and emotional fulfillment: "Women romance readers seem to derive a sustained level of sexual awareness and pleasure from the tension built into the development of this loving relationship *over time*, and it is the process of conflict and resolution that takes place between two wills and bodies that creates the necessary tension to turn the entire story into a psychogenic stimulus" (154). When this balance of body and emotion is achieved, even graphic sexual description can be accepted since the outcome subordinates biological drives to a perceived proper place in the relationship. For the romance novelist, the heroine's sexual longings and her willingness to engage with a hero who seems beyond control reflect an audacity and bravery that positions her as the real director of the relationship. The heroine must be willing to take risks in order to achieve her desires, and only a hero who represents a potential danger can be worthy of her efforts: "The heroine must put herself at risk with him if the story is to achieve the level of excitement and the particular sense of danger that only a classic romance can provide" (Krentz, "Trying to Tame the Romance," 109). These risks must also include the threat of hero's overpowering sexuality. Krentz, however, asserts that such "aggressive seduction," when set within the controlled environment of the romance, actually allows the reader the satisfaction of having her fantasy realized, to be the focus of such concentrated efforts by the hero to win the heroine's affections.

In the lesbian romance the concept of the aggressive seduction does not appear in the relationship that develops between the dominant couple. If the narrative traces the traditional plot of meeting, separation, and reunion, the seduction is more often mutual than one-sided. Lane and Diana, for instance, experience a simultaneous attraction on their first meeting and both women feel the same compulsion to explore these feelings. Variations on this scenario include one of the eventual couple's initial reluctance to acknowledge any attraction, especially if she has had either no previous experience or a negative one — Laura Kasdan in *The Deal* or Johanna Marshall in *One Summer Night*. Another version presents a woman who believes she is incapable of or no longer available for love — Veronica Cartwright of *Accidental Love* or Laura Harwood of *Carved in Stone*. Whatever the storyline, once the two characters who will become the romantic couple meet, their efforts parallel one another, and since this particular romantic plot requires the happy ending, their pursuits are rewarded. Over the narrative, of course, the characters will confront a range of frustrations, miscommunications, misinterpreted behavior, and delayed gratification, but it is their mutual desire for connection that overcomes these obstacles.

Typically the romantic hero can easily be seen as little more than a sexual predator, although romance writers are quick to defend his behavior as necessary to indicate the strength of the heroine's power.[9] Predatory sex does appear in lesbian romances; however, such behavior is generally given to characters who represent a negative conception of romance and who represent either one of the women's pasts or a model of passion that must be rejected. These women have failed; they cannot achieve real happiness because they will not, or cannot, accept the obligations of partnership. They are emotionally detached and do not understand another's insistence on connection or companionship. Dana Romano, from *Second Chances*, and Lacey Leigh Jaxon, from *Different Dress*, typify this character. Selfishness becomes their primary personal quality; it also becomes their motivation, most often expressed as jealousy, for interfering in the progress of the couple's romance. Dana, for example, has such an intense hatred for Alex Margulies that she spikes the drink of Regina Kingston, the woman Alex has become emotionally involved with. Dana represents an extreme illustration of the sexually aggressive character; Lacey's promiscuous sexual activity and emotional abuse of temporary lovers is the more common behavior attached to these characters. Some main characters in lesbian romances do enter their stories exhibiting behaviors that mimic the predatory qualities of the traditional romantic hero, and like him, these women will be brought to a new understanding of the value of commitment by the other woman. This typically happens early in the narrative, and for the rest of the novel, the reluctant lover is taught the importance of recovering her ability to express emotions. She comes to learn the value of vulnerability, risking a sense of self that she has come to see as flawed: however, for the other character, these hidden qualities are to be treasured and nurtured as the relationship develops. It is the recognition that remaining separate from intimacy is the source of her emotional pain that impels her to accept the offer of connection from the other woman. Surprisingly, like the heterosexual heroine, this character must be prepared to place the source of her power on the line if the relationship is to succeed. The difference between the lesbian and heterosexual character rests in the manner in which the balance of power is portrayed at the novel's conclusion: the previously emotionally remote woman engages fully with her new lover, as not only their reciprocal lovemaking continually demonstrates, but their social interactions as well. The previously remote woman comes to realize the importance and value of connection beyond the personal. The hero, while accepting his need to express his vulnerability, generally limits this revelation to his private relationship with the heroine.

In romances where both women have indentified as lesbians well before they meet, committing to the sexual component of their courtship sometimes requires a realignment of their desires. In some narratives one or both of the women who will become the couple usually enter the story having experienced some kind of loss of or denial of passion; the discovery that she is still capable of feeling the pull of desire is at first usually not sought or welcomed. Once she has experienced the freedom that comes with acknowledging and accepting her emotional needs, the character discovers an increasing pleasure in repeating them. These stories emphasize the importance for both women to understand the entirety of the experience of intimacy. Usually, one or both have compartmentalized the passionate aspects of their lives to accommodate the demands of career or family. Desire has been sidelined in the pursuit of other types of success, and such efforts, while materially or socially rewarded, do not give the characters any real sense of satisfaction:

> The relationship suited them both well. It meant that Isabelle didn't feel the tug of commitment and Maria, with her smouldering [*sic*] Spanish good looks, was free to pursue her other "interests" (quite of few if Isabelle's guess was correct). After all, Isabelle had reasoned, she herself had many things for their own sake. She had good friends and a good job. She was a member of a gym and a tennis club and had a secure home which she owned and loved. What was wrong with having a lover just for making love with? [*Carved in Stone*, 23].

For these characters the key moment in the developing romance is the relinquishing of control, particularly because being in command has allowed them to achieve the isolation of their private lives from any kind of intimacy. This epiphany may come after the woman undergoes an intense emotional crisis, one that calls into question her previous beliefs or behavior; in such instances the novels presents the romance narrative as a serious undertaking, involving more than finding a lover. The character often must also recover a sense of purpose and personal value: Alex

Margulies of *Second Chances* drives herself beyond her physical capabilities in an attempt to forget the death of her lover and her own failings, including an addiction to drugs facilitated by Dana. Through the persistence of Regina Kingston, who initially sees her attraction to Alex as just admiration and friendship, Alex's emotional equilibrium is restored. Over the novel, the two women will learn the strengths and weaknesses of one another; they will overcome outside efforts to diminish their relationship; they will discover the possibility of a future life together.

Sometimes the trigger is serendipitous, an accidental conflation of people, place, and events that propels the woman to reevaluate her views or actions. In such instances, the narrative takes on a more comic tone, painting the romance as an enriching and exciting discovery. *Carved in Stone* details the inadvertent romantic outcome of the efforts of Laura Harwood to save her family's estate from being sold to a commercial developer. Isabelle Perez, who is to put a value on the property, comes with preconceptions of the lady of the manor just as Laura has stereotypes of the London sophisticate. Isabelle's sudden illness during her visit, the accidental discovery of the restorative powers of a mineral spring on the Harwood property, and the shared desire of Laura and Isabelle to save the property contribute to the growing attraction between them. When Laura and Isabelle finally make love, their experience combines passion and comfort, since the various interruptions have given them the opportunity to consider the implications of this act. Like the traditional romantic comedy it is, all the misunderstandings are explained away as the couple declares their love:

> "I think I began to fall in love with you [Laura says] the very first time I set eyes on you. I think I loved you especially when you didn't die on me when you were ill ... and I knew, for certain, when I saw you get out of that ridiculous van in the rain that I didn't want to live without you. I don't expect you to feel the same — I know you've got Maria and that, to you, I'm probably a long one-night stand — but that doesn't alter how I feel" ... [Isabelle responds] "Laura, I'm sorry that I've put you through this. It's just — I don't ... Laura, I love you too" ... "for obvious reason, I didn't find you *terribly* attractive in the beginning.... But, as I grew to know you, I increasingly realised [*sic*] I couldn't imagine my life without you again" [279–180, emphasis and third ellipsis in text].

In both situations described above, the sexual component of the novel signals those points of release and discovery for both women that encourage each to believe in the possibility of finding love and provide the opportunity for a successful pursuit. Sex, on its own, does not guarantee compatibility, even if the sex is good. Sex must be contexted within a relationship that values those abstract qualities, honesty, empathy, and trust, that will insure the happy outcome. These particular lesbian sexual behaviors, after all, are intrinsic components of lesbian identity, and while the lesbian cannot be restricted only to sexual behavior, she cannot be denied her sexual expression. Audre Lorde, in her famous essay "Uses of the Erotic: The Erotic as Power," emphasizes the necessity for women to reclaim their connections to the erotic and its power to forge connections between the self and others, not only in sexual matters, but in every area of one's life: "Recognizing the power of the erotic within our lives can give us the energy to pursue genuine change within our world, rather than merely settling for a shift of characters in the same weary drama" (www.womenstemple.com/EroticAsPower-article.html). The purpose of the romance narrative, of course, is to offer its reader the ability to create a satisfying fantasy — the desire for an idealized partner and relationship, which must include the dream of giving and receiving sexual pleasure. As Lorde reminds her readers, though, the erotic "is a measure between the beginnings of our sense of self and the chaos of our strongest feelings. It is an internal sense of satisfaction to which, once we have experienced it, we know we can aspire." The couple in these romances discover they are capable of greater achievements, not just for themselves, but for the larger communities they will move in; this discovery is seen in the more recent romances that place the couple within a wider social environment and show the couple interacting with a diverse range of people, gay and straight, young and old, male and female.

To discover one's identity is as important as is the discovery of one's appropriate romantic partner in lesbian romantic fiction. Since the emphasis in these novels is partnership and a permanent relationship, most of these works end with the couple promising one another a long-lasting commitment; some even include an epilogue that pictures the couple some time after the main story to reinforce the promise the lovers have made. Sexual intimacy when undertaken with the right lover, as the genre requires, is always completely satisfying for both women, regardless of whatever experience they bring to the relationship. The couple, however, must also recognize that their sexual feelings are only one aspect of their developing relationship, and to gamble their happiness on sexual performance alone undermines their real desire. But, for the women to deny the sexual impulse and its role in creating their union, also diminishes the relationship. The successful lesbian couple balances the various expressions of desire and passion, longing and achievement, as they follow their hearts to the promised ending.

Chapter Five

PRACTICING ROMANCE

> In romance the success of an individual author is not based on how well she writes by conventional standards, but on how compellingly she can create her fantasy and on how many readers discover they can step into it with her for a couple of hours. This is equally true for the writers in other genres. Successful authors become successful not because of their conventional writing skills but because of how accessible they make their fantasies.
> (Jayne Ann Krentz, Introduction, *Dangerous Men and Adventurous Women*, 4)

> Auden had never awakened in the arms of a lover. She'd never had anyone touch her in passion or take her beyond herself to a place of only feeling. She'd read the passage over and over again, and felt far from foreign. She could see the two lovers, safe and secure in one another's arms, rejoicing in their love. Someday, she imagined that she would have a lover, but she hadn't formed an image of what that joining would be like. Friendship, companionship, affection — these things she could envision.
> (Radclyffe, *Lover's Masquerade*, 30)

This chapter connects the ideas previously discussed with the work of three well-known lesbian romance writers — Radclyffe, Karin Kallmaker, and Jennifer Fulton. The discussion of each author is based on a limited, but representative, number of her romances. My intent is to place the works against the ideas and issues raised in the preceding chapters in order to, first, show how they adhere to and stretch the requirements of romance; second, to examine how they represent the expectations of their particular set of readers; and third, to broadly trace the adaptations and adjustments made in the portrayal of lesbian experience. The selection of these authors also rests on certain shared aspects of their professional careers. Perhaps it seems obvious to state, but all three women express a strong sense of their awareness of writing for a specifically lesbian readership:

Radclyffe's statement that "I was initially drawn to and remain fascinated by the romance novel because I find it a powerful vehicle to present aspects of the gay and lesbian experience in an accessible and popular form" typifies each writer's sense of responsibility for providing lesbian readers with recognizable and believable stories and characters (personal communication, 12 Nov. 2008). Each author frequently addresses this understanding in blog comments, especially the importance of works, such as hers, being available for the lesbian reader: "For many women, even in 2008, the only community they can safely find is in fiction written by lesbians and for lesbians" (www.kallmaker.com). The authors express strong views on the value their books have and stress a commitment to representing as wide a range of lesbian experience as possible. The authors all indicate an awareness that they are part of a particular lesbian literary tradition, as well; all three have indicated reading early lesbian writers, Radclyffe Hall, for example, and all have indicated a debt to Katherine Forrest, not only as a practitioner of the genre, but as an editor of their own work. Forrest's *Curious Wine* is frequently cited as a model for plot, character development, and descriptive language. They also indicate, and this clearly ties in with their positions within the publishing field, a familiarity with other contemporary lesbian writers and their works. Based on the information that appears on their websites and in blogs, all three authors are part of a clearly defined and strong community of writers.

The next important criterion is the length and range of each woman's literary output. Each woman has published more than twenty novels and short story anthologies, as well as individual stories in other collections. In addition to writing romances, each author has written works in the other major genres as well: Radclyffe and Fulton have each written detective novels and have created serial characters and storylines. Radclyffe has both the Justice series, highlighting the investigations of a special police task force set in Philadelphia, Pennsylvania, and the political thriller focused Honor series, whose central character is a special agent of the Secret Service. While in these novels the crime or political threat dominates the plot, both series also trace the development of a romance between major characters — lead detective Rebecca Frye and consulting psychiatrist Catherine Rawlings and Special Agent Cameron Roberts and Blair Powell, the president's daughter whom she is assigned to protect. Fulton's first detective series featured Amanda Valentine, but unfortunately, she is no longer working with this character; her most recent series follows the investigative work of Jude Devine. She is also developing a new investigative series character — Portia Darling — utilizing the forensic format (personal communication, 14 Oct. 2008). Neither of Fulton's investigators are shown in the process of developing a romantic interest, although Devine does have an on again, off again relationship with Dr. Mercy Westmoreland. Interestingly, Kallmaker has not written in the detective/mystery genre, although she does write novels in the speculative/science fiction categories under a pseudonym.[1]

All three authors, adhering to what is now standard practice for writers, maintain individual websites with regular blog entries. These blogs become important conduits for responding to readers' questions and comments on specific works as well as general queries dealing with the authors' writing processes. Through the blogs each author keeps her readers apprised of her appearance schedule, posts works in progress, and provides links to other authors' sites. All three women, like many romance writers, take the time to respond to the comments and questions of their readers; the blog entries are posted sometimes weekly, but at least once a month and address specific reader issues or are used as the starting point for a longer commentary. In addition to connecting with their readers, Fulton, Kallmaker, and Radclyffe use their sites to link their readers to other writers, and often these writers will add their comments to a discussion thread. Kallmaker's site, for example, has a link to Bella Books, her publisher, which has separate links to discussions of authors and genre categories produced by Bella. What each author is doing is not only expanding the relationship between her work and her audience, but offering that audience a greater variety of reading choices. Besides responding to professionally framed questions and comments from readers, each writer uses her blog as a way of establishing more personal connections with the audience; Radclyffe, for example, will tell about her daily routine outside of writing or what's happening in her community; Kallmaker relates small stories of her children's activities. Readers are invited to share in aspects of the writer's life that go beyond the more formal relationship focused on the work. Only Fulton's site, actually a separate MySpace page, includes actual reader comments, including opinions about individual texts, Fulton's writing in general, and the impact of the work on them.

Besides their writing, Radclyffe, Kallmaker, and Fulton hold high-level editorial positions with their publishers: Kallmaker is the editorial director for Bella Books; Fulton, the senior editor/acquiring editor for Bold Strokes Books; and Radclyffe, holding the highest position, is the president and founder of Bold Strokes Books. Obviously, these positions give them multiple levels of expertise in the production of a text — from the business *and* the creative perspectives. Their profession also provides background material for the romances; Kallmaker and Radclyffe incorporate the publishing industry as the context for the romance that the novel tracks (Kallmaker's *Paperback Romance* and Radclyffe's *Love's Masquerade*). As with many romance novelists, Kallmaker's and Radclyffe's first profession had no relation to writing; Kallmaker in a November 2004 interview briefly mentions that accounting was her career before she became a writer (www.kallmaker.com). Not surprisingly, several of her characters have accounting or business backgrounds. Radclyffe, before taking up writing and publishing, was a surgeon, and many of her romances utilize the hospital setting to frame the romance narrative. Jennifer Fulton is the only writer of the three with an earlier connection to publishing/literature; on the main page to her website, Fulton relates her previous careers — "librarian, bookseller, literary critic and an editor" (www.jenniferfulton.com). To date, only Fulton's Gothic thriller, *Dark Dreamer*, has a main character who is a professional author.

While these three writers of romance use many of the standard techniques required by the genre, each writer also emphasizes particular narrative situations and character types, as well as incorporating themes or issues that reflect her own interests. Fulton, for example, in her several of her romances integrates an ecological awareness into the plot, usually a character who has an economical or corporate interest in taking over a currently pristine natural environment. This character's position changes over the course of the novel through her developing awareness of the harm her original focus will have on the environment; her growing romantic involvement with another character in the novel also contributes to this change in position. Radclyffe's narratives often focus on a character who is presented as emotionally damaged at the beginning of the novel; as the story develops she will come to discover that she is loved and that she can love, which allows her to move beyond the restrictions of the past. Kallmaker's novels include what is clearly an idiosyncratic detail; every novel has a character who seems to be addicted to chocolate, and this craving will be referenced, even if only in passing, over the course of the narrative. Often the reader, myself included, anxiously waits for its appearance in the story.

The reading of these three writers' romance novels that follows offers an interpretation built on theory and personal reaction, since I read these texts not only as a critic, but as a lesbian. With this caveat, this discussion illustrates the interconnections between genre conventions, reader expectations, and the writer's awareness of both in the crafting of a romance text that will satisfy that each makes to that outcome.

Jennifer Fulton

> I love writing romances.... Falling in love and finding happiness with another person is one of life's great adventures, and I want to celebrate that women share this adventure with one another.
> (www.boldstrokesbooks.com/review)

The opening chapter of *True Love* lays out the dominant romantic dynamics that Jennifer Fulton explores in her novels. The book opens with the narrator, Rosie Brooke, trying to understand what happened among a group of friends in their pursuit of true love and to reconcile the desires that impelled the behavior with the outcomes that sometimes satisfied those needs and sometimes failed. Each woman, with the exception of Anne, who is in a ten-year relationship, has attempted to find the woman who will satisfy all of her hopes for love; each woman hopes to find the elusive true love, although none of the group seems to believe in its existence. Over the dinner conversation in Chapter One, the women offer a variety of definitions of love: is it an instantaneous passionate connection or is this simply lust; is sex the only basis for a relationship or can it be built on something more? The key dilemma, as articulated by Julia, a woman who has enjoyed a wide experience of lovers, is "how in God's name are we supposed to recognize the real thing?" (9). Over the course of the novel these six friends will take a variety of positions on the possibility of finding a caring partner, whether such a thing as true love exists, and how one ends a relationship that is not working, among other topics. These searches pull them into a series of configurations that often undercut the assertions they have made about the all-encompassing power and desire of love. For most of the novel, Rosie and Nicole are pursuing a relationship, but each is willingly tempted, and acts on that temptation, with other members of the group. Even Anne, who believes most strongly in staying honest with one's partner, gives into the enticement of sex without commitment. Underlying the various match ups and break ups in the text, Fulton explores how these women have come to formulate their concepts and what are the implications and impediments such views have on their ability to experience true love.

The most interesting tension playing out in *True Love* connects to the women's awareness of how popular media — Mills & Boon romance novels, television, and Hollywood movies — as well as the dominant heterosexual culture shape their expectations of what constitutes real romance and how to achieve and nurture a relationship. That one of the group, Caroline, works in public relations, where crafting a client's or product's image for public consumption, is not surprising. Another indicator of how fiction impinges on reality is represented through Rosie's theatrical choices and performances: "This is one of the hazards of being an actor. People have difficulty separating you from your roles." However, Rosie, herself, seems to get caught up in the fantasy of the performance: "Playing Astra, I was astonished to find myself disdainfully taken for a prostitute by saleswomen in department stores" (98). Being able to distinguish between the prefabricated fantasies offered by popular media and those grounded in one's own experience is a theme that becomes more compelling to the characters, and for the reader, as the novel continues. The women attempt to reconcile their hopes for finding true love with the likelihood of attaining it as they move in and out of relationships among the group. Rosie toys with the idea of a relationship with Julia, but becomes involved with Nicole—who longs for Julia; meanwhile Zoe actively pursues Rosie, but has sex with Julia. Soon the reader has difficulty keeping up with who is having sex with whom. In fact, the pursuit of sex usually trumps a character's desire to find a lasting relationship, especially as jealousy becomes the dominant emotion these women feel and express during the weekly dinners. Gestures of tenderness quickly turn into foreplay; communication rapidly becomes confrontation: not surprisingly it is Zoe, the most sexually aggressive of the group, who says, "Let's not kid ourselves. We're not here to deal with the consequences, we're here to bury them. We're here for the Hollywood ending. This is about confessing and looking good, so we can let ourselves off the hook" (214).

However, Fulton does provide a happy ending, if a somewhat conditional one. The novel balances two dinners, the very first one in the opening chapter and the last in the next to the last chapter. The first meeting reveals a group of sophisticated, confident women who can laugh at the unrealistic notions they share about true love and romance and yet still willing to believe in their existence. At the last meal together, after the various couplings and uncouplings and the pain that accompanied them, it is Julia, the most superficially urbane, who sums up the lessons learned: "Darlings, I've come to a conclusion. I believe romance is ninety percent mystery and ten percent delusion—that's why it can't survive real life. If true love exists, it must be the rare exception, the kind of relationship that is enhanced, not destroyed, by what you know about your partner" (218). Her definition is full of conditions but does hold out the chance for hope. What romance and true love rest on is the communication and honesty one partner has with another. Only Anne, already in a relationship, appears to be able to achieve that success. As soon as Julia presents her views on love and romance, she returns to her standard practice of making an outrageous statement that undercuts the seriousness of her previous words. Julia first stuns the group by announcing that she is pregnant, then retracts it, but indicates she is thinking of donor insemination; after all, she says, "I want a Hollywood ending" (219). The reader comes away from *True Love* not with a typical romantic depiction of each woman finding the perfect mate, but a portrait of the fluctuations two women will experience as they test out their relationship, The reader glimpses the bargaining and compromises lovers make as they negotiate what the boundaries of the connection are and what each will allow or reject from one another as the relationship plays itself out.

The novel, then, could be seen as an anti-romance, and the background of the main story does contain references and allusions to very serious issues: family violence (Anne is a social worker and occasionally refers to the stress of dealing with families falling apart), sexual harassment (Rosie's current director expects the female members of the cast to sleep with him; Rosie does not and is blackballed from finding theatrical roles), and homophobia (Nicole's co-workers at one point spread rumors about her sexuality). Because the search for love and the fulfillment of one's desires does control the narrative, however, *True Love* must still be read as a romance novel because, even if only temporarily, members of the group, particularly Rosie and Nicole, do experience the thrill of finding a compatible lover. This represents for the reader a version of the traditional romantic fantasy: that a relationship, however it may be defined, can result if the women consciously direct their efforts to its creation and maintenance. Perhaps what is most important for the reader is that when possible the couple puts its greatest effort to ending the connection as gently as possible, although Rosie, whose quest for true love provides the central narrative focus, doesn't always achieve such equanimity. Although most of the women of the group end in the same situation — single — as they began the story, their experiences have given them new knowledge about their capacities, strengths, and weaknesses and as Rosie states,

> I often think about our dinners and feel proud of us. We made mistakes, but we survived. In the end, we loved one another.
> Today I wrote in my diary. *What is present becomes past and what is future becomes present, and my dreams have become my future. Knowing this, I feel hope. For while I dream of True Love, all is not lost* [224–225, emphasis in text].

Fulton's later romances adhere more closely to the traditional romantic framework, creating characters who embody standard fantasy elements, establishing storylines that set up conflicts between the women who will become the couple that are later resolved, and providing a satisfying happy ending. The major characters in Fulton's romances represent traditional opposed personalities and physical appearances: in *More than Paradise* Fulton introduces Ash Evans, a mercenary soldier working for an unsavory company in Indonesia, and Charlotte Lascelles, a botanist who is part of a research team exploring uncharted tropical forests. Ash and Charlotte fall into the typical lesbian dichotomy of butch/femme; in fact, on first meeting Ash, Charlotte mistakes her for a man, a mistake Ash, who is introduced as a woman of voracious sexual appetites, seems ready to play along with if it will help get Charlotte into bed. Charlotte is superficially femme, attentive to the details of dress and make-up. However, Fulton stretches these stereotypic portraits by giving each woman qualities not typically associated with them, turning the two-dimensional image into a more complex one; Charlotte, for example, exerts an authority and capability not usually connected with the traditional femme. She is quite capable of using threats of violence to intimidate her friend, Tamsin's, ex-lover and removes her from Tamsin's house; Charlotte also knows how to use a gun: "My dad taught me how to use his .347 magnum" (56). Charlotte's attitude towards romance is also more nuanced; a previous abusive relationship has made her cautious and careful; she views all ideas about love with the "conviction that [it] was overrated and not worth mutilating heart and soul for. In fact, she'd concluded that love virtually guaranteed bad decision-making" (20). The extreme adventures she participates in while on the research expedition intensify her emotional awareness and response, including her interactions with Ash.

Like Charlotte, Ash Evans embodies many typical butch qualities; she is tall, muscular, rather androgynous, brave, and emotionally distant. Like many romantic heroes, though, Ash carries a burden, although not the conventional one of a disguised past or wrongful accusation; her burden is the care of her physically and neurologically damaged sister. These injuries resulted from their father who, after murdering their mother, attempted to kill Emma. At the opening of the novel Ash has learned that Emma has suffered a stroke that has put her in a coma with the slimmest chance of any kind of recovery. The fear of loss and resulting loneliness that Ash hides come to the surface as she and Charlotte become more intimately involved.

The developing romance between Charlotte and Ash follows the classic romance pattern: initial antagonism, followed by growing interest as each woman inadvertently reveals the depths of her character, to an intense sexual encounter that calls forth unfamiliar emotions that must be confronted and reconciled before the couple can finally declare their passionate commitment; Charlotte must become willing to drop her fear of physical intimacy just as Ash must relinquish her freewheeling sexual past. The dangers of the expedition increase the women's sensitivity to one another's every action, and, of course, presents the opportunity for Ash to rescue Charlotte. The climax of the rescue helicopter crashing with Ash aboard follows a well-used plot device of the apparent loss of one of the lovers just as passion has been acknowledged and acted upon. Of course, Ash is alive, and the novel ends with the declaration of permanence, which for these women marks the impact the fulfillment of desire can accomplish. This same pattern appears in *Greener than Grass*; however, the contrasts of the main characters illustrates a common romantic variation. Here, the dilemma centers on a older woman, Blair Carroll, discovering a growing attraction to a much younger woman, Cassie Jensen. Blair must deal with her attraction and the age difference; the dramatic tensions are alleviated by the humor of the clashes of temperament and experience as Cassie and Blair deal with their growing attraction. For example, an impromptu pillow fight ends with Blair straddling Cassie on the bed, a situation that could easily turn into something else:

> She could feel Cassie's rapid breathing and smell her mild floral scent. The young woman was gazing up at her, the freshly applied eye shadow and plum-colored lipstick making her seem older, no doubt the desired effect. Cassie's mouth was slightly parted, revealing front teeth that over-lapped a little...
> They would kiss now, Blair thought, if this was the movies.... A more realistic alternative presented itself to Blair, The kiss, then Cassie bursts into tears and slaps her face. Promptly loosening her grip and moving aside, she allowed Cassie to sit up [67].

In this novel, too, Fulton introduces Australia as an important influence on the narrative: Cassie has come to Melbourne instead of going to university to earn money to help her mother maintain the family farm in the Outback; Blair has come to Australia to begin working on a new documentary and to escape from the memories of her failed relationship in New York. At the end of the novel, after Cassie's mother has come to accept and approve of her daughter's relationship, the rains come, ending a two-year drought. Fulton underscores the importance of the environment to her narratives: "Setting functions almost as a character in my novels — it has moods, it plays a role in the plot, it impacts on the characters in all kinds of ways" (www.boldstrokesbooks/review). Whether the lush rain forest of New Guinea, the frigid winter of Isleboro, Maine, or the beauty of Moon Island, the romance's setting establishes the physical atmosphere that reflects the emotional one. The setting also provides the narrative its drama; usually a character is trapped and must be rescued or she discovers a place that gives her the opportunity to examine her situation and achieve some resolution. A common feature of Fulton's settings is that, because they tend to be remote places, the characters are forced to confront their desires, determine what will satisfy them, and then act on those decisions. They literally cannot escape and avoid the consequences of acknowledging and articulating desire.

The impact of the setting is best seen in Fulton's Moon Island series, four novels that present the ongoing love story of Annabel Worth and Cody Stanton, the owners of the private, woman-only island, as well as trace, in each separate book, the romances of visitors to the island.[2] Annabel has become the owner of the island as part of the legacy of her aunt, an inheritance Annabel has had no awareness of. The island, in addition to being Annabel's legacy, also becomes the place where she will discover the answers to questions she has only been able to half articulate about her identity. In a sense the island is transformed into a guiding presence that offers all of the women who come to it a safe haven; Annabel, for example, feels this protective impulse as soon as she arrives: "Exploring the property, Annabel had been amazed and delighted at how immediately at home she felt there, how oddly familiar it all seemed. It was as though she belonged, as though in some strange way the island had been waiting for her" (*Passion Bay* 30). As the series continues this sense of the island as sanctuary becomes stronger. In the third and fourth novels Moon Island's mythic history plays an important role in the emotional healing of the visitors to the island. In book 3, *The Sacred Shore*, two visitors experience the otherworldly aspect of the island: Chris is lead into a cave that contains the skeletal remains of a sailor and the treasure from the ship that ran aground; Olivia, whose boat has overturned, is trapped by waves and currents, and just as she begins to drown is taken to a hidden cove and comes into contact with the island's mythic past, a vision of the goddess Hine te Ana. Most of the women who come to Moon Island have some pain or secret in their past that must be dealt with if the romantic feelings that have also been awakened are to flourish, and the island helps each wounded character to heal emotionally and to find new directions for their lives. Grace, who, in *Saving Grace*, comes to the island to assess its value as a hazardous waste dump, comes to appreciate its beauty, and works to undercut the efforts to buy the island. Lauren Douglas, a television star who, when outed, is fired from her series and shot by an irate fan. She has been sent to the island by her father to recuperate from the wound and to wait out the scandal of her sexuality being revealed. Once on Moon Island, Lauren undergoes a transformation from a typical self-centered star as the result of falling in love. After leaving the island, believing she will never see the woman she has come to love again, she eventually joins her mother, a doctor working in Africa, and comes to a new realization of her self:

> "I get embarrassed every time I think about how spoiled I was. You told me this was going to be tough, but I had *no* idea."
> "Are you sorry you came?"
> "God, no. It's the first really good thing I've done in my life" [*A Guarded Heart* 169, emphasis in text].

However, as with every romance, Lauren will be reunited with Pat, the woman she has come to cherish. The novel closes with Cody and Annabel receiving an invitation to their wedding.

Many of Fulton's characters do not fall into neat genre categories; Annabel, for instance, does have the extreme wealth of many romantic leads; however, she does not have the stunning physical beauty typical of such characters. Cassie from *Greener than Grass* neither looks nor behaves in the standard fashion of the ingénue; the group from *True Love* range from the beautiful — Julia — to the anorexic — Caroline — to the ordinary — Anne and Rosie. Other characters, of course, do adhere to the standards of appearance and behavior expected by romance readers; Ash Evans, as noted earlier, strides into the novel, a woman of large appetites and decisive actions. Rowe Devlin, the main character from Fulton's Gothic thriller *Dark Dreamer*, also exhibits conventional qualities, although in this case, two sets of genre expectations overlap — the Gothic and the romance. Rowe, a writer of horror stories, plays the role of the romantic hero, in that she becomes the object of Phoebe's desires; as the love story progress, these two women become attracted, initially hesitate to act on that attraction, and eventually take the step of commitment. Rowe also plays the role of Gothic heroine, in that she has unknowingly purchased a haunted house; however she does not believe in the ghosts, at least at the beginning of the novel. As she confronts ghostly dancers, knives that throw themselves at her, and reports of images of blood-stained floors, Rowe becomes convinced. She then determines to discover the reason for the hauntings and conducts research at the local historical society, scours the attic of the house to discover the previous owners' secrets, and becomes the target of one of the ghost's anger. Like the typical feisty Gothic heroine, Rowe braves the efforts of the spirits to defeat her search and succeeds in discovering the original crime that instigated the haunting. Phoebe also takes on dual roles in the novel; her gift of clairvoyance also marks her as a Gothic heroine, an innocent caught up by the demands of her ability. However, her ability also becomes the focus of the FBI and the CIA; both agencies want to use her talent to help in their investigations, making her the heroine of an adventure/thriller novel.

This blending of genre and conventional techniques has both positive and negative outcomes for the reader. When characters in the Moon Island series come in contact with the power of the island and its ancient history, the reader easily accepts their interactions; over the course of the series Fulton has prepared the reader by integrating and gradually increasing incidents that bring characters to the point where two worlds intersect as well as have visitors react to the atmosphere of the island and succumb to its power to awaken their desires. Fulton even plays with the mixing of genres; in the first novel in the series, *Passion Bay*, she has Cody reading a mystery thriller by an author named Rose Beecham; not only that, but Beecham makes an appearance in the novel and she and Annabel have sex during a hurricane. The inside joke here is that Rose Beecham is another of Fulton's pseudonyms. *More than Paradise* closely follows the framework of the romantic thriller, with its exotic setting, clash of opposing temperaments, heroic actions, and passionate lovemaking. Even the earlier novels — *True Love* and *Greener than Grass* — maintain the dominant pattern of the friendship novel and the initiation of a young lover narrative. In the case of *Dark Dreamer*'s combination of Gothic romance and psychic thriller, the blending of the genres is not as successful; when Phoebe is basically kidnapped by the CIA to help prevent terrorist attacks with her clairvoyant ability, the primary narrative suddenly stops and only picks up when Phoebe's assignment for the CIA is completed. Added to the mix is the developing romance between Cara, Phoebe's twin sister — a standard Gothic motif — and Fran. The reader has too many narrative threads to tie together, and while the reader can make the connections between the various formats, the logic of the connections is often strained. Despite this genre confusion, the reader's attention is still kept because Fulton stretches the romantic dynamics presented in the novel. Rowe is attracted to both Phoebe and Cara; they are identical twins, although they have created distinct personalities. Both Cara and Phoebe are attracted to Rowe and indicate their interest to her, creating a romantic dilemma for Rowe. Fulton gives Rowe the ability to channel her desire solely to Phoebe, but Fulton also makes narrative use of the accepted idea of twins, particularly identical twins, having an emotional and psychological bond not found in other siblings. Phoebe depends on Cara not only for protection from the wider world — her psychic ability clearly separates her from ordinary people — but the sisters also share an intense emotional connection and need for one another that seems to border on the incestuous. The novel ends with Rowe and Phoebe in bed when Cara enters; she wants to try to explain to Rowe the connection between her and Phoebe:

> "I don't want to leave," Cara said. "But I want to be fair to the two of you. If I'm here, I think things could get kind of crowded. Don't you?" She reached across Rowe and stroked her sister's hair. "It's hard to explain ... sometimes I feel like we can never be completely ourselves. It's like I don't know where she begins and I end."

Rowe comes to understand that "denying their bond was not the answer" and invites Cara to sleep with her sister, as the two have often done (189 ellipsis in text).

Rowe's last thoughts reflect her new understanding of the vagaries of love, but also that the ability to love, no matter its expression is the most important goal an individual can strive for. This emphasis, that finding true love, is not simply a romantic pipedream appears in all of Fulton's romance novels, even when she embodies this theme with standard genre frameworks. As noted above in the discussion of *True Love*, Fulton has the characters reference the impact popular concepts of love and relationship can have on the individual trying to achieve such a goal. In spite of their concern with discarding these influences, the power of popular representations cannot be easily discarded, and Fulton's constant referencing of them throughout her novels underscores this relationship between the fantasy construction of desire and fulfillment with the reality. Fulton is the only one of the three authors discussed here who deliberately plays with the tensions; surprisingly, though, the contrast allows the reader to become caught up in the genre representations while at the same time enjoy the inherent contradictions: "Mine [the romances] don't attempt to be anything but amusing romantic escapist entertainment" (www.boldstrokes books.com/review).

Karin Kallmaker

> I am of the opinion that lesbian romance novels are the only books where a woman can go to find affirmation of her hopes, her dreams and her choices in life. They contain the evolving nature of our relationships, friendships and community.
>
> (www.kallmaker.com/blog entry 1 Jan. 2008)

Over the course of her romantic fiction Karin Kallmaker has paid close attention to the importance of community within the pages of her novels. Her earlier works focus on one woman's coming to realize her need to establish a true connection with another woman; usually this woman, while enjoying public success, has isolated herself emotionally, either by denying any intimate relationship (Sydney Van Allen from *Wild Things*) or by pursing strictly sexual liaisons (Jessica Brian from *In Every Port*). Finding one's heart's desire, as required by the romantic narrative, takes precedence, but Kallmaker emphasizes that the couple belongs to a wider world and has a responsibility to acknowledge that relationship as well as the private. The representations of the expanded world will range from an increasing circle of intimate friends and neighbors, to discovering other lesbians or gay men within the main characters' social or professional environments, to connecting with an extended public awareness of the lesbian experience. This assertion is represented in a number of ways: 1978 San Francisco and the election, then assassination of Harvey Milk in *In Every Port*. The novel ends with Jessica and Cat joining the march to honor his memory. In *Car Pool* Anthea Rossignole, partially because of her growing desire for Shay (the woman she is becoming attracted to), but also because of her growing indignation at her company's disregard for its illegal actions that are negatively impacting the environment, provides Shay with damaging evidence that will force the company to pay heavy fines and face public disgrace. Both Jamie Onassis and Valkyrie Valentine become prominent entrepreneurs in their fields — chef/owner of an increasingly popular restaurant and the host of a nationally televised home improvement show — at the conclusion of *Making Up for Lost Time*.

Not every character in a Kallmaker romance achieves such prominent outcomes; just as important in terms of the couple's establishment of a supportive network are those novels that have them draw more limited boundaries that allow the women to explore and expand their understanding of intimacy. These are small groups of individuals who are at first living separate lives, but over the narrative they become connected by shared beliefs and ideals. More importantly, these people discover emotional links or the recognition of a shared identity that help the eventual lovers to resolve the tensions that threaten the happy ending. *Embrace in Motion*, for example, follows the romantic dilemma of Sarah MacNeil, who is drawn to the many artistic enthusiasms of Melissa Hartley and offers her emotional and financial support; as their relationship progresses, Sarah discovers that Melissa is incapable of following through on any of her grandiose plans; that, in fact, Melissa has manipulated Sarah's feelings to serve her own ends. As Sarah attempts to understand and support Melissa, another woman, Leslie Stuart, watches Sarah's efforts be continually thwarted by Melissa's selfishness. Leslie, of course, becomes attracted to Sarah, but holds back in expressing her desire: "Leslie knew she had Sarah's respect and genuine affection. If only, she thought. If only she could have more" (228). Once Sarah realizes the extent of Melissa's failures, not only in her creative pursuits, but, more importantly, in maintaining their relationship, she determines not "to believe in Romance anymore" (229). Resolutions like this in romance novels, however, are frequently overturned, and at the novel's conclusion Sarah comes to recognize and accept Leslie's influence and importance in her life.

Kallmaker describes her romance novel as one that "focuses on the character arc of one or two women, and culminates in the moment when the character(s) is the person she needs to be in order to have a probable chance at happy-ever-after with the woman she loves" (www.kallmaker.com/blog 7 Nov. 2008). Kallmaker's strength throughout her romances is the creation of credible characters who, although they must reflect the requirements of the genre, are given more down to earth personalities. Typically, one of the women who will become the center of the romance narrative enjoys a more prominent social and/or economic position; many of these characters, in fact, have a high position within the company they work for, or are in professions not usually given to romantic female characters: Toni Blanchard of *Just Like That* is a corporate turnaround specialist; Sydney Van Allen, from *Wild Things*, is an attorney pursuing a political career; Sarah MacNeil is a patent attorney for a software company; Alison McNamara is Carolyn Vincense's literary agent. As is standard with the romance, these women are usually very attractive, although not unrealistically stunning; this woman tends to be older than the other main character who will become her lover, but the age differences are not dramatic. Sometimes this character will be the more experienced of the two, but just as often the other woman has the necessary sexual and emotional knowledge that the other lacks. What Kallmaker establishes in the descriptions of these women is a more realistic balance of qualities and abilities so that when the two discover their growing attraction their eventual relationship makes sense, even beyond the genre's insistence on the sometimes unlikely pairing of lovers.

For example, *Embrace in Motion*'s Sarah MacNeil first meets Melissa Hartley while both are attending conventions held at the same hotel, and Melissa's flamboyant and assertive sexuality attracts and stimulates Sarah's sexual urges, given the rather dry world of patent law she generally inhabits. Sexual desire overrules Sarah's common sense and she continues her pursuit of Melissa despite already apparent indications of Melissa's lack of focus. In fact, Sarah even uproots her own life to accommodate Melissa and moves to California and a new job; at this point, Leslie, the co-owner of the company Sarah is now working for, enters the picture. The relationship that develops between Leslie and Sarah progresses slowly and naturally from professionally cordial to friendship to something more. Interestingly, the novel ends not with a declaration from either woman of undying love and promises of forever. There is promise as the story comes to its conclusion, but the promise is of contentment as well as passion, comfort as well as intimacy:

> They shared a similar smile, and Sarah's heart *settled into a calm, easy rhythym. How surprising, she thought. This love wasn't a tidal wave so much as the tide finally coming to the longed-for shore.* It poured into every part of her body and soul, washing away any fears still lingering, and leaving no room for doubts to creep in. She studied the promise in Leslie's eyes and anticipated the passion offered in her parted-lip smile [233, emphasis added].

Many of Kallmaker's novels utilize the same reasonableness in how characters meet and how the eventual commitment between the lovers comes about. Valkyre Valentine needs cooking lessons to clinch the television contract, and Jamie Onassis needs someone to do the required reconstruction of the restaurant in *Making Up for Lost Time*; Anthea Rossignole and Shay Sumoto both need to find a car pool and end up together.

As Kallmaker's statement above suggests, one or both of the main female characters comes to recognize or understand who she is; often this means claiming a lesbian identity and coming out. In *Wild Things* Faith Fitzgerald must finally acknowledge that her attraction to Sydney is more than admiration for her political abilities or her personality. Since Faith has been raised in a strict and conservative Catholic family, her declaration that she is a lesbian is met with anger and rejection: "Unnatural child! I should have had a half-dozen grandchildren by now, but instead you live under my roof and practice your filthy, perverted sins" (173). Not all of Kallmaker's characters who come out must confront such open hostility; more often, they have come to this awakening because of their discovery of intense feelings for another woman. For example, Carolyn Vincense from *Paperback Romance*, after the affair with Nicola Frost, begins to explore what being lesbian means. Her reading gives her the confidence to come out to her family and to admit her attraction to Allison. Leah Beck, a well-known painter, after an initially brief but intense affair with Jackie Frakes, has made explicit the lesbian imagery in her work. It is this rediscovered ability to love that has given Leah the freedom and inspiration seen in the new paintings: "I'm in love. I don't think she loves me back, but I can't think of any other way to prove it to her. And I need to prove it to myself. I'm afraid ... I'm afraid if I hide this work I'll forget that I could love someone again" (196). At least in the early stage of the romance, the other woman in these relationships often finds herself having to accept a secondary position because the first woman is already involved or has shut herself off from emotional connections. She must also come to the knowledge that her desires are legitimately felt and that her attraction, which seems dead-ended, will be satisfied, usually by being made to see that she is the only woman the other main character can love: "There have been lots of Jans. But I've never said I love you to anyone. To anyone. Ever. Not in my whole life. Only to you. Because until I met you I didn't know there could be more" (*Making Up for Lost Time* 221).

Throughout her romances Kallmaker illustrates the ways that lesbian experience and lives have developed over time. Since her works fall into the contemporary romance category, Kallmaker represents the various positions — social, ideological, economical — available to lesbians at the time described in the texts. As already noted, many of her main characters hold high-level positions in business or the law; surprisingly, in the works used for this analysis, none of the women have jobs in the fields traditionally associated with lesbians, for example, teaching or social work. Some of the characters work in fields stereotypically given to lesbian: Valkyrie Valentine knows her tools, although she is not described as butch; Jane from *Just Like That* can easily hoist irrigation pipe, but only as a way to support her painting. Kallmaker's depictions suggest her concern with portraying lesbians and their private and public choices as simply an illustration of what women, regardless of their sexuality, are capable of doing and being. Many of her characters have built complex lives that reflect varied interests that help stretch the genre's dependence on stereotypes. Kallmaker stresses that the romance writer's main concern and effort is "respect. Respect for the reader's hopes, dreams and choices in life. If your characters reflect these things for the reader in some way, your readers will follow you anywhere you take them..." (www.kallmaker.com/blog 4 Nov. 2008). Kallmaker may poke fun at some of her characters — seen in Melissa Hartley's glib articulations about lesbian creativity when she is incapable of creating anything herself— but this is not to be seen as blanket ridicule of any lesbian who works in a creative field. Several of her characters, in fact, are shown to be very successful: Leah Beck, Carolyn Vincense and Faith Fitzgerald have achieved critical and popular fame in their particular creative areas. Even in careers not usually considered creative, Kallmaker recognizes the talent needed to run a restaurant well or to turn grapes into a superior vintage.

Kallmaker also respects the reader's understanding that relationships take time and work if they are to succeed. The attraction between the women destined to become a couple is often immediate, but either cannot be acted upon or the couple's inability to articulate their desires accurately prevents the initial connection from being pursued. Communication is often shown to be an essential requirement for the romance to succeed: Leah feels that she has clearly conveyed her passionate feelings for Jackie through her paintings, but she fails to let Jackie see them before showing them in a gallery; after acting on their sexual feelings, Jamie retreats and refuse to deal with Valkyrie about the consequences of their lovemaking. Often in the story, the couple is shown giving way to these sexual urges before either truly understands the implications of their actions. At the ends of *Just Like That*, Missy tries to convince Toni, one of the women at the center of the romantic quest, of the importance of communication to a happy outcome:

> "You don't need luck," Missy said firmly. "You need to talk. Communicate. Be afraid of no topic."
>
> Toni laughed and pulled Missy against her for an affectionate squeeze. "I have to say I do not see you and Jane talking all that much."
>
> "We do." Missy's smile was impish. "We talk after. The best part is that it's hard to tell when the talking stops and the lovemaking begins again. Talking makes for great afterplay and it leads to more foreplay" [192–193].

A common scenario in Kallmaker's romances is the involvement of one of the women in a relationship that delays her connection with the right partner; the relationships between Sarah and Melissa or Toni and Mira illustrate two such narrative complications. Such connections are built on deception and manipulation by the inappropriate lover. Obviously, before the appropriate pairing can occur, these false romances must be dissolved, and this comes about when the woman who has been deceived discovers the truth about the other's actions. Making the right connection requires her to admit her initial misguided responses, and the admission of weakness presents her in a new, more human light, since many of these characters present a very self-controlled and defined image to the world.

Working beneath the romance plot, some of Kallmaker's novels reference social issues current at the time of a work's publication or during the period used as its setting: ecological destruction (*Car Pool*), the rejection of a lesbian daughter because of one's faith (*Wild Things*), the developing gay liberation movement (*In Every Port*), discrimination in the workplace (*Embrace in Motion*). Some of these topics become integral to the story — the dumping of contaminated waste that Anthea Rossignole helps to uncover — others serve as indicators of one or both of the characters' full engagement and commitment to her own identity — the commitment ceremony of Sydney Van Allen and Faith Fitzgerald and Sydney's public acknowledgement of their relationship when she accepts the Democratic Party's support for her candidacy for state senate. As with any romance, the details of establishing a household, the retaining of one of the partner's careers, and other compromises that couples usually make are left unexamined; this stems from the fantasy element necessary for the romance to succeed. After all, the mundane details of everyday life intrude upon the idealized world of the romance where such concerns take care of themselves. But surprisingly, Kallmarker, at least in the narratives used here, does not treat some of the dominant issues lesbians dealt with, particularly in the 1990s. For instance, none of the couples deal with the question of having children; Leslie, from *Embrace in Motion*, has a son from her previous marriage, but she is the only character who does. Families are made up of supportive parents and siblings and a circle of, usually gay or lesbian, friends.

Kallmaker's novels, like all lesbian romances, include concrete depictions of sex, which she believes is an important part of the romantic story. However, she has stressed in several blog entries the importance of placing the sex firmly within the developing relationship; the character's emotional connection is more important than sexual compatibility: "In romance the character's emotions come first, and the sex scenes must be part and parcel of the character" (www.kallmaker.com/blog 6 June 2006). When sex takes place because of uncontrolled physical desire only, the relationship will either fail (sexual lust is the only shared emotion between Sarah and Melissa) or take one or both women most of the narrative to integrate into their relationship (Leah and Jackie and Valkyrie and Jamie illustrate the false start of sexual passion overwhelming their emotions). Having sex affirms or reaffirms a character's identity, especially for those characters who come to realize that the attractions they have always felt for women has a name that they can claim; for example, Faith Fitzgerald and Jackie Frakes. Even for characters who know and understand their sexuality, sex gives them a way to embody that identity more completely; for Anthea Rossignole from *Car Pool*, her desire for physical intimacy with Shay and her sometimes clumsy, sometimes expert, experiences of sexual fulfillment help her gain greater self-confidence, to the point where she helps Shay steal the evidence that will bring the company's illegal chemical dumping to light. Becoming sexually active and comfortable with her lesbian identity gives Anthea the strength to confront the homophobia of her supervisor and out herself; not surprisingly, her fears of exposure are dissipated by several other employees also coming out and challenging the bigotry that Martin has just expressed.

Not all of the sexual encounters in Kallmaker's romances carry the burden of coming out or confrontation. When the women at the center of the romance finally achieve the sought for resolution — the discovery of one's true love — lust is transformed into fulfillment; sex is no longer simply a means to release pent up tensions, but a way to express the totality of the lovers' connection: "She wanted to hold part of herself aloof, to keep one last escape, just in case. *But a frozen moment of panic melted with the revelation that the only way to save her heart was to give it all.* She would be breaking it herself, this very moment, if she gave Toni anything less than the whole" (*Just Like That* 201, emphasis added). The descriptions of sex that appear in these novels represent what can be seen as conventional sexual practice; that is, the women rely on the use of mouths, tongues and hands to bring one another to orgasm. None of the love scenes include the use of sex toys or any other kind of enhancement to their lovemaking. The sex is also reciprocal, in that both women will bring the other to release during the scene; sexual dominance by one woman of the other does not appear either. The most exotic addition to a couple's lovemaking is Jamie's chocolate frosting:

> Val made a low sound that Jamie echoed as their mouths met, hungry for each other and tasting chocolate and passion with every movement of their tongues. They parted, gasping, and Jamie felt Val's chocolate-dipped fingers on her face, then they were smoothing across her throat. Then those fingers found their way under her apron, to her shirt buttons [*Making Up for Lost Time* 180].

In the last few years Kallmaker has begun writing explicit erotic lesbian romances because she notes there has developed "more openness about what lesbians really do in bed as well as greater acceptance in our community of what we really do in bed" (www.kallmaker.com/blog 6 June 2006). Kallmaker also points out that, for her, sex should involve more than mechanics; in a 2006 interview she states that she aims to combine the sexual and the emotional, "adding the romance to erotica, giving readers characters they identify with both in and out of bed" (www.kallnajer.com/blog 4 May 2006). She has also indicated in blog entries that erotic sexuality is not limited to fast living, single women who refuse to establish any kind of permanent relationship; such sexual practice is perfectly suitable for romances that concentrate on a couple. In addition, Kallmaker separates her erotica from her more traditional romances, publishing the erotic material under the Bella After Dark imprint.

Of the three authors considered here, Kallmaker is the only one who incorporates deliberate references to other literature; throughout *Wild Things* Sydney and Faith trade quotations from a wide range of literary references, from *Little Women* (73) to Lewis Carroll (219). In *Paperback Romance* once Carolyn accepts that she is a lesbian, she begins reading a number of lesbian works, from literary history to comics. Kallmaker also reveals a special fondness for Jane Austen's *Pride and Prejudice*, integrating the novel into the storyline of two of her romances. In *Embrace in Motion* Sarah turns to Austen's novel, "an old favorite," at the beginning of the story rather than join others in a night out (13). Later the novel appears at two important scenes: the first occurs when Sarah retreats to the bedroom to avoid dealing with Melissa and her radical friends; the second when Melissa comes in to invite Sarah to join their taking in a movie. When shown the book, Melissa says, "I could never get into Jane Austen ... too dry for me" (129). Her lack of appreciation clearly marks their incompatibility to become romantic partners. Throughout the novel Sarah longs to experience romance, so it should not surprise the reader to discover that when she thinks of romance she gives it a capital R. At the end of the novel, *Pride and Prejudice* is again referenced during the New Year's trip Sarah and Leslie have taken to Sarah's grandmother's cabin. Sarah is coming to the conclusion of Austen's work, with "the happy ending just in the offing" (221). That Sarah is finally able to dismiss all thoughts of Melissa and has begun to look at Leslie in a new way is no coincidence. Kallmaker's next reference to Austen's novel is her revision of its narrative in *Just Like That*. The first adaptation is Kallmaker's reinterpretation of Austen's famous opening line—"Everybody knows that a single woman with good money is in want of a wife" (1). The main male characters are recast as lesbians, including transforming Mr. Darcy into Toni Blanchard, who retains his dominant character trait of pride. Many of Austen's plot situations and devices—Darcy's explanatory letter to Elizabeth Bennett, for example—are kept and used to develop this modern romance. One could think Kallmaker has committed an act of hubris by taking such a classic work and turning it into a genre romance; however, Austen's text is just as much a story of the search for the proper partner, for true love, for the happy ending, as a comedy of manners, or social commentary, or any other of the many critical interpretations offered on Austen's work.

When asked why she choose the romance for her literary efforts Kallmaker said, "I think to write a good romance you have to believe in it yourself. You have to believe that a woman can create and shape her heart's desire" (www.kallmaker.com/blog 4 Nov. 2004). This statement can be read two ways: the writer must believe in her ability to produce a text that satisfies the demands of the genre as well as meet the expectations of the reader. She must understand how to achieve the happy ending without straining the reader's credulity too far; she must balance innovation and tradition in order to achieve a successful novel. To use Kallmaker's own term, the romance writer must respect both the reader and herself, because the attentive reader will recognize a writer who simply fills in the blanks. A careful writer, after all, has no intention of alienating her audience; her heart's desire has to be to have her creative efforts recognized and applauded. The second interpretation of Kallmaker's statement connects the reader more closely to the novel. Seeing the reality of her public and private lives in the pages of the romance allows the lesbian to imagine a similar outcome. The reader finds assurances that her desires are valid and deserve accurate representation, and Kallmaker's novel offer the reader a sympathetic understanding of those hopes through romances that portray lovers conquering fear and doubt as they declare their commitment to one another.

Radclyffe

> Romance fiction allows us to explore intimate interpersonal relationships — sexually, emotionally, and psychologically — to an extent that no other genre does, because in the romance novel, the relationship "is" the story.
> (personal communication, 12 Nov. 2008)

In a Radclyffe romance one or both of the main characters enters the story burdened by a past which impacts the present and which must be confronted and addressed if the character(s) will be able to pursue the relationship that has developed over the course of the narrative. Finding love for these women represents a freedom they have been searching for and that, because what has happened to them before the specific novel begins, has eluded them. Often these women deliberately turn away from the chance of finding connection because they feel their past will overwhelm any chance for happiness in a new relationship. Usually this stems from a sense of fear caused by some kind of loss, of a partner through death (Honor Blake) or breakdown of a previous relationship (Victoria King), of an emotional connection to others, especially to family (Tamar Whitley and Pearce Rifkin), of not accomplishing one's goals because of a physical impairment (Quinn Maguire or Haydon Palmer). They are trapped by the loss of hope and isolate themselves from acknowledging the need for emotion and connection, concerned that opening themselves up will prove to be illusionary: "What if it doesn't mean anything to her, Cath? What if it's all a mistake? How will I bury all these feelings again?" (*Safe Harbor* 176). For these characters the recovery of desire marks the moment of reclamation, and desire must be viewed as not only the expression of physical passion, but as the reawakening of understanding, that one cannot block or deny the need for finding other ways of connection. One must recognize that to be complete she needs to express her emotional desires openly, and she must reconnect with a community of others who can offer her the knowledge that she need not bear the burden of separation anymore: "Some of the most powerful themes in my work, which I revisit frequently, are redemption, healing, and self-acceptance. These are classic themes in romance fiction and the sex of the character has nothing to do with the emotional landscape of the character or the challenges she faces in accepting and giving love" (personal communication, 12 Nov. 2008).

In order for the two main characters to achieve this release, the narrative movement in many of Radclyffe's romances describes a series of increasingly intense engagements between them; several of the novels used for this analysis set up an initial antagonistic situation that guarantees these women will have to deal with two levels of feeling: an initial emotional reaction to the circumstances that bring the two characters together; and the developing awareness of deeper, more intimate emotions being able to be expressed. Two examples of the first response are Saxon Sinclair's hostility at being manipulated into accepting the documentary filmmaker Jude Castle (*Passion's Bright Fury*) or Honor Blake's anger at the new attending physician being hired at the hospital without her input (*Fated Love*). Of course, not all of these meetings are confrontational nor are the emotional responses based on dislike or distrust. In *Matter of Trust*, for example, JT Sloan, a computer security expert hired by Michael Lassiter to protect her systems, instinctively responds to Michael's sense of betrayal when her husband refuses to relinquish his claims on the business: "Sloan clenched her hands in her pockets, trying to ignore the almost irrational fury that pounded in her head" (52). Often it is just the stirring of feelings that one of the two major characters has denied, seen, for instance, in Tory King's refusal to acknowledge any interest in Reese Conlon to

Sally, her friend and nurse at the clinic where both work. It should be noted that the reasons for these characters to become acquainted is realistic and reasonable, but however the initial contact is made, from the moment these two women meet, they become intensely attracted to one another. In spite of their efforts to remain in control of themselves and the situation, both women find that their often unarticulated desires will determine the development of their relationship. What tends to result from this initial inability to communicate each other's needs and responses is that the women's sexual urges overtake them. However, the first exhilaration is often followed by anger, fear, or regret, and only when the couple is able to reach the second level of feeling can their romance become successful.

After the initial passion has been experienced, both women realize that they cannot return to their previous state of isolation; the acting on suppressed desire has opened them to an awareness of lack, and rather than retreat, they are willing to risk the pain of failure or rejection in order to continue to explore this new connection. Risk is present for both women, the one putting her emotional vulnerability on the line and fearing rejection, the other risking her happiness by offering herself and also facing the possibility of being spurned. After their first sexual intimacy Saxon expresses this fear to Jude who asks her to explain:

> Jude's stomach tightened when she realized that she might be alone in her desire for them to see more of one another, but if that were true, she needed to know, for her sanity. "Why? Why does it scare you?"
> "Because you make me forget everything," Sax whispered hoarsely, her eyes meeting Jude's. "You make me forget about everything except how warm you feel, and how..." She ran a trembling hand across her face and stared beyond Jude's shoulder into the past. "You make me feel ... so much" [*Passion's Bright Fury* 163, ellipses in text].

Since one of the couple is frequently portrayed as the stereotypic strong, silent loner, such moments of revelation represent essential moments of clarity. As with Kallmaker's characters, the ability to speak from the heart signals the turning point in the romance, and only the realization that she is capable of loving and being loved allows one woman to tell her truth to the other. Interestingly, in several Radclyffe romances both of the main characters must achieve this moment of deliberate self-revelation: Quinn must reveal the heart condition that has stymied her career goals and Honor must recognize that being able to love again does not diminish her connection to Terry, her lover who died in a construction accident; Drew must accept that she could not protect Dara from the vicious attack that killed her and Sean must acknowledge that she is in love with a woman. The recognition that one needs to articulate one's most personal secrets to another means that the woman deliberately risks her happiness if the other refuses that declaration, and since the conventions of the romance require that the emotionally damaged character will be healed by love, the characters discover that only by exposing themselves will they find the sought for feelings of peace and belonging they have been missing.

Developing strong and believable characters, for Radclyffe, is the starting point for the story: "In a romance, character should always be central" (personal communication, 12 Nov. 2008). Her main emphasis centers on creating not just attractive fantasy figures, but on giving her characters honest emotional lives that reflect their personal and public experience. This honesty must be part of the individual's make-up; the character needs to behave and respond consistently with the personality the author has given her. Reese Conlon, who has served in the military for fifteen years, embodies those ideals of honor, duty, and respect, and she brings them into every interaction described in *Safe Harbor*, regardless of an individual's social or economic status, age, or gender. These qualities, in fact, provide her with a structure that has allowed her to make the dramatic break with her past that she must reconcile to insure the happy ending with Tory. Romances, however, are about the formation of a couple, which requires the individual to form an emotional bond with another, and Radclyffe stresses, "Two essential ingredients — attraction/conflict. Everything about character and story has to believably relate to those emotional elements" (www.radfic.com/Blog, 13 Mar. 2008). Since both women bring their private history into the relationship, they will confront a number of differences in beliefs, expectations, and actions that have the potential to prevent the relationship from developing. These obstacles may be as straightforward as the age difference between Tanner Whitley and Adrienne Pierce or the initial differences in literary tastes between Auden Frost and Haydon Palmer. Of course, more serious tensions exist that can have more devastating implications for the couple, particularly when one of the women is introduced as straight. Several characters, Wynter Thompson, Sean Gray, Auden Frost, and Michael Lassiter, face the greatest emotional crisis in their narratives. As with other lesbian romances, the linking of passion and the discovery of one's sexuality intensifies the emotional tensions that develop between the women. Discovering new feelings can lead the one woman into reckless behavior — Wynter's increasing willingness to allow Pearce to touch her, for example — but Pearce's recognition of what Wynter cannot yet fully understand forces Pearce to restrain her own increasing longing for connection. When Wynter's hesitation dissipates, the two immediately realize a need neither has felt before, and for the rest of *Turn Back Time*, they explore the meanings of these new feelings. The characters caught up in this situation must confront the shifting pull of desire and fear until the moment when they discover that simply being committed to each other offers the relationship its best hope of survival:

> Wynter raised her head, her eyes dreamy. "Will you stay, then?"
> "For how long?" Pearce breathed.
> "Always." Wynter kissed her gently. "Always."
> "I don't have very much practice at ... this." Pearch waved at the room uncertainly.
> "*No one ever really does, until you do it.*" Wynter kissed Pearce's throat. "You're doing just fine. You're great with Ronnie. And I adore you" [273, ellipsis in text, emphasis added].

Radclyffe's characters bring out strong reactions in her readers; several blogs entries deal with the author's response to readers' interest in when characters will be brought back or what they would like to see happen to favorites or how she develops them. According to Radclyffe, reader demand was a major factor in the continuation of her Honor series (personal communication, 12 Nov. 2008). Several of Radclyffe's characters cross over from one romance to another; for example, Saxon Sinclair and Jude Castle, from *Passion's Bright Fury*, make an appearance in *Fated Love*. Michael Lassiter and JT Sloan of *A Matter of Trust* become regular characters in the second book of the Justice series. However, these appearances are not random; when Quinn's defibrillator malfunctions, she returns to New York City so that her personal cardiologist can deal with the problem. The hospital she is taken to is the one at which Saxon works. At one point in her investigation Det. Rebecca Frye requires specialized computer skills, which is how she meets JT Sloan. Like Jennifer Fulton's Moon Island Series, Radclyffe has also developed a serial romance saga — the Provincetown novels — which extends the story of Reese Conlon and Tory King, and like Fulton, in each subsequent novel, the original couple's relationship is repositioned to allow a new romantic narrative to take precedence. As noted with the discussion of Fulton's series, these novels must accomplish two different goals; the first requires satisfying the reader's interest in following the development of a new romance. The second is to present the continuation of the original love story in a way that does not interfere with the progress of the new relationship. Radclyffe achieves this balance by "us[ing] the setting as the unifying factor between books, allowing me to present a new romance in each subsequent novel while incorporating continuing secondary characters. Each novel in the series focuses on a new romantic pairing, maintaining the central elements of the romance while continuing to explore common themes and developing relationships" (personal communication, 12 Nov. 2008). Kallmaker, interestingly, does not write series romances, although several of her characters from her novels appeared in a collection of short stories. Kallmaker asserts that once the happy ending is achieved "a sequel would be, to my mind, anticlimactic," although she does accept that in a romance with a strong mystery, fantasy, or thriller background, the possibility of a continuation of the romance is reasonable (www.kallmaker.com/blog, 7 Jan. 2008). Both the Honor and Justice series incorporate such frameworks; the dominate plot typically involves criminal activity (the Justice novels) or political intrigue (the Honor books), but the relationship between the main characters of each series is also continued, especially in how their personal relationship and desires confront and accommodate the public demands made on the lovers. Currently, the Provincetown Series includes four additional novels.

Like the other two novelists, Radclyffe allows the couple to experience intense sexual intimacy over the course of the novel, and as with the other writers such scenes engage the reader's imagination in several ways. The first, of course, is the representation of intimacy as experienced between women, and each writer expresses a sense of responsibility in portraying these moments in the narrative: "I also think it's important that we present some of the complexities of human relationships within the context of loving, positive emotional sexual encounters" (Radclyffe personal communication, 12 Nov. 2008). Sex illustrates the shared desire of both women for connection, and Radclyffe, like other lesbian romance writers, gives the women a number of such opportunities to explore the multiple levels of meaning such sharing calls up for them. The sex should not just be presented as a technique manual for the reader; rather, these present key turning points for the characters, especially when, in the heat of passion, a character will be able to experience physical *as well as* emotional release. After several intense sexual encounters with Jude, Saxon feels vulnerable, but safe enough to confess her yearning to be connected; she is also able to reveal the medical issues and resulting drug dependency that forced her into psychiatric treatment (pages 162–167). What the reader sees is a reconfiguring of sex as more than just an expression of pure physical need; the characters who do treat sex in such a way — Pearce Rifkin or Tanner Whitley — come to recognize the psychological emptiness that accompanies this behavior. It cannot be coincidental that these women, particularly, discover what is lost by denying the emotional component of such intimacy. Early in *Tomorrow's Promise*, for instance, Tanner has begun to feel an attraction to Adrienne; unfortunately she can only relate this feeling by initiating physical contact. She kisses Adrienne, but it quickly turns from a gesture of affection into lust which is broken off by Adrienne. Adrienne's reaction brings Tanner to the beginning of a self-analysis that she has previously shunted aside:

> And though Adrienne had made it clear she wanted nothing from her, she almost didn't care. *Something had happened here on this beach—for one brief instant they had touched upon one another's secrets....* Remembering brought another wave of desire coursing through her. Not lust like the sex she had known, although her flesh cried simply to be touched, but a wild hunger to know and be known, to nourish and be filled. Fleetingly, she had felt it and, close upon it, suffered the loss like blood leaving her veins [68, emphasis added].

Tanner cannot yet separate the two drives and returns to her "normal" sexual behavior, indulging in one-night stands. However, it is Tanner's sexual ability that restores Adrienne's own sense of self-worth, because through Tanner's obvious desire not only to make love, but to protect her, Adrienne's fears of rejection because of her mastectomy are laid to rest. The predominant portrayal of sex in Radclyffe, and the other lesbian novelists, shows its healing potential and it as a source of connection and completion for the lovers.

The depictions of sex in *Love's Masquerade* offer an extension of the representations of desire and fulfillment. Not surprisingly, the chief mechanism for this portrayal is the printed word. Auden Frost, who knows nothing of romance, let alone lesbian romance, is hired as the director of the lesbian fiction division of Palmer Publishing, and as a way of learning about the genre, Auden starts reading books from her friend's collection of such texts. Immediately, Auden finds herself responding to the books in a way she has not before, which begins the process that will end with her acting on romantic impulses she has never experienced before:

> "Then what in the world am I doing thinking about publishing romances? Not just romances, *lesbian* romances. I really don't know anything about either."
>
> But then she thought of the book that had quickly captured her imagination the night before and realized that wasn't exactly true. The scene of a woman awakening to only memories lingered powerfully in her mind still [30].

The novel is one written by one of Palmer Publishers' authors, Rune Dyre, whose latest work Auden will be bringing out. As Auden reads the manuscript, she finds it uncannily reflects and articulates her own previously unacknowledged feelings. This stems from the fact that Rune Dyre is the penname of Haydon Palmer, who is transcribing her relationship with Auden in the fiction. For Haydon writing becomes the only way to express her own emotional longings because of her fear that her leukemia denies her any hope of a relationship. Their courtship for the first part of the novel is carried out through email and the submissions Rune/Haydon sends to Auden. Once the two declare their love, they continue to use their correspondence in a more deliberately playful way of communication. These are not the only written representations of sex that appear in this novel. Another of Palmer Publishing's author's work also appears throughout the story, but Thane Cutlass' stories describe highly charged, erotic situations that act as a counterbalance to the more sensuous romantic narrative of Rune Dyre. Her stories describe lovers who engage in consensual acts of bondage, domination and submission, and graphic sex. What the novel seems to suggest is that passion, in all of its forms, provides lovers insights into their relationships that are not available through any other means, and that the visual representation of that passion, through words on a page or screen, lets the reader/lover experience the sensations on more than one level. In the text, once Auden learns the real identity of Rune Dyre, she and Haydon use the texts of their emails to send coded messages telling of their desires; while reading Thane's erotic story of shower sex, her lover becomes aroused, and the two women act on that arousal as Gayle reads the text. The reader sees the lovers actively controlling the naming and practice of their feelings for one another and becomes a part of the experience, perhaps inserting herself into the scene. This fantasy is actually shown in the novel itself when Auden, reading Rune's manuscript, subconsciously changes the names of the characters: "Gasping, she fixed on what she had just read. *Kyle and Dane. Kyle and Dane. Not Hays and...*" (170, emphasis and ellipsis in text).

The fantasy elements in Radclyffe's novels greatly influence a reader's engagement with the characters and stories; for example, major characters in the novels are strikingly attractive and tend to work in the higher levels of their particular profession — Haydon Palmer is the owner of Palmer Publishing; Adrienne Pierce, Reese Conlon, and Drew Clark are officers in the particular branch of the military in which they have served; Tanner Whitley is the daughter of privilege and wealth. Often a character will come from a socially prominent family: Saxon Sinclair's father is the president of a Fortune 500 company and her grandmother is a famous actress. Besides having the heightened physical qualities, most of the central characters have abilities and skills that allow them to act quickly and decisively, sometimes literally making life and death decisions. However, Radclyffe situates these characters in settings that demand just such abilities; several of the romances discussed here — *Passion's Bright Fury*, *Turn Back Time*, and *Fated Love* — are set in hospitals or have characters involved in the medical profession like Dr. Victoria King of *Safe Harbor* and psychologist Sean Gray in *Love's Tender Warriors*. The immediate communities in which the major characters pursue their romance also reflect a strong fantasy element; most of the people who interact with the main characters are lesbian or gay or totally accepting of their sexuality. Family members who are directly involved with a major character are also supportive, although Pearce Rifkin's father is not. Even in situations beyond the immediate world of the couple, people willingly accept them and their relationship. When Haydon is in the hospital to receive a transplant, Auden openly declares that she is Haydon's lover, an announcement that causes no other reaction than the doctor's "Pleased to meet you" (*Love's Masquerade* 303). At the same time, Radclyffe takes care to establish the reality of the settings and describe characters' profession competently; novels set within the medical field reflect her own background. Before becoming a writer and publisher, Radclyffe was a surgeon; as she noted in a blog entry on January 22, 2008, "Contemporary romance writers or mystery authors also have to create a believable world, and a great deal of that authenticity often centers around the occupation of the main characters" (www.radfic.com). This balance of reality and fantasy, typical for a successful romance, gives the readers the opportunity to enter into the lives of the characters and establish points of connection between what happens in the text and their own experience. If the reader is unable to make such a link between her own expectations and the text, the author has failed to satisfy the most important relationship of all, and Radclyffe, like any romance writer, acknowledges the interest of her readers: "I definitely pay attention to what readers have to say about what they would like to read more of" (personal communication, 12 Nov. 2008).

This attention paid to readers' interests and concerns reflects more than good public relations. Radclyffe, like Kallmaker and Fulton, understand the value their work offers to their particular readers, that through their fiction, lesbians find representations of their lives that are treated honestly and accurately: "Our literature provides support and validation and very often, a lifeline, for members of our community throughout the world" (www.radfic.com). Radclyffe acknowledges that genre fiction provides a set of guidelines through which the writer can frame and order the narrative (www.radfic.com, 7 Nov. 2008). The reader of genre, who is knowledgeable of those guidelines, willingly engages with the world, people, and actions created by the writer, looking for the desired resolution to the problems and tensions presented, and genre offers a system that makes it possible for those conflicts not only to be resolved, but to be integrated into the reader's expectations of what occur. The desire to see a successful outcome, particularly in the romantic narrative, keeps the reader attentive to the lovers' efforts to achieve the happy ending. Lesbian readers, as well, want to see their lives and relationships given the same success and support, and the romances of authors like Jennifer Fulton, Karin Kallmaker, and Radclyffe reassure them that such desires are achievable. Lesbian romance writers have continually reimagined the experiences of the women in their pages for the women who read these stories; from the self-loathing of the pulps to the celebration of two women's commitment to one another, lesbian readers have seen their fantasies given tangible form and been encouraged to imagine that a happy ending is possible.

Chapter Six

READING BETWEEN THE SHEETS

> The happy ending of lesbian romance fiction is a gesture of faith and hope even more idealistic — and courageous — than its counterpart in the heterosexual romance. In the teeth of homophobia and sexism, the reality of the social world, lesbian romances propose that an alternative way of being, living, and especially loving exists and can flourish, to have an effect on the world at large. The lesbian fantasy of true love is particularly insistent that gender matters: that being a woman, not a man, is central to self-identity as it operates privately and publicly.... For the lesbian reader, the romance story is more. It lets you know you are real in a world that would hide you; it lets you know you are right in a world that calls you wrong.
> Suzanne Juhasz, *Reading from the Heart*, 240–241

> "I don't like your final scene for *Drumbeat*," Diana says. "Vonny and Diana should end up together." ...
> I put down the receiver with a sigh. I have to acknowledge it's excellent editorial advice. Naturally my audience would want a happy ending, so of course Velda and Davina should end up together.
> Then my heart takes a gigantic leap. I hear Diana's voice as though she's in the room. Vonny and Diana. *Vonny* and *Diana!* I snatch up the phone and punch in her direct line. "Diana?"
> "Yes?"
> "You said ... you made the connection..."
> Claire McNab, *Writing My Love*, emphasis in text, 185

Perhaps no other genre is said to call for such a complete suspension of disbelief as the romance. Once a reader accepts the premise that life exists on other planets or that time travel is possible, science fiction novels make sense. While coincidence often plays a role in the solution to a crime, as long as the investigation adheres to the particular rubric of its type of mystery, a reader will accept the investigation's outcome. Romances, however, are seen as asking their readers to willingly overlook the reliance on extreme yet limited stereotyped characters, highly contrived plots, overwrought themes, and unrealistic outcomes, and when the reader does accept the romantic narrative at face value, she is often castigated for being too susceptible to the false assertions that finding true love is possible. Not surprisingly, then, romantic stories are still more likely to be censured by critics while other genre texts receive extensive analysis and commentary, and although more positive scholarly criticism of the romance has begun to appear, popular romance does not quite enjoy the academic cachet of other genre texts. Yet, the romance still remains the most often sold and read of all the popular genres.[1] The essential question remains: what does the romance novel offer its readers so that, in spite of its reliance on convention and cliché, the love story compels attention?

The reader's importance to the success of the romance novel cannot be overlooked; every examination of the genre, whether critical or popular, emphasizes the impact readers' expectations of and responses to the texts not only has on their own preference, but on the writers of these works as well: "Romance readers are linked by their interest in the genre. They love to talk to each other about their favorite romance titles and authors. They exchange books and opinions and make recommendations wherever they meet..." (Linz, "Setting the Stage" 13). Not surprisingly, romance novelists give their readers greater respect and autonomy in terms of the relationship that is established between writer and reader. Although the earlier view of romance readers as easily swayed by the unattainable fantasy of a happy ending, has begun to diminish, some critics still see the power of the romance to have a potentially detrimental effect on the reader: "The success of formula romance ... would, indeed, suggest that for literally *millions* of women, romantic love still promises salvation. In the face of existential crisis, a newly sexualized form of romantic love appeared to offer a way out; but it was ... more often the way to the self, and not to the other; the way to (orgasmic) oblivion, rather than meaningful relationality" (Pearce, emphasis in text, 136). What Lynne Pearce suggests here is that genre romance, in spite of the narrative emphasis on union between lovers, focuses the reader's attention on her own desire to experience a subliminal denial of connection with another. The source for the reader's acquiescence to this restricted vision of the ending is tied to her compulsion to accept the promised fantasy as an achievable reality.

This concept of the romantic fantasy has been considered the hallmark of the reader's relationship with the text by every critic of the genre, although there has been much discussion of the nature, extent, and value of this element. The constituent parts of fantasy can be organized along two major lines of discussion: the way the conventions of the genre work to establish a framework in which various representations of the fantasy can be expressed and the larger theoretical contexts in which critics describe the make-up of reader fantasy. The first, and perhaps most commented on, fantasy component of the romance is its insistence on the happy ending — the coming together, after a series of trials and separations, of the heroine and hero. However, the ending requires more than just an immediate or future wedding; the couple must recognize their suitability for one another. No one else could be an appropriate partner as each brings to the relationship those qualities and opinions that balance one another. In effect, the whole — the new couple — is greater than the sum of its parts. All of the romance novelists who contributed to Jayne Ann Krentz's anthology, *Dangerous Men and Adventurous Women*, reiterate the importance of the happy ending: Suzanne Guntrum's view is typical; it is also important to note that Guntrum speaks not only as a writer of romances, but as a reader of them as well:

> Why do we, the readers, enjoy these books so much? Obviously we enjoy reading about challenging men and gutsy heroines. We also read romance novels because they're fun. Because they give us immense pleasure and joy. Because in the end there is no ambiguity, no tragedy, no defeat. There is ambiguity enough, tragedy enough, defeat enough in real life. We do not read romances to be reminded of these realities.
>
> In a romance novel we know that, whatever the odds against them, the hero and heroine will come together in the end and live happily ever after. Indeed, if the above is *not* true, then either the book is flawed or it isn't a romance [152–153, emphasis in text].

Besides giving pleasure, the happy ending presents to the reader the process of the heroine overcoming the public and private obstacles that delay the satisfaction of her desires, what Pamela Regis identifies as the "two great liberations": freedom from whatever has restrained her progress and freedom to become united with the hero (15). The reader of the heroine's struggle recognizes that effort and applauds the successful outcome; rather than being overwhelmed by the personality of the hero, the heroine retains this independence especially as it is expressed through her uncoerced choice to accept the hero. Critics who see harm in this emphasis on the cliché that each person will fall in love with her or his soul mate stress the negative implications of the image. Such a view creates the false notion that "a good romance focuses on an intelligent and able heroine who finds a man who recognizes her special qualities and is capable of loving and caring for her as she wants to be loved.... Such an ending [says] that female independence and marriage are compatible rather than mutually exclusive" (Radway 54). The contradictory expectations of the heroine's acceptance of masculine (patriarchal) control while simultaneously experiencing a sense of autonomy are said to present the reader within an unachievable outcome. She can be seen as capable of determining her own position in the world but at the same time willing to cede that control and allow the hero to determine the progress of her/their life. As paradoxical as this intention is, the organization of the narrative enables this goal to be achieved within the pages of the novel.

The typical romance adheres to a very limited narrative framework, but one that must be maintained if the text is to be called a romance. Whatever variations in certain elements — settings, character descriptions and attributes, or social contexts — the novel's basic storyline cannot alter the emphasis on the courtship and the union of the couple. Most romances open when the characters destined to become lovers meet, are attracted to one another, but, for a number of reasons, are unable or unwilling to respond to that attraction. Through a series of plot twists, the hero and heroine will be temporarily united and separated; their actions and motives will be misinterpreted; other characters will deliberately or misguidedly interfere. All of these obstructions to the couple's eventual union will be overcome usually due to the deliberate efforts of one or both of the couple to correct the false image or ideas that have influenced how they respond to one another.[2] Each new plot situation places the hero and/or heroine at a point of decision; they must choose whether to continue the pursuit of a relationship or call a halt. However, the contrivances of the plot prevent the second choice from being finalized, although either of the couple may temporarily believe that electing not to pursue the relationship is the wisest course of action. This fear of desires unrealized is what keeps the reader attentive to the working out of the romantic plot, in spite of her familiarity with the basic outlines. Although she knows that the lovers will reach the understanding that they belong together, the reader engages each specific romance as the particularized expression of the search for idealized love and responds to the trials and emotional tension of that text. However, the reader also re-contextualizes the individual text within her larger reading experience and recognizes the inevitable positive outcome (see McCracken 98).[3]

In addition to this standard narrative movement, the romance novel also utilizes a limited set of characters who are given recognizable personalities, and it is their narrative positions that determine how they will behave. As Lynne Pearce attests, "It is usually the narrative itself that answers the question: that is, the 'hero' will always be the person who assumes *the hero's narrative function* and not simply 'the nice guy' (13, emphasis in text). The hero will always be larger than life, combining the seemingly impossible ultra-masculine attributes of physical strength, decisive action, intelligence, and the ability to command any situation while at the same time, be able to express tenderness and empathy for the heroine. Whatever superficial alterations in his make-up, the hero's contradictions will never prevent the heroine from accepting him as her ideal mate. Likewise, the heroine will adhere to a particular base set of criteria: that is, although her physical attributes, career, social status, and other external descriptions will follow the fashion of the day (particularly in contemporary romances), her emotional live — her desires and the ability to articulate and achieve them — will remain constant. She will be beautiful, but her beauty is balanced by an open, generous personality; she will be intelligent, but not bookish; resourceful, but not always deliberative (see Heinecken, "Changing Ideologies in Romance Fiction," 151–158). These frameworks must be kept not only because romance readers expect them, but, as romance writers themselves acknowledge,

> The author of a romance novel and her audience enter into a pact with one another. The reader trusts the writer to *create and recreate* for her a vision of a fictional world that is free of moral ambiguity, a larger-than-life domain in which such ideals as courage, justice, honor, loyalty, and love are challenged and upheld.... The romance writer gives form and substance to this vision by locking in language, and the romance reader *yields herself to this alternative world in the act of reading*, allowing the narrative to engage her mind and her emotions and to provide her with a certain intensity of experience [Barlow and Krentz 15–16, emphasis added].

This compact assures the reader that her expectations will continue to be met.

Once the personalities of the couple have been established, the novel presents the various barriers that must be overcome if they are to achieve the requisite happy ending. Of course, the nature of these obstacles depends on the text's particular sub-genre; a Regency romance may have the heroine confused by her attraction to a man who is most unsuitable only to be won over by his ability to understand her deepest longings; a contemporary novel may have the heroine coming back to her small home town to uncover the truth about her parents' deaths, a quest set in motion by the frantic contact of an old friend, who is murdered. The hero, at first, is reluctantly pulled into her investigation, but becomes more consumed in helping her solve the mystery, partly because of his attraction, but partly, too, because of his desire to see justice done.[4] During these confrontations the suitability of the couple is tested, and, since the goal of the narrative is to illustrate that the proper outcome has been achieved, both characters discover that initial impressions prove faulty; that what appears as insurmountable conflicts are actually incidental to their compatibility. This, of course, is the essential fantasy, that what seems to be an individual's flaws are actually one's strengths, that one's physical beauty does, indeed, reflect one's inner qualities, and that one's emotional and sensual needs can and will be fulfilled by the only one other individual, whose efforts are aimed towards the same goals.

These narrative contradictions are hallmarks of most generic texts, and romances, particularly, build their plots on oppositional situations, often what seems to be harmful is proven to be beneficial for the development of the romance, and characters, including hero/villain, heroine/seductress, adversary in love/devoted friend. This dependence on stark contrasts underscores the importance of the reader's ability to imagine reconciliation of these opposing narrative components. In essence, having one's cake and eating it too can only occur if there are clear distinctions presented that allow the reader to pull desired qualities from both to create a new whole. Because the romance novel's "form is stable," the reader can concentrate on the emotional content and outcome; after all, the plot exists to facilitate the emotional awakening of both hero and heroine (Regis 205). The often cliched representation of characters encourages the reader to position herself within the narrative, not as voyeur but as participant: "Reader identification is subjective: the reader *becomes* the character, feeling what she or he feels, experiencing the sensation of being *under control* of the character's awareness" (Kinsale, "The Androgynous Reader," 32, emphasis in text). However, it is this intense sense of connection that allows the reader to accept the overt incompatibilities between the main couple and that establishes the point of entry for the fantasy to materialize with the working out of the plot. Since the romance is also a conservative genre, one that reinforces traditional conceptions of gender behavior, the tensions that are established in the plots reinforce mainstream social attitudes about the appropriateness of the wished for fulfillment. The hero, for example, may at first sight seem totally unsuited to the heroine's deepest needs, although she may find herself attracted to his physical qualities; his actions, past and present, suggest a dangerous, uncontrollable personality that poses a threat to the heroine's physical and emotional safety. For much of the narrative his actions seem motivated by self-interest rather than altruism or affection, and his decisions can place the heroine in jeopardy.

Often, secondary characters will voice their objections, calling the heroine's own behavior and decisions into question since these figures frequently reflect traditional views of what is socially appropriate and acceptable. Only the determination of the heroine, her belief, finally, in the rightness of her feelings and in her pursuit of happiness, brings the romance to its expected conclusion. The hero, too, will express misgivings about his attraction to the heroine and sometimes take steps to distance himself from any deeper involvement, but since an essential purpose of the romance is to permit the hero to acknowledge his own emotional desires, he will finally cede his social position for the personal intimacy of a relationship with the heroine. This acquiescence of the hero to a restriction of his world is another aspect of the fantasy provided by the ending; after all, the heroine must become his entire world.

Georgette Heyer's Regency romance, *Lady of Quality*, illustrates these conventions. Annis Wychwood enjoys a high social status, sufficient wealth to provide for her own household, and a sterling public reputation. Her only flaw, according to the circle in which she moves, is that at twenty-nine she is still unmarried. Although she has received numerous offers, she has rejected them because she did not love any of the suitors. Through a series of comic misadventures, she becomes the temporary chaperon of Lucilla Carleton, the ward of Oliver Carleton, a member of the same social set, but who has the reputation of being the most uncivil man in all of England. Here are the typical contrasts that establish the romance's trajectory. Annis and Oliver originally clash over the responsibility of monitoring Lucilla's behavior; as the novel continues they begin to find points of commonality in how they view their community and its expectations. It is at this point that Annis begins to find herself attracted to Oliver in spite of his lack of civility; Oliver Carleton treats Annis as the capable, intelligent adult she is, a response she rarely finds in her closest connections. He also intuitively recognizes her need for independence and will allow her to retain it. Surprisingly, neither of these characters shows the least reticence in discussing Carleton's sexual past and both talk openly about his behavior towards his mistresses. In fact, at the point in the novel when both have declared their feelings, this subject becomes a key component in the final disposition of the relationship as he acknowledges that for the first time that "I have never in my life wanted anything more than I want to win you for my *own*—to love, and to cherish, and to guard—Oh, damn it, Annis, how can I make you believe that I love you with my whole heart and body, and mind?" (284, emphasis in text). His recognition of her ability and her understanding of his past ensure that despite all of the objections offered by friends and family, this will be the perfect match. What Heyer's text shows is the balance of opposites that makes the fantasy ending possible.

What the romance's fantasy ending also achieves with this reconciliation of opposites is the reiteration and normalization of a conservative social construction of heterosexual relationships. While Radway's description stresses the negative implications of this process for the reader, her analysis does highlight the all-encompassing impact of the ending:

> The romantic narrative demonstrates that a woman must learn to trust her man and to believe that he loves her deeply ... the fantasy's conclusion suggests that when she manages such trust, he will reciprocate with declarations of his commitment to her.... Once she responds to his passion with her own, she will feel as the heroine does, both emotionally complete and sexually satisfied. In short, she will have established successfully an external connection with a man whose behavior she now knows how to read correctly [149].

By correctly interpreting the outward behavior of the hero, the heroine accomplishes the fulfillment of her desires and insures the continuation of the fantasy. What is guaranteed in such instances is the belief that every individual can find the ideal partner; of course, the ideal mate must also offer the necessary sexual balance. If one accepts the importance of contrasts to the romance novel's narrative structure and of their reconciliation during the story's development, then the final couple must also reflect that contrast. Mainstream romance continually affirms that the expression and achievement of desire belongs to heterosexuals.

Jill Ehnenn provides a useful foundation for examining how narrative fantasy plays out in lesbian romance. She acknowledges that

> the practice of reading the lesbian romance does reflect the regulatory nature of the existing sex/gender system, but also allows for the resistance to that system.... In other words the expectations and desires of lesbian consumers ... significantly resist, yet are simultaneously contained by, a genre which is always already steeped in heteronormative ideologies. The conflicting readings intersect in the realization that while heterosexual romance provides a social sanction for "normal" female sexuality, lesbian romance insistently celebrates a female sexuality which is doubly dangerous since its object of desire resides outside of patriarchal boundaries [126].

Like the typical mainstream romance, lesbian romances follow the expected narrative and character conventions fairly closely; the intended couple make initial contact; there is an intuitive attraction and sense that this is the meant to be lover; some separation of the women is detailed, involving sometimes dangerous, sometimes comic interactions; after the women have reunited the story ends with the promise of a committed relationship. The major characters in lesbian texts also replicate the concept of contrast; one woman tends to exhibit more recognizable "masculine" qualities — self-assurance, a high social status, physical strength, and a commanding personality but emotionally isolated — the other woman often complements these qualities by presenting a more "feminine" aspect — more empathetic and/or creative, a less aggressive manner, an often lesser social status, but more socially adept. These characters also present contrasting physical appearances, as the discussion of the Xena/Gabrielle couple in Chapter Three indicates. However, just as often as lesbian romances follow tradition genre guidelines, the authors frequently and deliberately overturn such expectations. Typically the Xena-based character does take the dominant position; she is the woman who rescues the object of her affection (*Accidental Love*); she has the physical, financial, or social resources to determine that the couple will be secure in their future (*Second Chances*). But, in other romances, the Gabrielle-based character is shown to be the one controlling if not the outer lives of the couple their more important inner lives. Christine Hanson in Maggie Ryan's *The Deal* represents such an overturning of the model; it is the small, blond who decides to pursue Laura Kasdan, and on discovering Laura's emotional and sexual inexperience, determines not only to continue the pursuit, but to support Laura throughout the process. Christine continually reveals her own feelings for Laura over the course of the novel, until Laura is confident and comfortable enough to reciprocate, not the feelings, which Laura has privately acknowledged, but to verbalize them. Christine allows Laura to control the progress of the romance, even though this frustrates her, so that Laura will not retreat from their rowing attachment.

While lesbian romances retain the basic outlines of the heterosexual romantic plot and characters, they incorporate important variations that represent a specific lesbian sensibility, since these are written for a specifically lesbian audience. For example, the main characters do not always embody a rigid set of contrasting qualities; in Forest's *Curious Wine* both Lane and Diana are described as extremely attractive and feminine. Neither woman can be considered to represent the lesbian stereotype of the butch. Even though Lane is a lawyer, the reader never sees her engaged in her profession; this is partially due Diana having the novel's central viewpoint, but also to the closed narrative space of the story — the developing romance between the women is the only story being told. Both women, since they are simultaneously coming out, are shown to be hyperattentive to one another, responding to the slightest alterations in looks or behavior. They become aware of the things that connect memories and desire to one another and experience a sudden sensual response previously unanticipated: driving to a Reno casino, Lane becomes distracted as Diana's look calls up memories of recent lovemaking—"It's hard for me to drive when you're looking at me"—or Diana, during the agreed-to separation spending days searching for the exact perfume Lane wears (113). What Forrest can be offering her readers is a primer of response for lovers, using the story of Lane and Diana to provide idealized models for the reader to imagine engaging in. In addition, Forrest places this romance within a larger emotional context by using the work of Emily Dickinson, not only for the work's title, but to highlight moments when the women recognize their shared attraction. Forrest may have been responding to late 1980s feminist criticism that began to reevaluate Dickinson's sexuality, with its emphasis on the strong homoerotic sensibility that threads through many of her poems. Even if the reader is not aware of critical movements, simply placing well-know words, like the ones that close the novel—"The Soul selects her own Society—/Then—shuts the Door"—as the coda to the passion reunion and commitment of two women encourages the reader to reinterpret standard ideas of finding one's perfect community (160).

Another text that plays with the romance's narrative conventions, illustrating the ways lesbian writers by deliberately manipulating them is Julia Watt's *Wedding Bell Blues*, a comic romance that begins when Lily, in order to retain custody of her dead partner's biological child, agrees to a sham marriage with her gay neighbor, who has his own family issues. Although the premise sounds decidedly unfunny, the potential for tragedy is overwhelmed by the frenetic machinations of Lily and Ben to help Lily keep custody of Mimi, prove Ben's heterosexual credentials to his parents, deal with the classic tension of urban sensibility clashing with Southern rural life; when both Lily and Ben find themselves falling in love with residents of Faulkner County, the complications are multiplied as both now must worry that their presentation of heterosexual marriage is, indeed, false. Of course, the snooping of Ben's family reveals the truth, and the custody fight also becomes a referendum on "homosex-yoo-ality" (204). Here, Watts uses the techniques of slapstick romantic comedy to comment on the meaning of family as well as relationships, particularly as Ben's parents express a surprisingly laissez-faire position on Lily and Ben's sexuality. Watts insures that Mimi will stay with the best parents when a court ordered DNA test reveals that Ben, in fact, is her actual biological father, not Dez, whom everyone involved in her conception believed to be. Here, Watts expands the comic narrative complications to include the process of pregnancy that has become a dominant issue within the lesbian and gay community. The novel's publication date —1999 — positions this narrative component within the whole issues of gay parenting, covering viewpoints ranging from the political, economic, moral, and procedural, and by framing the story between Mimi's conception and the outcome of the custody hearing, Watts also expands the parameters of the reader's fantasy. The novel ends with a celebratory party at Ben's parents' house; among the guests are Ken, Ben's new lover, and Mick, Lily's new lover, both apparently welcomed with open arms. What the inclusiveness of the party also implies is that finding true love, between parents and children as well as lovers, can defuse hostility and support a shared happy ending.

The impact of the heterosexual paradigm in the definition of a successful romantic outcome can be seen in the novels' maintaining of the notion that each woman has, and can find, her one true soul mate, thus encouraging the lesbian reader to imagine, at least during the reading of the novel, that such an achievement is possible. Whatever obstacles confront the women, their innate awareness that they are meant for one another will enable them to succeed; Bonnie Zimmerman call this approach "the *domestication* of the lesbian novel" (227). Zimmerman feels such a movement in lesbian novels, especially romances, undercuts their potential power; she further asserts that the normalizing of lesbian relationships such novels describe actually diminishes the visibility and distinction of the lesbian; these texts succeed in "destigmatizing lesbianism so thoroughly that, were the sex of the protagonist's love interest changed it would make virtually no difference to the story" (227). Such a negative view does raise key questions about the positioning of the lesbian within her larger society, particularly around concerns of the creation and assertion of one's identity.[5] Of course, sexual expression, in terms of behavior and object choice, carries with it the most transgressive potential for any individual as such public display automatically challenges the dominant preconceptions of correct gender behavior. Zimmerman's position can be countered by stressing that lesbian romances are adamant in their insistence that two women are articulating and achieving their intimate desires. Characters who have had previous heterosexual relationships have already discarded them before the particular events presented in a text; characters whose sexual awakening is described do not regret their discovery that it is the longing for another woman's affection that compels their searches; characters who believe that they have lost any opportunity for intimacy and relationship do not isolate themselves from situations that hold out the potential for romantic renewal and that their choice will be a woman.

This determination is especially prominent in romances that often blend genres, typically combining the love story with adventure (Belle Reilly's *High Intensity*), mystery (C. C. Devize's *Misplaced People*), or gothic (Karin Kallmaker"s *Christabel*).[6] Such narrative frameworks present often extremely dramatic situations that the main couple must confront in order to achieve the desired outcome. Several characters bring dangerous pasts with them that they must confront and correct over the development of the story (Jo Madison, from *Heart's Passage*, used to be the executioner for a criminal ganglord; Conn Stryker, of *First Instinct*, runs a computer firm, but also engages in national security undercover work). Other characters, usually the object of the first woman's desires has become involved, usually by accident, with some potentially harmful and life-threatening situation: for example, Carson Garret, in *The Bluest Eyes in Texas*, is reluctantly convinced to act as a spy for a government investigation of the firm in which she works as a paralegal. At the novel's climax she has been kidnapped and physically beaten before being rescued. The developing love story frequently provides needed scenes of calm and normalcy for the couple; at these moments the women are allowed to explore the meanings of their growing attraction and are encourages to imagine a live together beyond the immediate pressures. As with traditional heterosexual romances, before the real ending is achieved, the couple's chance for happiness appears to be denied. Often the more dominant woman — the one who must resolve her past — is violently removed from the narrative; she is often presumed to have been killed, placed in protective, but isolated, custody, or voluntarily removes herself from the scene, believing her lover cannot overlook her past behavior. However, whatever trials and tensions the couple experiences during the narrative, the reader's apprehensions are balanced with her understanding that the couple will be reunited, that any potentially damaging influences from the past have been overcome by their present resolution and the promise of a shared future. The seriousness of this concept of the finding the right lover tends to dominate stories that limit any comic treatment of the quest for love. This is not to suggest that lesbian romantic comedies deny the belief in the right couple attaining the happy ending. Indeed, given that even the concept of a successful lesbian relationship is discredited by mainstream society, the serious treatment of the search of one woman for emotional and physical fulfillment with another woman becomes reasonable. Comic romances, however, place the romantic quest within a supportive community and presents that search as a series of inadvertent blunders and missteps, confusions and misunderstandings that are easily reconciled when these false assumptions are stripped away. More serious romances underscore the potential for loss and denial in the couple's search for connection; this reinforces the importance of the fantasy of success because the reader understands that there are two lines of potentially harmful influence on that happy ending — mainstream condemnation as well as the breakdown of the romance itself, regardless of external pressures. Any reader wishes to see some indication that her desires are valid and valuable, and lesbian readers are no different. Suzanne Juhasz, in *Reading from the Heart*, stresses the importance the idea of "mutual recognition" has for the lesbian reader, that moment of not only seeing herself in the text, but also seeing someone else who is the same as she is in the text (209).

The romantic plot, then, facilitates the reader's acceptance of the fantasy of reconciliation and union, that the right couple is together at the end, and that their commitment will not only last, but ultimately receive social approval. The expression of this fantasy remains as true for lesbian romances and their readers as for heterosexual ones. But, even more important to the fantasy of happy endings for the lesbian reader, is the consistent iteration that two women have the same right to the happy ending as the straight couple. Whether serious or comic, the lesbian reader becomes a witness to the working out of the couple's hesitancy, fear, and, frustration and participate in their happiness and success. The repetition of this outcome "allows the construction of the couple as a unique lesbian subject who together realign the traditionally dichotomous narrative spaces" of conventional mainstream romances (Farwell *Heterosexual Plots & Lesbian Narratives*, 142). The fantasy encouraged by the romance for its readers involves more than narrative conventions; as mentioned earlier, critics of the genre identify deeper aspirations and desires in the relationships readers develop with the romantic text.

These connections involve trying to define the reader's essentially subconscious, subjective experiences felt during the reading of the romance. The first, and most common position of the critics, uses different psychological theories centered on the linking of the individual's desire with the experience of lack, typically of the mother's love. One broad synopsis of this situation, which is based on Freudian concepts, states that the "infant's realisation [*sic*] that it is separate from the mother induces a sense of lack that includes just a trace of the memory of satisfaction. The gap is filled by fantasy ... which provides the means by which the child can imagine a sense of wholeness" (McCracken 89). Feminist reinterpretations of this relationship, especially those based on Nancy Chodorow, emphasize the girl child's inability to develop a complete sense of individuality due to the inability to distinguish a separate sense of self because of the complete similarity between her and the mother; both see themselves as extensions of the other since they share the same gender. This failure to achieve complete separation then impacts the daughter's attempts to develop independent sexual relationships: "The girl becomes erotically heterosexual but at the same time carries an internal emotional triangle into adulthood, a triangle that is completed by her continuing need and desire for her mother. This finally produces in women a continuing wish to regress into infancy to reconstruct the lost intensity of the original mother-daughter bond" (Radway 136). These theoretical positions are much more complex than presented here, but the reader's identification with the text is closely tied to connecting the heroine's, and the focus of this theory is generally limited to her experience, fantasy with a desire for nurture and complete emotional support from the hero.

The accepted breakdown of this version of the nurturing fantasy provided by the romance novel places the heroine in a passive position; although she may express longings, her actions to achieve any satisfaction are severely limited. Despite heroines who are described as combative, daring, or courageous, she rarely acts in her own best interests. At best she may run away from the threats — real or imagined — embodied by the hero. In her delineation of the ideal romance Radway notes that its "narrative logic" only requires the heroine to respond to the hero's overtures and actions (150). The one self-directed decision made by the heroine, according to Radway, occurs when she chooses to reinterpret the hero's previous behavior, reimaging his hostility, distance, or superiority as affection, connection, and equality. Here is the reader's fantasy made tangible — that "when the heroine retroactively reinterprets the hero's offensive behavior as equivalent expressions of his basic feeling for her, the reader is encouraged to engage in the same rereading process ... the romance perpetuates the illusion that, like water into wine, brusque indifference can be transformed into unwavering devotions. Its value derives from its offer of a set of procedures that will accomplish the transformation" (151). This general pattern of passivity may explain the dominance of the numerous implicit and explicit rape scenes in many romances and explains the strong negative response of many critics who find the heroine's acceptance of her physical and emotional subordination disturbing, not only in the text, but in the reader's frequent anticipation of such situations (see Beverly Clark, Karen Bernier, Michelle Henneberry-Nassau, et al. "Reading Romance, Reading Ourselves"). The heroine's need to find a supportive relationship, one that promises her complete care to substitute for the mother's loss, encourages her to accept whatever form the hero chooses to express it. The heroine dreams of being able to abandon all ties to society, to loose herself in the love on one man, and in the fantasy world of the romance, the hero comes to realize these feelings and reciprocate them, becoming the tender, nurturing companion.

The one problematic aspect of these theories of the romantic fantasy resting on a dream of returning to an infantile state of pure and total mother love appears when sex enters the narrative. Standard psychological theory stresses that to achieve an independent identity the daughter must come to transfer her desires for the mother's love to a suitable object — the male. The first such figure for the daughter would be her father, but here social taboo condemns and punishes those who would act out such desires. Since the father is unavailable for the daughter to act out her sexual feelings, she must redirect those longings to a more suitable person, a man who literally and figuratively takes the father's place. This substitution helps explain the age difference between many romantic couples. The heroine's sexual awakening by the hero represents the complement to the fantasy of complete emotional surrender and support; as noted throughout Chapter Four, the role sex plays in the development of the romance is key since it marks the totality of the couple's commitment and suitability for one another. However frequently sex occurs within the novel, the couple achieves complete release and satisfaction; the heroine, even if she has been raped, comes to anticipate continued intimacy with the hero. The heroine's virginity becomes proof of her value, and in the typical narrative movement the moment when she offers her innocence to the hero marks that desired transformation in him as he recognizes the import of the offer. Not all heroines are virgins, but even sexually experienced heroines have generally reserved the complete surrender of their passion for the right man:

> Women romance readers seem to derive a sustained level of sexual awareness and pleasure from the tension built into the development of this loving relationship *over time*, and it is the process of conflict and resolution that takes place between two wills and bodies that creates the necessary tension to turn the entire story into a psychogenic stimulus [Thurston 154, emphasis in text].

More recent critical comment on genre romance highlights the alterations in the heroine's character that bring her awareness of and ability to act on her own sexuality, and this reevaluation alters the framing of the fantasy for the reader. Instead of being forced into sexual knowledge by the hero, she often takes control of this component of the romance. Not surprisingly, many modern romance writers find this type of heroine more appealing since she presents a more decisive personality, one that places more control and responsibility for the progress of the romance in her hands. In her introduction the *Dangerous Men and Adventurous Women* Jayne Ann Krentz emphasizes this point:

> Romance novels invert the power structure of a patriarchal society because they show women exerting enormous power over men. The books also defy the masculine conventions of other forms of literature because they portray women as heroes.... The romance novel is the only genre in which readers can routinely expect to encounter heroines who are imbued with the qualities normally reserved for the heroes in other genres: honor, courage, and determination.... The hero falls in love with the heroine because he sees something of himself in her — he sees the *hero* in her [5].

How this heroic position transfers beyond the pages of the text is open to question, but the romance's insistence on the importance of female power in bringing about the happy ending cannot be overlooked. Another point modern romance writers emphasize is the increasing need for reciprocity between the hero and heroine in matters of the heart. The hero comes to realize that he must admit to his emotional needs and that only the heroine is capable of providing him the means of satisfying them. Here is the revision of the more traditional fantasy of the female being taken care of; now the hero discovers the same lack of nurture and looks to her to fill that lack. As Dawn Heinecken notes, "Relationships are no longer based on sexuality and male dominance but on mutuality and equality. In turn, this emphasis on mutuality further changes the meanings of sexual relations, as well as gender and gender roles" (165). The idea of shared power must be balanced with shared responsibility if the romance is to progress smoothly to its desired outcome; without this acknowledgement from both partners, the promise of the ending will be undermined. For the reader the representation of a true sharing of all aspects of the relationship offers the temporary belief that such outcomes can be attained. What makes such a desire so compelling, of course, is the notion that the exchange of autonomy for integration enables the couple to close off the rest of the world in the creation of the entity of the coupe. They become totally self-sufficient and directed, so instead of moving back into the wider society, the couple disengages, suggesting that nurturing one another is enough. Given the importance of social approbation for the instigation of the narrative, the ending appears to resign social interest to the periphery. This escape from the pressures and interference of the wider world will provide the couple with the environment needed to allow the relationship to thrive.

For many readers, the primary fantasy offered by the romance is the temporary escape the book offers from everyday live and the brief glimpse of a world outside their ordinary experience: "Women use romances for escape—*to* another time or new experience and *from* the constant demands being made of their time, attention, and energy" (Thurston 132). For critics, the concern rests on the reader's attachment to the idea of leaving the complexity of the real world for one where difficulties can be overcome through the exertions of a hero whose only focus is to rescue and protect the heroine, especially since the text invites the reader to identify with the heroine's own desire for such an outcome. The main concern with overindulgence for critics is the likelihood that the reader will develop an "addictive" need to recapture the freeing experience promised by the romantic narrative; the feared result is the development of false expectations about gender which will be transferred from the fictional realm to the real world. The reader looking for the happy ending will always face disappointment since personal and social relationships cannot operate according to the dictates of genre literature. Janice Radway addresses the complexity of this question of the implications of the escape fantasy for readers; she notes that for the Smithton women escape carries a double meaning—literally a chance to put aside the demands of career, home and family to indulge in an enjoyable activity and, figuratively, a disengagement from the reality of their lives to engage with the basic nurturing fantasy (97). Escapism carries a negative connotation, and many romance writers take the critics to task for assuming their readers are so easily swayed:

> Of course the readers can tell the difference. They do not expect the imaginative creations of romance to conform to real life any more than they expect the fantasies of any other genre to conform to the real world. Like all the other genres, romance is based on fantasies and readers know it. Readers and writers alike get disgusted with critics who express concern that they may not be able to step back out of the fantasy. They do not appreciate being treated as if they were children who don't know where one stops and the other begins [Krentz "Introduction," 2].

However, even romance writers acknowledge the power of the fantasy to transport the reader to an ideal world of the heroine's empowerment and the hero's admission of desire for her.

When lesbians read their romances, do they read first as women and then as lesbians or as lesbians first and then as women? To answer this question demands an expertise in the psychology of human sexual development and the sources of sexual difference that go beyond the scope of this analysis. What critics of the genre do reference are basic theoretical concepts that help them contextualize their interpretations of the connections readers develop with the narratives. It is, perhaps, not surprising that an essential fantasy that lesbian and straight readers share is the desire to discover in the beloved a source of unconditional, completely nurturing love. The essential difference, of course, is the source of that love; for the lesbian reader wishes to experience, like the characters in the novels, the discovery that only another woman will be able to provide her the completeness she is seeking. That the figure of the mother should be seen as the first representation of a totally nurturing relationship is not unreasonable; Suzanne Juhasz, referencing the work of Lizzie Thynne, states that "the earliest love between mother and infant, which sets the tone and the template for all subsequent love relationships (be they heterosexual or homosexual), is of great importance to the manner in which lesbian lovers play out their relationship" ("Lesbian Romance Fiction and the Plotting of Desire" 72). The ideal mother acts as a facilitator to the daughter's growth, offering images of acknowledgement and support that enable the daughter's own identity to develop; the mother becomes the model of a continually satisfying relationship where needs are not only met, but anticipated and where both mother and child participate in such reciprocity. Of course, this presents an idealized situation; many lesbians, especially once they have come out to family, experience a complete withdrawal of affection and support. Like her heterosexual counterpart, then, the lesbian character will seek this emotional support by substituting the mother with another source. Here, again, that object of desire will be a woman, because although the mother is no longer available, the experience of female centered love is, and the character will use this as a gauge in her search.[7]

The lesbian reader, then, shares the chief romantic fantasy of lovers finding the perfect partner. What changes is the delineation of the search for and finding of true love. Many lesbian romances end, as mainstream ones, with the couple shutting out the larger world and retreating to a utopian situation where their love will flourish unimpeded. Here the isolation is emotional, a metaphoric cocoon that enhances the couple's desire to concentrate solely on one another. *Curious Wine* typifies this scenario. Other novels give the couple an actual physical distance between the relationship and the couple's activities with a larger society: at the conclusion of *Class Reunion* Heather and Jennifer live on a large ranch well outside of Phoenix; in *Rebecca's Cove* Hobie and B. J. reside on a private island off the Florida coast. However, many lesbian romances do not end with the couple turning away from social engagement and connection; in fact, the couple takes deliberate steps to show their love to a wider community. In *Horizon of the Heart,* Danni, the character who at the moment she accepts that she loves Jenny also accepts that she is a lesbian, makes her declaration in the parking lot of the town's grocery store, puts Jenny on the handlebars of a bike, and as they pedal towards home, kisses Jenny on the lips while at a stoplight. The fantasy of finding love includes the corollary fantasy that love, even lesbian love, can overcome social stigma. Many of these characters, because of the social and/or economic status within them, could face potential ostracism, but the romance insures that the declaration of love is sufficient to the couple's well-being. More importantly, the recognition that in spite of the sexual orientation of one's partner, love transforms social expectations. Not surprisingly, then, the communities in which the main characters move generally accept and support the new couple. Portraying lesbian love as legitimate and showing that the couple in, essential ways, does not challenge conventional ideas of relationship highlights the transgressive aspect of the lesbian romance.

Of course, the lesbian couple *does* challenge standard ideas of the romantic relationship. The typical romantic resolution, as has been noted, highlights the creation of the couple, but also keeps the couple a separate and distinct entity. The hero and heroine are shown as sufficient to themselves, and while not completely severing all connections to a wider society, capable and desirous of narrowing the limits of the relationship to their own needs. Lesbian romances consistently place the couple's relationship within a circle of social connections that will provide them variations of the private nurture they find in one another: the "romance formula ... develop[s] a fantasy in which a world structured by feminosocial bonding will become normative rather than aberrant, central rather than marginal" (Juhasz, "Lesbian Romance Fiction and the Plotting of Desire," 78). Juhasz's feminosociality combines a full range of female connections and influences, including familial, social, and romantic, and these relationships establish a series of environments that allow women to recognize and act on their own wants as well as provide the necessary support systems that will encourage their success. The most clear-cut way this widening of the fantasy of approval and support appears in the lesbian romance is the way concepts of family and community are integrated into the happy ending.

Family for the lesbian romance begins with the characters' family of origin; parents and siblings will express either support for the lesbian woman or reject her. The first issue to be confronted deals not with a romantic search by this character but her own search for identity. Many of the main characters come into their narratives completely independent of any familial ties often because they have been literally or emotionally cast out. This rejection has occurred earlier in the character's life, usually before the events chronicled in the narrative, and sets up the woman for the belief that she is incapable of establishing any beneficial relationship with another person; if her family cannot love her, how can she be loveable. During the progress of the romance, as described previously, the woman, coming to realize her own sexual identity, also comes to accept that she is someone who can give and receive love. The restoration of social balance has been a consistent thread in criticism of the romance, and for lesbian readers this restorative aspect contributes to the fantasy of inclusion and acceptance.[8] Some romances illustrate this equilibrium when the creation of the lesbian couple also opens the door to the family reuniting; often this is shown with one of the couple introducing her lover to her relatives. Not all families disassociate themselves from the lesbian daughter; often one person — frequently a sibling — offers emotional support for the woman and will encourage her to pursue her heart's desires. For example, in *Class Reunion* Sally, Jennifer's sister, notices the growing attraction between Jennifer and Heather. She asks sometimes embarrassing questions about what's happening, and calls Jennifer to task for not admitting her feelings: "What are you going to do about Heather?" (145).

A variation of the realignment of the biological family that supports the fantasy of inclusion appears in novels that bring the lesbian couple more intimately into the process of creating a family. Many novels present one of the eventual couple as a parent — Heather in *Class Reunion*, Hobie in *Rebecca's Cove*, Eliot Barron in *Forty Love* — and the progress of the romance requires the other woman to broaden her understanding of relationship and desire to include the child. At first, the woman expresses reluctance, not so much that she dislikes children, but that she has no experience with them; often this character has no siblings or is much older than they. There are novels that do have this woman as part of a large family, but she has removed herself from intimacy with them. Over the course of the story, however, the reluctant character discovers an affinity with the child; she can communicate effectively with the child — interestingly the gender of the child does not seem to matter. Often, too, the child becomes the instigator for bringing the couple back together. In *Forty Love*, for example, Morgan, Eliot's daughter, sends a frantic message to Julia about her father's attempts to ruin her mother's reputation; this precipitates Julia to approach her own mother and ask for assistance in preventing this outcome. What the acceptance of the child illustrates is the humanizing of the one woman, who before this has presented a public image of control, distance, and coldness, and since the child embodies qualities that have attracted the one woman to the child's mother, her growing attachment to the child further qualifies her as the proper partner. *Wedding Bell Blues* presents a telling variation on this model since Mimi is not Lily's biological child, but the daughter of her partner as a result of artificial insemination. Much of this novel follows the custody battle for Mimi, since Lily's lover's parents are suing to take Mimi away from Lily. DNA testing proves that Ben — the gay neighbor Lily has married to facilitate the custody issues — to his surprise is, in fact, Mimi's biological father. What could have been a tragic outcome is turned through the comedy of multiple inseminations and Ben's substitution of his sperm one day to give Dez a breather into the expansion of family at the narrative's conclusion. In some novels the child's needs for a stable family influence the decisions made by the two women in the developments of their own relationship. In *Shaken* Lily Stewart becomes the custodian of her nephew and worries how it will impact the growing connection between her and Anna; however, her fears prove unfounded when, at the romance's conclusion, Anna tells Lilly, "Honey, I want Andy to live with us. We should ask for custody so that he gets to stay. We can even adopt him if you want to, both of us" (385).

Many lesbian romances do not use children as a signifier of a couple's true attachment; rather, they move the couple into an expanded community which indicates an increasing involvement with others. Such a repositioning presents a major shift in the idea of the couple being totally self-sufficient in terms of satisfying one another's needs. What such scenarios suggest is that while the couple can offer one another certain levels of fulfillment, especially the satisfaction of sexual desire, by themselves, the couple cannot provide complete emotional support; to attempt to be the all and everything sets up the relationship to fail. In fact, some lesbian romances include relationships where a character attempts to dominate one of the eventual couple, believing that only she can provide what the other woman really wants; in *Heart's Passage*, for example, Cadie Jones' obsessive lover refuses to admit that Cadie no longer has feelings for her and tries to sabotage the developing relationship between Cadie and Jo Madison. These maneuvers may be harmful or comic, but the inclusion of such contrasts reinforces the idea that the fantasy of total integration of the couple offers no benefit either for each individual woman or the couple. The greatest threat is the loss of an individual sense of self and of agency; the controlling partner determines the ability of the other to function. Since this situation too closely reflects real life abusive relationships, the romance narrative brings about a definitive resolution for the character who will become part of the appropriate couple at the novel's end. Cadie's former lover, a United States senator, uses one last ploy to keep Cadie's affection, by offering her the chance to pursue her career and to announce publically that they will have a child together. However, Cadie is able to manipulate the senator's own fear of negative publicity to achieve the desired separation from her control. Many times the efforts needed to rescue the dominated woman are undertaken by the woman who will be the right partner. She has the necessary social, monetary, or legal connections to force the dangerous woman out of the picture, or she has the skill and strength to bring about this removal on her own. Once the rescue has been affected, the new couple establishes a relationship built on an understanding that they must allow each to remain independent if their union is to succeed. Each woman must recognize she has a responsibility not only to one another, but to herself as well in order to bring to the relationship a maturity and ability that guarantees the permanence of the relationship: "the mature woman is a person who operates in relationship authentically and with agency — that is, she is distinct (has viable self-boundaries) and connected (functions in healthy relationship — to individuals and society as large)" (Juhasz *Reading from the Heart*, 18).

The importance of achieving this balance often takes precedence over the more intimate aspects of the romance; many novels even reduce the importance of the couple's sexual pleasure to their engagement with a wider community. The number of novels that conclude with a large celebration underscores this shift in the delineation of the fantasy of nurture: the cast party for the high school musical in *The Light Fantastic*, the family Christmas in *Accidental Love*, the wedding in *Heart's Passage*. The makeup of the lover's new community includes family and friends whose numbers will vary; however large or small the community, its operation rests on total acceptance and support of the new couple. Nurturing is no longer the function of the couple in the revised fantasy; their relation is improved, in fact, with their acceptance of their social role. Just as the couple accepts responsibility to support one another, they also accept the responsibility of their communal obligations. They also discover that they play important roles in this community and that the community benefits from their participation. The creation of these wider ties will sometimes function as a bridge for the completion of the couples' romance, providing them a point of reference for maintaining their relationship during the final stages of it completion. For instance, in *Carved in Stone*, even though Isabelle and Rose have acknowledged their commitment, circumstances at the end of the novel prevent an immediate joining of their lives. Developing the potential of the natural spring well requires Isabelle's presence in London as Rose remains in the north to deal with the practical issues of the renovations of the estate. However, as Rose reminds Isabelle, "I shall ... insist that Roger assign me a Public Relations person, I mean woman. That's your background, isn't it? ...And after that, I'm sure I can think of endless little ruses to get you back up here *on business*— he doesn't need to know it's the business of our hearts that he's supporting, does he?" (281, emphasis in text). Rose will not feel abandoned not only because she is sure of Isabelle's feelings, but because of the support of a small circle of intimates who have encouraged Rose in following her desires. Yet, it is important to note that even though the immediate union of the couple is not shown, that delay is a temporary one. The narrative clearly implies that Isabelle and Rose, and other similar couples, will ultimately join households as well as affections.

Building or joining this community becomes part of the couple's desire for connection and support. In the communal romances discussed in Chapter Three, for the central character, who either comments on the interactions of the group or whose romantic efforts dominates the narrative, keeping the entire community together is as necessary to the couple's success as it is to the group's itself. Interestingly, a member of the particular community who expresses a need for exclusivity — at the expense of the smooth functioning of the group — is perceived as threatening. Distinguishing between real threat and momentary disruption depends on the motives of the women involved in a developing relationship and on who might be hurt by their actions. In other instances the threat comes from outside the specific community itself. Disruptions, however, are smoothed over as the power of shared affection and support prevents the group from splintering; newcomers, even those who are welcomed, particularly as lovers, must recognize the various threads that hold the community together:

> David sat down beside [Laura] and shook his head.
> "I don't get it."
> Laura smiled.... "You don't get what?"
> He nodded his head in the direction she was looking. "Them. You'd think they never saw each other. Ryan spends more time with Tori than he does with me." ...
> "They're a breed apart, David. We'll never understand them, they're different from us. They're Sirens, and we hear their call. We're attracted to them for their fire, their energy, and then we try to tame it out of them." She shook her head. "We can't do it, and if we could, we wouldn't like what they'd become" [Stevens 244].

This particular community of firefighters and emergency medical technicians presents a special circumstance in terms of its various relationships. Other groups usually share some level of background, either work (*It's in Her Kiss*), residence (*Paxton Court*), or interests (*Between Girlfriends*). What the expansion of the private fantasy of acceptance and love to a community of like-minded people offers the lesbian reader is the possibility of her finding a similar world of openness and open-mindedness, where coming out and expressing one's love will not be ridiculed or denied.

As necessary as the fantasy of nurture is for the lesbian reader, the fantasy of sexual fulfillment cannot be overlooked. Romantic love has always included passionate expression, both verbally and bodily; lovers communicate desire and commitment as the level of intimacy deepens. Lovers want support, but first they need ecstasy:

> The first touch was exquisite, enough to send both women out of their minds with lust. Baylor used her lips, tongue, and teeth to drive Hobie higher and higher. She alternated between breasts, and when she had her mouth on one, she used her hands to knead and massage the other. Slipping the tip of her tongue into the small gold hoop, Baylor tugged gently, pulling harder once Hobie's breathless moans encouraged her [Maas 267].

In the romances lovers always know what to do to satisfy one another; even when the lovemaking represents the initiation of one of the couple, there is an instinctual awareness of what she can do to satisfy the other. Hesitancy on the novice's part quickly dissipates as she becomes more assured and bolder in her sexual overtures; several romances include numerous scenes of lovemaking that trace the couple's intensifying desire for one another. Often their passion becomes almost out of control as the slightest touch, sometimes, even a glance, is enough to initiate the sex. Such appetites, however, do not mark either of the couple as incapable of controlling their sexual drives. Christine Hanson of *The Deal* must continually delay her own physical gratification until Laura signals her willingness; once that barrier is broken, however, the two thoroughly enjoy exploring one another's body and the ways to bring each other to satisfaction. Lane imposes a month long moratorium on any contact between her and Diana, as *Curious Wine* moves to its conclusion, as a way for them to test their feelings and commitment. Obviously, what the reader sees portrayed here is the idealized image of pure and continual gratification; sexual intimacy can be engaged in any time, will always be mutually satisfying, and retains the intensity of the first embrace. Sexual contact remains safe, even in the decades after AIDS.

No matter the age of the couple the ability to enjoy sex must be included in the narrative if the romance is to satisfy the reader's fantasy, explicit sex scenes appear frequently in lesbian novels.[9] Not surprisingly, though, most characters' ages in lesbian romance novels appear to range between the mid-twenties to mid-thirties, when they are best able to respond at a physical peak. In some more recent romances, those texts appearing in the twenty-fist century, the age of one or both of the partners has crept up a bit, perhaps as a way of reassuring the reader that sexual desire does not fade with age. Whatever the age of the characters, lesbian readers, according to Jill Ehnem, enjoy the inclusion of concrete depictions of sex between lovers and "reported that they wanted more love scenes with explicit sexual detail" (124). This suggests that lesbian readers do not equate the graphic descriptions of sex with pornography or see them as gratuitous; rather, the insistence that lesbians have sex offers the lesbian reader the chance to see women not only enjoying sex, but also see women having sex as a normal expression of their very being. While the constant display of sexual activity may be seen as supporting the negative stereotype that sex, and sex alone, defines the lesbian individual, the lesbian reader is shown women reveling in this aspect of their identity. The novels privilege lesbian sexual expression and make it an intrinsic component of who these characters are. The characters, in fact, celebrate their ability to enjoy the physical aspect of the relationship, and while the sexual desire and fulfillment represent an essential aspect of the couple, sex without the emotional nurturing proves insufficient to sustain any relationship. The ultimate fantasy the lesbian reader discovers in her romance reading illustrates that love between women is possible, that its expression can balance physical and emotional intimacy, that the relationship benefits both women in all ways, and that the larger world will see no threat in their commitment to one another.

Conclusion: Escape Clause

> Whilst it could be argued that there are no limits to the permutations of perverse *desire*, love ... endures on account of principles and boundaries that can be pushed but never broken.
> (Lynn Pearce, *Romance Writing*, 22, emphasis in text)

> The sun broke out of low clouds and green leaves turned copper in the light. Sandra pushed open the window and reached to touch rough bark. She stayed for a moment leaning into the air, balanced between hills and bay, certain of an edge on which she had found plenty of room to stand.
> (Lisa Shapiro, *The Color of Winter*, 201)

Above all else, romance novels retain the distinction of being viewed primarily as escapist reading. Women, and the majority of readers remain women, it is said, turn to romances as a way to put aside the pressures of everyday life for a little while, as a chance to dream of having a tall, dark hero sweep them up and take them to a world of luxury and sensuality. For many critics the central dilemma focuses on the implications of the reader's interest in using the romantic text to separate herself from the mundane and seek some level of solace. Critics who see this behavior in a negative light comment on the compensatory nature of the reading experience: "In effect, romance reading provides a vicarious experience of emotional nurturance *and* erotic anticipation and excitation" (Radway 105, emphasis in text). Not only is the reader seeking some kind of tenuous sense of connection and satisfaction with the heroine's search for love and fulfillment, but she must rationalize her reading to defend her continued engagement and enjoyment. The difficulty with such a position is that defining what a reader might be escaping from and /or escaping towards remains subjective. That readers find a momentary sense of freedom in identifying with a heroine whose exploits provide her with a lover who will ease her social, economic, and emotional burdens should not seem unreasonable. Most of us wish that we could transfer the stresses of everyday life to someone else, at least for a short time. Such a wish clearly supports those critics who emphasize the psychological desire of an individual to return to a pre-oedipal state of complete immersion in the mother's love. However, a reader indulging in these fantasies of complete surrender suggests, according to these critics, that she will also cede her autonomy to her lover in exchange for that support.

Romance writers, of course, find that such comments demean the ability of the reader to distinguish between the fantasy world of the text and her daily life:

> [Romances] are often harshly judged, but their appeal makes sense to me. In this fantasy, you don't have to earn love. There are brighter people in the world, prettier, more glamorous people, but you are the one who is loved.... And nothing for anyone to get upset over. This is all taking place in the realm of fantasies. We should not assume that fantasies are necessarily goals, things people actually want [Seidel "Judge Me by the Joy I Bring," 163].

The writers continually stress the influence their readers have on the creation of romantic characters and plots and how quickly they respond to aspects seen as too incredible to be accepted. This relationship between producer and consumer can be viewed strictly in pragmatic terms — give the reader what she wants to insure continued sales — but authors reveal a real sense of responsibility to their readers' concerns and interests; in fact, the relationship between romance writers and readers represents a very different model than that between other authors and their audience. Through websites, blogs, and conventions the interaction between the writer and reader is initiated and maintained through constant conversation and feedback. This strong attachment between the two encourages writers to pay close attention to the nuanced interests of the readers and incorporate these concerns in their novels. Readers turn their interest in following the exploits of the hero and heroine into producing the very texts they have enjoyed; many of the writers collected in Krentz's anthology read romances before they became authors. (See Judith Arnold's, Doreen Malek's and Susan Phillips' essays.)

Critics who view the romance reader's engagement with the novels from a positive perspective also highlight this reciprocal engagement. Pamela Regis points to the value for the reader of experiencing a strong emotional response to the triumph of the heroine's narrative, and, as she notes, "Romance novels, are, therefore, profoundly out of step with the prevailing contemporary high culture simply because of this emotional sensibility" (206). Happy endings are considered suspect since they make promises that cannot be kept beyond the pages of the novel. The pursuit and maintenance of love is more complex than is described in the romance, and social expectations impinge on the couple's attempts to establish a private life more strongly than they do inside these narratives. Yet, most of us would probably prefer the happy ending to the tragic one; not many women would see the lives of Anna Karenina or Isabelle Archer as ones to emulate. The assumption that romance readers willingly discard their grasp on reality when they take up a novel undercuts their knowledge of the genre itself and their interactions with writers and works. Both Carol Thurston and Janice Radway, even with their differing interpretations of the data, reveal through their extensive surveys that romance readers hold strong opinions about what contributes to a novel's success of failure, that they take and make recommendations seriously, and that they continue to read this literature because they enjoy it. Such a degree of deliberateness suggests that rather than romance readers being swept away by the passion of the story they are able to balance their experience of both worlds.

Although lesbian readers have not had their romance reading choices examined as often or extensively as straight readers, Ehnenn's small sample indicates this same level of conscious engagement with the text. They actively seek out stories that provide them with entertainment as well as idealized descriptions of sex and relationships that offer temporary escapes from the homophobia of mainstream society. Ehnenn does question the whether some lesbian romances simply reiterate the dominant heterosexist concepts of relationship or offer a transformation of them. Her sample indicates that most lesbian readers do not appear upset that the love of two women follows the pattern of the typically straight romance. However, acceptance of a version of human relationships, as Ehnenn indicates, does not signify allegiance to those standards. Although she feels that the romance does not effectively confront or reinscribe the dependence on mainstream representations of lesbians, she does applaud such novels' depictions of a lesbian desire and the attainment of that desire. In the end, it is this reaffirmation of one's experience that encourages the momentary suspension of disbelief necessary for the reader to experience the happy ending offered by the romance.

For the lesbian to see one woman successfully articulating, pursuing, and achieving an intimate relationship with another is a heady experience. As I have discussed throughout these chapters, the lesbian romance novel describes a narrative movement that positions the lesbian at its center and reframes her marginal status; this allows her to escape the stereotypic and homophobic depictions of the lesbian as deviant, disordered, and demonic. Her sexuality is celebrated as she is encouraged not only to claim it, but to express it; she discovers a lover who satisfies her sexual and emotional needs and who allows her to provide the same fulfillment; she becomes part of a supportive community that offers advice or criticism as needed to facilitate the successful outcome of her romance:

> Everyday reading, then, is a story about need, sometimes satisfied, sometimes not.... [And] the importance both of our need for true love and of fantasies we create about getting it.... The stories revolve around fantasies not because they are the opposite of life but because they are integral to life. One way, if not the only way, to address the need is to imagine how it might be fulfilled. We may give shape to the fantasies with words and characters and plot. We may take part in the fantasy by reading these novels. Fiction can make these dreams of love and identity come true — for the characters; for the reader who is participating wholeheartedly in their story; for the author [Juhasz *Reading from the Heart*, 249].

For the duration of the romance the lesbian, like any reader, can put aside the pressures of dealing with the typical demands of family or career; more importantly, she can also momentarily experience the fantasy of complete acceptance, dreaming of the possibility of its achievement. Like Sandra, who is pictured looking out of her window in the headnote to this conclusion, the lesbian reader balances between dreams and reality, the possible and the actual. What appears to be reaching for the insubstantial, "leaning into the air," is proven to be solid since love experienced gives her "plenty of room to stand." This, perhaps, is the greatest value of the romance, giving the reader the freedom to imagine her happy ending.

Chapter Notes

Introduction

1. The popularity of the romance novel has been noted from the earliest critical studies of the genre. See, for example, Tania Modleski, *Loving with a Vengeance: Mass-produced Fantasies for Women* (New York: Methuen, 1982); Janice A. Radway, *Reading the Romance: Women, Patriarchy, and Popular Literature* (Chapel Hill: University of North Carolina Press, 1984); Pamela Regis, *A Natural History of the Romance Novel* (Philadelphia: University of Pennsylvania Press, 2003). How these, and other authors, respond to such popularity is tied to their position on the value of the romance as literature. Regis regards romantic fiction in a positive light, seeing it as detailing "women's freedom" (xiii). Others view the romance as debilitating to its readers by encouraging unrealistic ideas about love and lovers.

2. Interestingly, critics of the mystery novel, science fiction, and other genre literature do not emphasize as strongly the disconnect between the fictive expression and real world behavior. Of course, some genres, such as horror and science fiction, have no corollaries with the everyday. The mystery novel, however, does have close ties to the ways that crime and its investigations are carried out; one of the mystery novel's requirements is that it adhere to actual procedural standards, especially those works that present police, forensic, and specialty detective investigations.

3. In *Romantic Conventions*, ed. Anne K. Kaler and Rosemary E. Johnson-Kurek (Bowling Green, OH: Bowling Green State University Popular Press, 1999), Anne Kaler, in her introduction to this collection of scholarly examinations of the genre, emphasizes this view of the importance to the genre of the writer's "mastery" of its conventions (4) She compares these conventions to the vowels of the English language, the "primal glue, the building blocks, the carriers which shape a human story into a recognizable form or genre" (5).

4. The history of the romance can be found, in varying degrees of completeness, in Eileen Fallon, *Words of Love: A Complete Guide to Romance Fiction* (New York: Garland, 1984); Pamela Regis, *A Natural History of the Romance Novel*; Carol Thurston, *The Romance Revolution: Erotic Novels for Women and the Quest for a New Sexual Identity* (Urbana: University of Illinois Press, 1987).

5. This listing of romance sub genres comes from Eileen Fallon.

6. See, for example, Dawn Heinecken's "Changing Ideologies in Romance Fiction," in *Romantic Conventions*.

7. See Chapter Seven, "Updating the Kama Sutra," in Carol Thurston's *The Romance Revolution*.

8. In her 1998 article, "Desperately Seeking Susan Among the Trash: Reinscription, Subversion and Visibility in the Lesbian Romance Novel," Jill Ehnenn indicates that Naiad Press, the premier publisher of lesbian fiction, was "earning 1.9 million dollars," which indicates a steady interest (122). Since the article's publication Naiad Press has dissolved, although many of its authors have continued to be published by Bella Books.

9. Like the romance writers, supportive critics open their examinations with their personal histories as romance readers. My own reading of genre romances is a late development, partially coming from my teaching courses in popular/genre literature. My reading of lesbian romances has to be linked to my coming out, when I was looking for images of lesbians and lesbian life as well as models of behavior. At first, I felt slightly embarrassed to be purchasing such books; as I became more secure in my identity as a lesbian, I found that these works provided moments of escape from a hectic teaching schedule and opportunities to indulge in the fantasy of ideal partners and relationships. As a critic I have found that these texts trace a particular vision of lesbian experience that allows the reader to position herself as both observer of varied possibilities for imagining a romantic relationship and as a vicarious participant in creating that connection.

10. See essays by Laura Kinsale and Linda Barlow in Krentz's *Dangerous Men and Adventurous Women*.

Chapter One

1. This concern with clarifying the definitions of romance texts can also be found in David Shumway's *Modern Love: Romance, Intimacy, and the Marriage Crisis* (New York: New York University Press, 2003). In addition to discussing the various genre representations and meanings of the term romance, Shumway also distinguishes between romance and intimacy, a point which I will examine in a later chapter.

2. It is beyond the scope of my discussion to offer more than an overview of this history. My summary is based on the work of several scholars and critics whose work has resulted in a more complete understanding of the position of lesbian writers and their place in literary history. This list is by no means complete: Terry Castle, *The Apparitional Lesbian: Female Homosexuality and Modern Culture* (New York: Columbia University Press, 1993); Emma Donoghue, *Passions Between Women: British Lesbian Culture, 1668–1801* (New York: HarperCollins, 1993); Jeannette H. Foster, *Sex Variant Women in Literature* (1956. Tallahassee: Naiad Press, 1985); Lillian Faderman, *Surpassing the Love of Men: Romantic Friendship and Love between Women from the Renaissance to the Present* (New York: William Morrow, 1981) and *Odd Girls and Twilight Lovers: A History of Lesbian Life in Twentieth-Century America* (New York: Columbia University Press, 1991); James Gifford, *Dayneford's Library: American Homosexual Writing, 1900–1913* (Amherst: University of Massachusetts Press, 1995); Carroll Smith-Rosenberg, "The Female World of Love and Ritual: Relations Between Women in Nineteenth-Century America," in *Disorderly Conduct: Visions of Gender in Victorian America* (New York: Oxford University Press, 1985); Jane Rule, *Lesbian Images* (Garden City, NY: Doubleday, 1975).

3. Of course, a single reference cannot fully support a wide public acceptance and usage of the term. However, Donoghue's research offers a broader sense of how a community (however defined) utilized the language available to identify itself. Interesting, too, is Donoghue's interpretation that "[l]esbian does not have the specific connotations of such terms as tribade, hermaphrodite, romantic friend, Sapphist and tommy, and so can encompass them all" (7).

4. The history of the popular romance novel has been discussed in a number of critical studies, some that take a condescending position such as Herbert Ross Brown's *The Sentimental Novel in America, 1789–1860* (Durham: Duke University Press, 1940) and Q. D. Leavis' *Fiction and the Reading Public* (London: Chatto & Windus, 1932). With Frank L Mott's *Golden Multitudes: The Story of Best Sellers in the United States* (New York: Macmillan, 1947) and Helen Waite Papashvily's *All the Happy Endings: A Study of the Domestic Novel in America, the Women who Wrote It, the Women who Read It, in the Nineteenth Century* (New York: Harpers, 1956) popular fiction, including the romance, became the subject of more serious study. The emphasis of such criticism ranged from descriptive histories—Margaret Dalziel's *Popular Fiction 100 Years Ago: An Unexplored Tract of Literary History* (Philadelphia: Dufour Editions, 1958) and James Hart's *The Popular Book: A History of America's*

Literary Taste (Berkeley: University of California Press, 1950) — to specifically theoretically based examinations — Nina Baym's *Woman's Fiction: A Guide to Novels by and about Women in America, 1820–1870* (Ithaca: Cornell University Press, 1978); Madonne Miner, *Insatiable Appetites: Twentieth-Century American Women's Bestsellers* (Westport, CT: Greenwood Press, 1984): Les Boshon and Meredith Goldsmith, eds., *Middlebrow Moderns: Popular American Women Writers of the 1920s* (Boston: Northeastern University Press, 2003).

5. The history of the obscenity trial of *The Well of Loneliness* is detailed in Sally Cline's *Radclyffe Hall: A Woman Called John* (Woodstock, NY: The Overlook Press, 1997), particularly pages 253–264.

6. See, for example, the "Introduction" to Julie Abraham's *Are Girls Necessary?: Lesbian Writing and Modern Histories* (New York: Routledge, 1996). Throughout these pages, Abraham contends that the lesbian novel continually butts up against the conventionality of the heterosexual plot and that as a result of that confrontation "to become or not become a lesbian is to be coming from or going to a heterosexual relationship. Consequently, in the lesbian novel the lesbians are always in circulation in a system that remains heterosexual" (13). Wachman does reference *The Well of Loneliness*' replication of certain popular motifs common to popular romances of the time — racial purity, a rural aristocracy, patriotism, and Christian imagery — but sees these as illustrative of the dominance of a conservative political ideology.

7. The impact of Hall's novel cannot be overlooked. Many women have indicated the impact the work had on them. See, for example, Ann Bannon's Introduction to *Odd Girl Out* (San Francisco: Cleis, 2001): Paula Christian's Introduction to *Amanda* (New Milford, CT: Timely Books, 1981); a 1974 interview with Barbara Gittings quoted in Marilyn Schuster's *Passionate Communities: Reading Lesbian Resistance in Jane Rule's Fiction* (New York: New York University Press, 1999).

8. It is impossible to claim that all readers of lesbian pulp fiction were women who identified as lesbian. Many of the pulps were geared to male readers. See, for instance, Yvonne Keller, "'Was It Right to Love Her Brother's Wife So Passionately?'": Lesbian Pulp Novels and U. S. Lesbian Identity, 1950–1965" *American Quarterly* 57.2 (2005):385–410.

9. See Diane Hamer, "'I am a Woman': Ann Bannon and the Writing of Lesbian Identity in the 1950s" in *Lesbian and Gay Writing: An Anthology of Critical Essays*, edited by Mark Lilly (Philadelphia: Temple University Press, 1990); Angela Weir and Elizabeth Wilson, "The Greyhound Bus Station in the Evolution of Lesbian Popular Culture," in *New Lesbian Criticism: Literary and Cultural Readings*, edited by Sally Munt (New York: Columbia University Press, 1992); and Stephanie Foote, "Deviant Classics: Pulps and the Making of Lesbian Print Culture," in *Signs* 31.1.

10. See Suzanna Danuta Walters, "As Her Hand Crept Slowly up Her Thigh: Ann Bannon and the Politics of Pulp" in *Social Text* 23 (Autumn-Winter, 1989): 83–101; Christopher Nealon, "Invert-History: The Ambivalence of Lesbian Pulp Fiction," in *New Literary History* 31(2000): 745–764.

11. To get to this point in the text, Beth has gone through a cross-country trip from California, where she has had an affair with the owner of a modeling agency whose feelings for Beth have become dangerous, to New York. Once in the city, she meets Jack and discovers that he and Laura are married with a child, although they have agreed to allow each other to have affairs as long as both continue the marriage. Beth has also met Beebo and has had sexual encounters with other women. The rescue comes when Vega, the agency owner, tracks Beth down and confronts her in a hotel room with a pistol. Vega kills herself, but Beth is arrested and only released through the efforts of Laura, Beebo, Vega's brother, and, surprisingly, Charlie, Beth's husband.

12. Meredith Miller in "Secret Agents and Public Victims: The Implied Lesbian Reader" discusses the impact of the pulps, and other mass-market books, for many lesbians. Surveys of readers are quoted that indicate their pleasure in finding literature that provided them with a sense of connection to others like them: "The process of seeing oneself in print in a mass-market format provides a kind of identification which carries the mark of a subcultural identity and the authority of a mass-cultural reality." Miller's examination also

indicates the double-edged quality of such representation, in that the images of lesbian identity, particularly found in the pulps, emphasized the dominant social viewpoint of them as diseased.

13. Mavor's book, since it is biography, does not fit smoothly into the framework of my analysis; however, the work's appearance in 1971 does indicate an increasing interest in closer examinations of the lives of women who defied traditional social norms.

Chapter Two

1. I make no claim of any expertise in the field of linguistics, whether practical or sociological. My attempts at defining language and describing the function of language are, at best, superficial. The summary is based on the work of such experts, including Robert Hooper, *Gendering Talk* (East Lansing: Michigan State University Press, 2003); Deborah Cameron and Don Kulick, *Language and Sexuality* (New York: Cambridge University Press, 2003); Suzanne Romaine, *Communicating Gender* (Mahwah, NJ: Lawrence Erlbaum, 1999); Kevin Kopelson, *Love's Litany: The Writing of Modern Homoerotics* (Stanford: Stanford University Press, 1994); R. Jeffrey Ringer, ed., *Queer Words, Queer Images: Communication and the Construction of Homosexuality* (New York: New York University Press, 1994): A. C. Liang, "Conversationally Implicating Lesbian and Gay Identity," in *Reinventing Identities: The Gendered Self in Discourse*, Mary Bucholtz, A. C. Liang, Laurel A. Sutton, eds. (New York: Oxford University Press, 1999); Anna Livia, "'I Ought to Throw a Buick At You': Fictional Representations of Butch/Femme Speech," in *Gender Articulated: Language and the Socially Constructed Self*, Kira Hall and Mary Bucholtz, eds. (New York: Routledge, 1995); and Jane Ussher, "The Meaning of Sexual Desire: Experiences of Heterosexual and Lesbian Girls," *Feminism and Psychology* 15.1 (2005): 27–32.

2. The connection of romantic love with pain finds one of its most cogent discussions in Denis de Rougemont's *Love in the Western World* (1940. New York: Harcourt, 1966). The lovers suffer because of the forbidden nature of their feelings (de Rougement analyzes the Tristan and Iseult story as the paradigm of such a relationship), their inability to declare their feelings openly, the constant struggle to achieve physical and emotional union, and the eventual death of one or both of the lovers. This model of tragic romance appears in much of the world's classical texts, from poetry to drama to prose. Genre romance, however, rejects this tragic configuration for the happy ending.

3. This very terse summary of a set of complex theories is based on discussions of the psychological foundations of romance found in Lynne Pearce's Introduction to *Romance Writing* (Cambridge: Polity Press, 2007): Chapter Three of Scot McCracken's *Pulp: Reading Popular Fiction* (Manchester: Manchester University Press, 1998); and Chapter Five of Deborah Cameron and Don Kulick's *Language and Sexuality* (Cambridge: Cambridge University Press, 2003); David R. Shumway's *Modern Love: Romance, Intimacy, and the Marriage Crisis* (New York: New York University Press, 2003).

4. Shumway notes the ubiquitousness of the love story in most cultures; from classic texts to popular formats, such stories are told over and over, permeating a person's consciousness to the point where one "assume[s] that all these representations of love are themselves a response to people's natural concerns and therefore a reflection of reality" (2). Such stories, with their particular culturally situated representations of what a romance should look and sound like, can be said to infiltrate one's understanding and expectations of pursuing and achieving romantic fulfillment.

5. Although Radway's tone seems to undercut the sophistication of the Smithton women's interpretation and understanding of the romance novel's linguistic component, she does acknowledge that "although it is true that readers never discover meanings in or behind the words they find on the page but actively attribute significations to the verbal structure from their own linguistic repertoire, it is nonetheless clear that Dot and her women read the romantic text *as if* such simple discovery of meaning was possible" (emphasis in text, 189).

6. Regis' reference to the barrier that the romance heroine must overcome is a major

component of her analysis of the structure of the romance novel. See Chapter Four, "The Definition Expanded," of *The Natural History of the Romance Novel.*

   7. See Chapter Four of Regis' study and Chapter Four, "The Ideal Romance: The Promise of Patriarchy," in Radway's *Reading the Romance: Women, Patriarchy, and Popular Literature* (Chapel Hill: University of North Carolina Press, 1984) for a more complete discussion of these stages in the typical romance narrative.

   8. For the writers of romance novels the importance of the heroine and hero being able to talk correctly actually supersedes the tendency of much negative criticism to emphasize the potential of intimidation based on the hero's physical presence. Pamela Regis and several of the authors in *Dangerous Men and Adventurous Women* reference Austen's *Pride and Prejudice* as the model for the role verbal skill plays in the narrative's development.

   9. Throughout the essays in *Dangerous Men and Adventurous Women*, the romance novelists continually stress the importance of the heroine "taming" the hero:

This powerful man, confident in his standing and his masculinity, sure of himself, competent and trustworthy, discovers during the course of the romance that without the heroine he is no longer able to enjoy his life. *He needs her.* He may kidnap her, he may force her into marriage, he may coax or intimidate her into his bed, but eventually he learns that her physical presence, even her sexual surrender, is not enough. He needs her to come willingly to him, not as a slave to be conquered but as an equal in all respects [Robyn Donald, "Mean, Moody, and Magnificent," emphasis in text, 83].

   10. It is interesting to note how many supportive critics of the romance novel reference Jane Austen's *Pride and Prejudice* as the source and best illustration of these behaviors. See, for example, Regis's Chapter Eight, "The Best Romance Ever Written," and Juhasz's Chapter One, "Becoming a Romance Reader."

   11. In their analysis of language and desire in Chapter Five of *Language and Sexuality* Cameron and Kulick examine this concept of how certain forms of the expression of an individual's desire will break social taboos, usually by the inappropriateness of the words chosen to describe the feeling, the situation in which the language occurs, and who is speaking. See pages 114–119.

   12. These quotations come from CN Winters' *Contract for Hire*, page 116–117, emphasis in text; Ann O'Leary's *The Other Woman*, page 211; LJ Maas' *Rebecca's Cove*, page 274; and Janet E. McClellan's *Winter Garden*, page 180.

Chapter Three

   1. I will be using the term gesture to represent the range of physical cues and behaviors characters will use and respond to in the novels under discussion in this chapter.

   2. Another area of critical focus on the use of gestures can be found in the study of body language and its applications in the self-help arena. A number of texts have popularized the practice of reading other people's actions and body gestures to help the individual understand their "true" motives and responses in order to position oneself more effectively in negotiating for desired outcomes. Such works also present to the reader ways of manipulating dress and behavior in order to achieve a particular goal. Not surprisingly, many of these texts address the world of business. However, many gay and lesbian humorists also utilize this type of reading of visual and behavioral cues to ground their comic descriptions of choosing potential dates, the art of dating, how to live together, and the like.

   3. O' Sulivan's article appeared in the 1994 essay collection *The Good, the Bad and the Gorgeous*; however, these questions and concerns over the representations of lesbians in mainstream media are still debated. The show *The L Word* has reignited these debates, and in a recent collection of essays and interviews—*Reading the L Word: Outing Contemporary Television*, Kim Akass and Janet McCabe, eds. (London: I. B. Tauris, 2006)—Susan Wolfe and Lee Ann Roripaugh succinctly state the issues:

[Contemporary reviews of the show] reveal a consistent sense of anxiety about lesbian representation: assimilationist visibility vs. marginalized invisibility, identitarian "authenticity" vs. Revlon revolution "passing," second-wave vs. third-wave feminism, lesbianism vs. post-lesbianism, and policing of commodified mainstream image making vs. the policing of negative stereotypes [45].

4. I accept as given that a distinct lesbian culture does exist, has always existed. At times this culture has developed along parallel lines to the mainstream and at others it has achieved a prominent position. My position is based on the historical work of Lillian Faderman, George Chauncey, and Martha Vicinus among others, as well as the work of literary historians such as Terry Castle, Emma Donoghue, Sherri Innes, Jeannette Forster, and many others.

5. Beginning in the late 1990s and continuing to the present is the ongoing practice of paying authors for mentioning a specific manufacture's product, a form of product placement similar to the film industry's practice.

6. Interestingly, the profession of choice in recent lesbian romances is builder/contractor; see, for example, Marianne Martin, *Love in the Balance* (Tallahassee: Naiad, 1998); Cynn Chadwick, *Girls with Hammers* (New York: Harrington Park Press, 2004), and C N Winters, *Contractor for Hire* (Monroe, MI: Baycrest Books, 2004). Other professions include police officers, usually beat officers, and a commercial lobsterman.

7. In some of these novels, interestingly, one of the best friends of the main character is a gay man: Harold in Paula Martinac's *Chicken* and Peter in Sharon Stone's *All the Bold Days of My Restless Life*. Perhaps the authors are playing with the stereotypic gay male sensibility and experience with dating.

8. For a fuller discussion of the butch, see Sally Munt, *Heroic Desire: Lesbian Identity and Cultural Space* (New York: New York University Press, 1998; Judith Halberstam, *Female Masculinity* (Durham: Duke University Press, 1998) and *In a Queer Time & Place: Transgender Bodies, Subcultural Lifes* (New York: New York University Press, 2005); Marjorie Garber, *Vested Interests: Cross-Dressing & Cultural Anxiety* (New York: Routledge, 1992); and Judith Butler, *Undoing Gender* (New York: Routledge, 2004). In addition to these theoretical studies, the butch's history can be found in Lillian Faderman, Emma Donoghue, and Elizabeth Kennedy and Madeline Davis' *Boots of Leather, Slippers of Gold: The History of a Lesbian Community* (New York: Penguin, 1994).

9. One of the most compelling portraits of the butch remains Leslie Feinberg's *Stone Butch Blues* (Ithaca: Firebrand, 1993). When the main character comes to understand her identity as butch, the novel traces how she comes to understand the social expectations of that role and the means through which she accommodates those pressures in the creation of her private self. This same commitment of the butch to the butch image also appears throughout the pulps.

10. See Martha Geber, *Entertaining Lesbians*, pages 37–41.

11. Discussions of the butch figure have dominated lesbian criticism, whether from literary, historical, sociological, or psychological perspectives, including the butch's transgressive position, her defiance of social norms, and her role in sexual situations. The overwhelming attention paid to the butch also reflects an assumption of the dominant culture that the butch represents all lesbians. For a succinct overview see Sherrie Innes' "GI Joes in Barbie Land," in *The Lesbian Menace: Ideology, Identity, and the Representation of Lesbian Life* (Amherst: University of Massachusetts Press, 1997).

12. The concept of Xena as a representation of camp appears in several examinations of the series. Joanne Morreale, quoting Susan Sontag's definition of camp as "a failed seriousness, a love of exaggeration and artifice, the privileging of style over content and a being alive to the double sense in which things can be taken," points out the self-consciously formulated and referential expansions of gender identification and behavior in many of the episodes ("Xena: Warrior Princess as Feminist Camp"). This notion of the show's deliberately tongue in cheek stretching of the boundaries of acceptable character/gender behavior can also be found in critical studies by Robin Silverman and Elyce Rae Helford.

Chapter Four

1. Scott McCracken in *Pulp: Reading Popular Fiction* contends that the romance reader does not see each new romance as an individual text, but rather part of an extended, continuous story. He cites Helen Taylor's assertion that the "relationship between reader and text is not between a 'fixed book and a generalizes universal reader,' but 'a relationship between an active, critical reader, and a text, with all its literary, historical and cultural references'" (89).

2. As Thurston notes, however, these adaptations can also quickly become clichés to be easily exaggerated and mocked. Her example of the typical language of the erotic romance follows:

> The reverently worshipful kiss on chastely sealed lips has been displaced by plundering tongues that lap and lick, dart and delve — his from the warm moist cavern of her mouth to the pink shell of her ear, then to the pulse in her throat before descending to the rosy crest of a passion-swollen breast and across her creamy belly to the nest of silky curls, there to find its sheltered secret; hers paints a wet trail across one muscular shoulder before discovering the tiny brown nub hidden in the wiry hair that arrows downward, to disappear below the belt of his pants, after which pants are quickly done away with and she teases a tortuous path down his firm abdomen to the warm granite of his need [143].

3. See, for example, Dawn Heinecken's essay "Changing Ideologies in Romance Fiction," in *Romantic Conventions*, eds. Anne K. Kalor and Rosemary Johnson-Kurek (Bowling Green, OH: Bowling Green University Press, 1998), as well as many of the writers collected in *Dangerous Men and Adventurous Women*.

4. Both Radway and Thurston note that in spite of the sometimes explicit content of modern romances, readers prefer to support those texts that "advance the ideology of romantic love, insisting thereby that marriage between a man and a woman is not an economic or social necessity or a purely sexual affiliation but an emotional bond freely forged" (Radway 170).

5. The conflation of sexual orientation and sexual behavior has been a controversial issue both in heterosexual as well as homosexual contexts. Many straights refuse to separate the gay or lesbian person from what happens in the bedroom, giving them the opportunity to categorize the lesbian or gay man as deviant. Obviously, such biased views allow the mainstream society to marginalize and penalize the individual whose sexuality is seen to contravene social norms. For some gay and lesbian theorists the separation of sexual behavior from sexual identity is seen as an attempt to deny the importance of sex as a component of the complete person. Teresa de Lauretis in *The Practice of Love: Lesbian Sexuality and Perverse Desire* (Bloomington: Indiana University Press, 1994), presents such a view: lesbians' "self-definition, self-representation, and personal and political identity are not only grounded in the sphere of the sexual, but actually constituted in relation to a *sexual* difference from socially dominant, institutionalized, heterosexual forms" (xii, emphasis in text). This debate also focuses on the attempts within the lesbian and gay communities to regulate sexual acts; some seeing certain types of sexual behavior and settings, like the bathhouse or cruising areas of public parks, as a necessary part of one's homosexual being, while other view such behavior as legitimizing homophobic reactions, from legal sanctions to gay-bashing. Theorists root the more abstract aspects of this on-going debate within a number of fields, including psychology, sociology, politics, philosophy, and gender, among others; their ideas are complex and beyond the scope of this analysis. Some authors who engage this topic include Lynda Hart, *Fatal Women: Lesbian Sexuality and the Mark of Aggression* (Princeton: Princeton University Press, 1994); Judith Roof, *A Lure of Knowledge: Lesbian Sexuality and Theory* (New York: Columbia University Press, 1991); and Sally R. Munt, *Heroic Desire: Lesbian Identity and Cultural Space* (New York: New York University Press, 1998).

6. These quotations come from Ann O. Leary, *Julia's Song* (Tallahassee: Naiad, 1998), 168; Shelley Smith, *Horizon of the Heart* (Tallahassee: Naiad, 1986), 168; and Diana Simmonds, *Forty Love* (Tallahassee: Naiad, 1997), 273.

7. Recently, there has been a movement in lesbian romance writing to stretch the boundaries of sexual description. Some publishers, like Bold Strokes Press, have added imprints that present a much more graphic depiction of the sex between characters; these books also develop plots that have the characters explore the more provocative expressions of sexuality, including S/M, role playing, and the explicit use of sex toys.

8. Critical attention on the nature of the engagement between reader and the work centers more on the feelings the reader experiences after the act of reading itself. See *Reading the Romance*, Chapter Three "The Act of Reading the Romance." However Radway does indicate that during the actual reading of the novel, the reader will experience a "vicarious emotional nurturance by prompting identification between the reader and a fictional heroine whose identity as a woman is always confirmed by the romantic and sexual attentions of an ideal male" (113). Radway separates the female reader from the male character, but romance novelists themselves emphasize that the reader is able to, in fact must be able to, experience the progress of the romance as both hero and heroine do. Krentz's view is typical:

> This twist on the basic seduction fantasy is not a simple matter of the writer structuring the scene so that the reader switches back and forth between viewpoints. It cannot be summed up or explained by saying that the seduction is witnessed first through the heroine's eyes and then through those of the hero. In a really good romance, the experience for the reader is that of being in both the heroine's mind and the hero's *at the same time*. The reader knows what each character is feeling, what each is sensing, how each is being affected [110–111].

9. This is a recurring theme throughout the essays in *Dangerous Men and Adventurous Women*. See, for example, the essays by Doreen Malek, Robyn Donald, Elizabeth Lowell, Jayne Ann Krentz, and Stella Cameron.

Chapter Five

1. It is not surprising to note that all three writers use pseudonyms; in fact, the names that appear throughout this chapter are themselves pseudonyms. However, Radclyffe is the only writer of the three who retains the same name for all of her production, regardless of genre. Fulton is the name this author uses to identify her romantic works; her mysteries appear under the name Rose Beecham. Kallmaker is also pseudonymous and appears under the titles of her traditional as well as erotic romances. She has used an additional alias — Laura Adams — for gothic romances, but she has reissued a previous title, *Christabel*, under Karin Kallmarker; other Gothic romance titles for 2009 will be issued with the name Kallmaker. Neither Kallmaker's nor Fulton's real name appears anywhere on their websites.

2. Fulton is not the first romance writer to continue the stories of characters readers strongly connect to or identify with. Ann Bannon's pulp novels may be considered the first to serialize the lives and loves of the characters in the novels that make up the Beebo Brinker Chronicles. In the Introduction to the 2001 Cleis edition of *Odd Girl Out*, Bannon remembers the advice of her publisher. "Go back to the people you love and breathe some life into them" (viii). Bannon indicates that this was the impetus for her continuing to explore the relationships of Laura, Beth, Beebo, and Jack.

Chapter Six

1. The most recent statistics, according to the Romance Writers of America Website, indicates that in 2007 romance novels generated $1.375 billion in sales and that 8,090 romance titles were released; of all those who read in 2007 1 in 5 were estimated to have read a romance novel.

2. The importance of the narrative framework to the romance novel is reiterated by both Regis and Radway, and each presents an outline of the sequence of events that will

result in the happy ending. See Radway, Chapter 4, "The Ideal Romance," page 148–150, and Regis, Chapter 4, "The Definition Expanded." Of course, each critic organizes her reading of this plot based on the implications the development of the story has for its readers; Regis emphasizes the role the wider society plays in the development of the heroine's identity and the eventual relationship with the hero; Radway focuses on the social isolation of the heroine and her developing dependence on the hero to provide her with a sense of security and identity.

3. McCracken's view stresses what he sees as the reader engaged in "one long saga, where the happy ending is constantly rejected for a new, unhappy beginning" (98). This suggests that the anticipation and positive response to the happy ending can only be temporary for the reader. However, Regis and other supportive critics emphasize that the reader's continued consumption of the romance lies in her identification with the heroine's attainment of her desires; the reading is not to concentrate on separation, but on the conclusion — the union.

4. These, broadly sketched, are the plots of Georgette Heyer's *Lady of Quality* and Jayne Ann Krentz's *All Night Long*.

5. Zimmerman's analysis of lesbian writing was published in 1990 and reflects issues and debates circulating at the time, one of which involved questions of assimilation into the mainstream — especially as a response to the AIDS crisis and the beginnings of a wider popular representation of a "gay lifestyle" — versus separation.

6. The blending of genres is not a new phenomenon, but in recent years the tendency has become more common. At the 2008 Popular Culture Association/American Culture Association Conference in San Francisco, several panels were devoted to a range of explorations and discussions of the methods, implications, and expectations in the combining of sometimes compatible, sometimes less easily merged, genres. One common question dealt with how to categorize such texts, especially when the text integrated different compositional methods which challenge reader expectations and engagement with the work.

7. Mothers appear in a number of lesbian romances and perform a range of functions, from the homophobic, distant woman who refuses to deal with her daughter's sexuality and has cut off all contact, for example, Veronica Cartwright's in *Accidental Love*. Other mothers are shown to be hesitant about their daughter's lesbianism, but over the course of the novel come to see the harm the daughter's denial of her identity has caused them both; such texts end not with the mother's full acceptance, but an expressed willingness to learn, Sara D'Amico's in *The Light Fantastic*. Not surprisingly these novels include some kind of reunion between mothers and daughters, as well as other family members. Finally are mothers who often are aware of their daughters' sexuality before their children; they frequently look forward to, sometimes try to arrange, the daughter's meeting with a woman whom she believe will help her daughter reconcile her public and private lives. In *Rebecca's Cove* B. J. Warren's grandmother instigates the romance, but clearly she serves the same nurturing function.

8. This critical position reflects the classic description of the function of romance presented by Northrop Frye in *Anatomy of Criticism: Four Essays* (Princeton, NJ: Princeton University Press, 1971). Frye's discussion centers on the mythic/archetypal implications of romance beyond the particulars of genre. However, Pamela Regis in her study of the popular genre romance also stresses the importance of the couple's reintegration in society as essential to the happy ending.

9. Of the novels used to illustrate this analysis only Diane Salvatore's *Paxton Court*, set in a retirement community, presents the various relationships of a group of older lesbians. The lack of sexual intimacy between couples reflects the loss of desire or physical impairments.

Works Cited

Abraham, Julie. *Are Girls Necessary?: Lesbian Writing and Modern Histories*. New York: Routledge, 1996.
Ames, Lynn. *The Price of Fame*. Gainesville: BookEnds Press, 2003.
Arnold, Charlotte. *Carved in Stone*. Barcelona: Editorial EGALES, 2003.
Arnold, Judith. "Women Do." In *Dangerous Men and Adventurous Women: Romance Writers on the Appeal of the Romance*. Ed. Jayne Ann Krentz. Philadelphia: University of Pennsylvania Press, 1992.
Avery, Gillian. "The Very Pink of Society." In *Georgette Heyer: A Critical Perspective*. Ed. Mary Fahnestock-Thomas. Saraland, AL: Prinny World Press, 2001.
Bannon, Ann. *Beebo Brinker*. 1962. San Francisco: Cleis, n.d.
_____. *I Am a Woman*. 1959. San Francisco: Cleis, 2002.
_____. *Journey to a Woman*. 1960. San Francisco: Cleis, 2003.
_____. *Odd Girl Out*. 1957. San Francisco: Cleis, 2001.
_____. *Women in the Shadows*. 1959. San Francisco: Cleis, 2002.
Barlow, Linda. "The Androgynous Writer: Another Point of View." In *Dangerous Men and Adventurous Women: Romance Writers on the Appeal of the Romance*. Ed. Jayne Ann Krentz. Philadelphia: University of Pennsylvania Press, 1992.
_____, and Jayne Ann Krentz. "Beneath the Surface: The Hidden Codes Of Romance." In *Dangerous Men and Adventurous Women: Romance Writers on the Appeal of the Romance*. Ed. Jayne Ann Krentz. Philadelphia: University of Pennsylvania Press, 1992.
Baym, Nina. *Woman's Fiction: A Guide to Novels by and about Women in America, 1820–1870*. Ithaca: Cornell University Press, 1978.
Beers, Georgia. *Too Close to Touch*. New York: Bold Strokes Books, 2006.
_____. *Turning the Page*. Nederland, TX: YellowRose Books, 2001.
Berzon, Betty. *Permanent Partners: Building Gay and Lesbian Relationships That Last*. New York: Penguin, 1988.
Boshon, Les, and Meredith Goldsmith, eds. *Middlebrow Moderns: Popular American Writers of the 1920s*. Boston: Northeastern University Press, 2003.
Brandt, Kate. *Happy Endings: Lesbian Writers Talk about Their Lives and Work*. Tallahassee: Naiad, 1993.
Brooke, Gun. *Course of Action*. Philadelphia: Bold Strokes Books, 2004.
Brown, Herbert Ross. *The Sentimental Novel in America, 1789–1860*. Durham: Duke University Press, 1940.
Brown, Rita Mae. *Rubyfruit Jungle*. 1973. New York: Bantam, 1988.
Cameron, Deborah, and Don Kulick. *Language and Sexuality*. New York: Cambridge University Press, 2003.
Carpenter, Alison. *Cold*. Nederland, TX: Renaissance Alliance Publishing, 2003.

Carrera, Juliet. *Inside Out*. New York: Harrington Park Press, 1999.
Castle, Terry. *The Apparitional Lesbian: Female Homosexuality and Modern Culture*. New York: Columbia University Press, 1993.
Cawelti, John G. *Adventure, Mystery, and Romance: Formula Stories as Art and Fiction*. Chicago: University of Chicago Press, 1976.
Chadwick, Cynn. *Girls with Hammers*. New York: Harrington Park Press, 2004.
Chauncey, George. *Gay New York: Gender, Urban Culture, and the Making of the Gay Male World, 1890–1940*. New York: Basic Books, 1994.
Christian, Paula. *Amanda*. 1965. New Milford, CT: Timely Books, 1982.
———. *Edge of Twilight* 1959. New Milford, CT: Timely Books, 1983.
Clark, Beverly Lyon, et al. "Reading Romance, Reading Ourselves." In *Women and Romance: A Reader*. Ed. Susan Ostrov Weisser. New York: New York University Press, 2001.
Cline, Sally. *Radclyffe Hall: A Woman Called John*. Woodstock, NY: Overlook Press, 1997.
Cooper, Blayne, and T. Novan. *First Lady*. Falls Church, VA: Cavallier Press, 2003.
Crist, Linda. *The Bluest Eyes in Texas*. Austin: Fortitude Press, 2001.
Dalziel, Margaret. *Popular Fiction 100 Years Ago: An Unexplored Tract of Literary History*. Philadelphia: Dufour Editions, 1958.
Dean, Elizabeth. *Between Girlfriends*. New York: Kensington Publishing, 2003.
———. *It's in Her Kiss*. New York: Kensington Books, 2002.
de Lauretis, Teresa. *The Practice of Love: Lesbian Sexuality and Perverse Desire*. Bloomington: Indiana University Press, 1994.
de Rougemont, Denis. *Love in the Western World*. 1966. New York: Harcourt, 1940.
Devize, C. C. *Misplaced People*. Gainesville: Intaglio Publications, 2005.
Donoghue, Emma. *Passions between Women: British Lesbian Culture, 1668–1801*. New York: HarperCollins, 1993.
Ehnenn, Jill. "Desperately Seeking Susan Among the Trash: Reinscription, Subversion and Visibility in the Lesbian Romance Novel." *Atlantis* 23.1 (Fall/Winter 1998):120–27.
Ennis, Catherine. *Up, Up and Away*. Tallahassee: Naiad, 1994.
Faderman, Lillian. *Odd Girls and Twilight Lovers: A History of Lesbian Life in Twentieth-Century America*. New York: Columbia University Press, 1991.
———. *Surpassing the Love of Men: Romantic Friendship and Love Between Women from the Renaissance to the Present*. New York: William Morrow, 1981.
Fallon, Eileen. *Words of Love: A Complete Guide to Romance Fiction*. New York: Garland Press, 1984.
Farwell, Marilyn R. *Heterosexual Plots and Lesbian Narratives*. New York: New York University Press, 1996.
Feinberg, Leslie. *Stone Butch Blues*. Ithaca: Firebrand, 1993.
Fisher, Philip. *Hard Facts: Form and Setting in the American Novel*. New York: Oxford University Press, 1987.
Foote, Stephanie. "Deviant Classics: Pulps and the Making of Lesbian Print Culture." *Signs* 31.1 (Autumn 2005). *ProQuest*. 9 July 2007 http://proquest.umi.com.
Forrest, Katherine. "Acts of Individual Valor." *Lambda Book Report* Feb. 2002: 6–9.
———. *Curious Wine*. Tallahassee: Naiad Press, 1983.
———. *An Emergence of Green*. Tallahassee: Naiad, 1987.
Foster, Jeannette H. *Sex Variant Women in Literature*. 1956. Tallahassee: Naiad, 1985.
Frantz, Sarah S. G. "'Expressing' Herself: The Romance Novel and the Feminine will to Power." *Scorned Literature: Essays on the History and Criticism of Popular Mass-Produced Fiction in America*. Eds. Lydia Cushman Schurman and Deidre Johnson. Westport: Greenwood Press, 2002.
Frye, Northrop. *The Anatomy of Criticism: Four Essays*. 1957. Princeton, NJ: Princeton University Press, 1971.
Fulton, Jennifer. *Dark Dreamer*. Port Arthur, TX: Yellow Rose Press, 2005.

———. *Greener Than Grass*. Tallahassee: Naiad, 1996.
———. *A Guarded Heart*. Port Arthur, TX: Yellow Rose Press, 2005.
———. *More Than Paradise*. New York: Bold Strokes Books, 2007.
———. *Passion Bay*. Tallahassee: Naiad, 1993.
———. *The Sacred Shore*. Port Arthur, TX: Yellow Rose Press, 2005.
———. *Saving Grace*. Tallahassee: Naiad, 1993.
———. *True Love*. Tallahassee: Naiad, 1997.
Garber, Marjorie. *Vested Interests: Cross-Dressing & Cultural Anxiety*. New York: Routledge, 1992.
Garvey, Ellen Gruber. *The Adman in the Parlor: Magazines and the Gendering of Consumer Culture, 1880s to 1910s*. New York: Oxford University Press, 1996.
Gelder, Ken. *Popular Fiction: The Logics and Practices of a Literary Field*. London: Routledge, 2004.
Gever, Martha. *Entertaining Lesbians: Celebrity, Sexuality, and Self-Invention*. New York: Routledge, 2003.
Gifford, James. *Dayneford's Library: American Homosexual Writing, 1900–1913*. Amherst: University of Massachusetts Press, 1995.
Guntrum, Suzanne Simmons. "Happily Ever After: The Ending as Beginning." In *Dangerous Men and Adventurous Women: Romance Writers on the Appeal of the Romance*. Ed. Jayne Ann Krentz. Philadelphia: University of Pennsylvania Press, 1992.
Halberstram, Judith. *Female Masculinity*. Durham, NC: Duke University Press, 1998.
———. *In a Queer Time & Place: Transgender Bodies, Subcultural Lifes*. New York: New York University Press, 2005.
Hall, Radclyffe. *The Well of Loneliness*. 1928. New York: Anchor Books, 1990.
Hamer, Diane. "'I am a Woman': Ann Bannon and the Writing of Lesbian Identity in the 1950s." In *Lesbian and Gay Writing: An Anthology of Critical Essays*. Ed. Mark Lilly. Philadelphia: Temple University Press, 1990.
Hart, James. *The Popular Book: A History of America's Literary Taste*. Berkeley: University of California Press, 1950.
Hart, Lynda. *Fatal Women: Lesbian Sexuality and the Mark of Aggression*. Princeton, NJ: Princeton University Press, 1994.
Heinecken, Dawn. "Changing Ideologies in Romance Fiction." In *Romantic Conventions*. Eds. Anne Kalor and Rosemary Johnson-Kurek. Bowling Green, OH: Bowling Green University Press, 1998.
Helford, Elyce Rae. "Feminism, Queer Studies and the Sexual Politics of *Xena: Warrior Princess*." In *Fantasy Girls: Gender in the New Universe of Science Fiction and Fantasy Television*. Ed. Elyce Rae Helford. Lanham, MD: Rowman & Littlefield, 2000.
Heller, Dana. "How Does a Lesbian Look? Stendhal's Syndrome and *The L Word*." In *Reading The L Word: Outing Contemporary Television*. Eds. Kim Akass and Janet McCabe. London: I. B. Tauris, 2006.
Hermes, Joke. "Sexuality in Lesbian Romance Fiction." *Feminist Review* 42 (Autumn 1992):49–66.
Heyer, Georgette. *Lady of Quality*. 1972. Naperville: Sourcebooks, Inc., 2007.
Hill, Gerri. *Behind the Pine Curtain*. Tallahassee: Bella Books, 2006.
———. *One Summer Night*. Tucson: Rising Tide Press, 2000.
Hill, Linda. *Class Reunion*. Tallahassee: Naiad, 1997.
Hollander, Anne. *Sex and Suits: The Evolution of Modern Dress*. New York: Kodansha International, 1994.
Hollows, Joanne. *Feminism, Femininity and Popular Culture*. Manchester: Manchester University Press, 2000.
Hooper, Robert. *Gendering Talk*. East Lansing: Michigan State University Press, 2003.
Innes, Sherrie. *The Lesbian Menace: Ideology, Identity and the Representation of Lesbian Life*. Amherst: University of Massachusetts Press, 1997.

Juhasz, Suzanne. "Lesbian Romance Fiction and the Plotting of Desire: Narrative Theory, Lesbian Identity, and Reading." *Tulsa Studies in Women's Literature* 17.1(1998): 65–82.
———. *Reading from the Heart: Women, Literature, and the Search for True Love*. New York: Penguin, 1994.
Kaler, Anne K., and Rosemary E. Johnson-Kurek, eds. *Romantic Conventions*. Bowling Green, OH: Bowling Green State University Popular Press, 1999.
Kallmaker, Karin. *Car Pool*. Tallahassee: Naiad, 1993.
———. *Christabel*. 1998. Tallahassee: Bella Books, 2008.
———. *Embrace in Motion*. Tallahassee: Naiad, 1997.
———. *In Every Port*. 1989. Tallahassee: Naiad, 2001.
———. *Just Like That*. Tallahassee: Bella Books, 2005.
———. *Making Up for Lost Time*. Tallahassee: Naiad, 1998.
———. *Painted Moon*. Tallahassee: Naiad, 1997.
———. *Paperback Romance* Tallahassee: Naiad, 1992.
———. *Watermark*. Tallahassee: Naiad, 1999.
———. *Wild Things*. Tallahassee: Naiad, 1996.
Keller, Yvonne. "Pulp Politics: Strategies of Vision in Pro-Lesbian Pulp Novels, 1955–1965." In *The Queer Sixties*. Ed. Patricia Juliana Smith. New York: Routledge, 1999.
———. "Was It Right to Love Her Brother's Wife So Passionately?" Lesbian Pulp Novels and U. S. Lesbian Identity, 1950–1965." *American Quarterly* 57.2 (2005):385–410.
Kennedy, Elizabeth Lapovsky, and Madeline D. Davis. *Boots of Leather, Slippers of Gold: The History of a Lesbian Community*. New York: Penguin, 1994.
Kinsale, Laura. "The Androgynous Reader: Point of View in the Romance." In *Dangerous Men and Adventurous Women: Romance Writers on the Appeal of the Romance*. Ed. Jayne Ann Krentz. Philadelphia: University of Pennsylvania Press, 1992.
Kopelson, Kevin. *Love's Litany: The Writing of Modern Homoerotics*. Stanford, CA: Stanford University Press, 1994.
Krantz, Judith. *Scruples*. New York: Bantam Books, 1989.
Krentz, Jayne Ann. *All Night Long*. New York: Jove Books, 2007.
———., ed *Dangerous Men and Adventurous Women: Romance Writers on the Appeal of the Romance*. Philadelphia: University of Pennsylvania Press, 1992.
———. "Introduction." In *Dangerous Men and Adventurous Women: Romance Writers on the Appear of the Romance*. Ed. Jayne Ann Krentz. Philadelphia: University of Pennsylvania Press, 1992.
———. "Trying to Tame the Romance: Critics and Correctness." In *Dangerous Men and Adventurous Women: Romance Writers on the Appeal of the Romance*. Ed. Jayne Ann Krentz. Philadelphia: University of Pennsylvania Press, 1992.
Lake, Lori. L. *Different Dress*. Nederland, TX: Regal Crest Enterprises, 2003.
Leach, William. *Land of Desire: Merchants, Power, and the Rise of a New American Culture*. New York: Pantheon, 1993.
Leavis, Q. D. *Fiction and the Reading Pubic*. London: Chatto & Windus, 1932.
Liang, A. C. "Conversationally Implicating Lesbian and Gay Identity." In *Reinventing Identities: The Gendered Self in Discourse*. Eds. Mary Bucholtz, A. C. Liang, Laurel A. Sutton. New York: Oxford University Press, 1999.
Linz, Cathie. "Setting the Stage: Facts and Figures." In *Dangerous Men and Adventurous Women: romance Writers on the Appear of the Romance*. Ed. Jayne Ann Krentz. Philadelphia: University of Pennsylvania Press, 1992.
Livia, Anna. "'I Ought to Throw a Buick At You': Fictional Representations of Butch/Femme Speech." In *Gender Articulated: Language and the Socially Constructed Self*. Eds. Kira Hall and Mary Bucholtz. New York: Routledge, 1995.
Lorde, Audre. "Uses of the Erotic: The Erotic as Power." www.womenstemple.com/EroticAsPower-article.html. Accessed 21 July 2008.
Lowell, Elizabeth. "Love Conquers All: The Warrior Hero and the Affirmation of Love."

In *Dangerous Men and Adventurous Women: Romance Writers on the Appeal of the Romance*. Ed. Jayne Ann Krentz. Philadelphia: University of Pennsylvania Press, 1992.
Lynes, Russell. *The Tastemakers*. New York: Grosset and Dunlap, 1972.
Maas, LJ. *Rebecca's Cove*. Port Arthur, TX: Yellow Rose Books, 2003.
MacGregor, K. G. *Shaken*. Gainesville: BookEnds Press, 2005.
Malek, Doreen Owens. "Mad, Bad, and Dangerous to Know: The Hero as Challenge." In *Dangerous Men and Adventurous Women: Romance Writers on the Appeal of the Romance*. Ed. Jayne Ann Krentz. Philadelphia: University of Pennsylvania Press, 1992.
Martin, Della. *Twilight Girl*. 1961. San Francisco: Cleis, 2006.
Martin, Marianne. *Love in the Balance*. Tallahassee: Naiad, 1998.
Martinac, Paula. *Chicken*. Ferndale, MI: Bella Books, 1997.
Mavor, Elizabeth. *The Ladies of Llangollen: A Study in Romantic Friendship*. New York: Penguin, 1973.
McClellan, Jane E. *Winter Garden*. Tallahassee: Naiad Press, 1998.
McCracken, Scott. *Pulp: Reading Popular Fiction*. Manchester: Manchester University Press, 1998.
McNab, Claire. *Silent Heart*. Tallahassee: Naiad Press, 1993.
———. *Under the Southern Cross*. Tallahassee: Naiad Press, 1992.
———. *Writing My Love*. Tallahassee: Bella Books, 2006.
Meyer, JLee. *First Instinct*. New York: Bold Strokes Books, 2006.
Miller, B. L. *Accidental Love*. Tacoma: Justice House Publishing, 1999.
Miller, Isabel. *Patience and Sarah*. 1969. New York: Ballantine, 1983.
Miller, Meredith. "Secret Agents and Public Victims: The Implied Lesbian Reader." *Journal of Popular Culture* 35.1 (Summer 2001). *ProQuest*. 14 April 2005 http://proquest.umi.com.
Miner, Madonne M. *Insatiable Appetites: Twentieth-Century American Women's Bestsellers*. Westport, CN: Greenwood Press, 1984.
Modleski, Tania. *Loving with a Vengeance: Mass-produced Fantasies for Women*. New York: Methuen, 1982.
Morgan, Claire [Patricia Highsmith]. *The Price of Salt*. 1952. Tallahassee: Naiad, 1991.
Morreale, Joanne. "Xena: Warrior Princess as Feminist Camp." *Journal of Popular Culture* 32.2 (Fall 1998). http://proquest.umi.com.
Mott, Frank L. *Golden Multitudes: The Story of Best Sellers in the United States*. New York: Macmillan, 1947.
Munt, Sally. *Heroic Desire: Lesbian Identity and Cultural Space*. New York: New York University Press, 1998.
Nealon, Christopher. "Invert-History: The Ambivalence of Lesbian Pulp Fiction." *New Literary History* 31 (2000): 745–764.
Norris, Lynne. *Second Chances*. Nederland, TX: Yellow Rose Books, 2002.
O'Leary, Ann. *Julia's Song*. Tallahassee: Naiad, 1998.
———. *The Other Woman*. Tallahassee: Naiad Press, 1999.
O'Sullivan, Sue. "Girls Who Kiss Girls and Who Cares?" In *The Good, the Bad, and The Gorgeous: Popular Culture's Romance with Lesbianism*. Eds. Diane Hamer and Belinda Budge. London: Pandora, 1994.
Packer, Vin. *Spring Fire*. 1952. San Francisco: Cleis, 2004.
Palmer, Diana. "Let Me Tell You about My Readers." In *Dangerous Men and Adventurous Women: Romance Writers on the Appeal of the Romance*. Ed. Jayne Ann Krentz. Philadelphia: University of Pennsylvania Press, 1992.
Papashvily, Helen Waite. *All the Happy Endings: A Study of the Domestic Novel in America, the Women who Wrote It, the Women who Read It, in the Nineteenth Century*. New York: Harpers, 1956.
Pearce, Lynne. *Romance Writing*. Cambridge, UK: Polity Press, 2007.
Phillips, Susan. "The Romance and the Empowerment of Women." In *Dangerous Men and*

Adventurous Women: Romance Writers on the Appeal of the Romance. Ed. Jayne Ann Krentz. Philadelphia: University of Pennsylvania Press, 1992.

Rabine, Leslie. *Reading the Romantic Heroine: Text, History, Ideology.* Ann Arbor: University of Michigan Press, 1985.

Radclyffe. *Fated Love.* Gainesville: BookEnds Press, 2004.

―――. *Love's Masquerade.* Gainesville: BookEnds Press, 2003.

―――. *Love's Tender Warriors.* Gainesville: BookEnds Press, 2002.

―――. *A Matter of Trust.* Port Arthur, TX: Renaissance Alliance Publishing, 2003.

―――. *Passion's Bright Fury.* Port Arthur, TX: Yellow Rose Books, 2003.

―――. *Safe Harbor.* Port Arthur, TX: Yellow Rose Books, 2001.

―――. *Tomorrow's Promise.* Gainesville: BookEnds Press, 2002.

―――. *Turn Back Time.* New York: Bold Stroke Books, 2006.

Radford, Jean. "An Inverted Romance: *The Well of Loneliness* and Sexual Ideology." In *The Progress of Romance: The Politics of Popular Fiction.* Ed. Jean Radford. London: Routledge, 1986.

Radway, Janice A. *Reading the Romance: Women, Patriarchy, and Popular Literature.* Chapel Hill: University of North Carolina Press, 1984.

Regis, Pamela. *A Natural History of the Romance Novel.* Philadelphia: University of Pennsylvania Press, 2003.

Reilly, Belle. *High Intensity.* Port Arthur, TX: Renaissance Alliance Publishing, 2002.

Renault, Mary. *The Friendly Young Ladies.* 1944. New York: Random House, 2003.

Ricker-Wilson, Carol. "Busting Textual Bodices: Gender, Reading, and the Popular Romance." *The English Journal* 88.3, Genderizing the Curriculum (Jan. 1999): 57–64. *JSTOR* 7 Aug. 2007 http://links,jstor.org.

Ringer, R. Jeffrey, ed. *Queer Words, Queer Images: Communication and the Construction of Homosexuality.* New York: New York University Press, 1994.

Romaine, Suzanne. *Communicating Gender.* Mahwah, NJ: Lawrence Erlbaum Associates Publishers, 1999.

Roof, Judith. *A Lure of Knowledge: Lesbian Sexuality and Theory.* New York: Columbia University Press, 1991.

Rule, Jane. *Desert of the Heart.* 1964. Tallahassee: Naiad, 1985.

―――. *Lesbian Images.* Garden City, NY: Doubleday, 1975.

Ryan, Maggie. *The Deal.* Tacoma: Justice House Publishing, 2001.

Salvatore, Diane. *Paxton Court.* Tallahassee: Naiad, 1995.

Schuster, Marilyn R. *Passionate Communities: Reading Lesbian Resistance in Jane Rule's Fiction.* New York: New York University Press, 1999.

Shapiro, Lisa. *The Color of Winter.* Tallahassee: Naiad, 1995.

Shields, Trish. *Inferno.* Monroe, MI: Baycrest Books, 2003.

Shumay, David. *Modern Love: Romance, Intimacy, and the Marriage Crisis.* New York: New York University Press, 2003.

Silverman, Robin. "What Xena Giveth, *Xena* Taketh Away." *The Gay & Lesbian Review* 8.5 (Sept.–Oct. 2001):32–34.

Snitow, Ann. "Mass Market Romance: Pornography for Women Is Different." In *Women and Romance: A Reader.* Ed. Susan Ostrov Weisser. New York: New York University Press, 2001.

Simmonds, Diana. *Forty Love.* Tallahassee: Naiad, 1997.

―――. *Heart on Fire.* Tallahassee: Naiad Press, 1996.

Smith, Shelley. *Horizon of the Heart.* Tallahassee: Naiad Press, 1986.

Smith-Rosenberg, Carroll. "The Female World of Love and Ritual: Relations between Women in Nineteenth-Century America." In *Disorderly Conduct: Visions of Gender in Victorian America.* New York: Oxford University Press, 1985.

Stevens, R. L. *The Best of Friends.* New York: Kensington Books, 2005.

Stone, Sharon. *All the Bold Days of My Restless Life.* Los Angles: Alyson Books, 2005.

Swannell, Cate. *Heart's Passage*. Nederland, TX: Regal Crest Enterprises, 2003.
Swirski, Peter. *From Lowbrow to Nobrow*. Montreal: McGill-Queen's University Press, 2005.
Tasker, Yvonne. "Pussy Galore: Lesbian Images and Lesbian Desire in the Popular Cinema." In *The Good, the Bad, and the Gorgeous: Popular Culture's Romance With Lesbianism*. Eds. Diane Hamer and Belinda Budge. London: Pandora, 1994.
Taylor, Valerie. *The Girls in 3-B*. 1959. New York: Feminist Press, 2003.
Thurston, Carol. *The Romance Revolution: Erotic Novels for Women and the Quest for a New Sexual Identity*. Urbana: University of Illinois Press, 1987.
Tucker, L. A. *The Light Fantastic*. Nederland, TX: Yellow Rose Books, 2003.
Ussher, Jane M. "The Meaning of Sexual Desire: Experiences of Heterosexual and Lesbian Girls." *Feminism and Psychology* 15.1 (2005): 27–32.
Wachman, Gay. *Lesbian Empire: Radical Crosswriting in the Twenties*. New Brunswick, NJ: Rutgers University Press, 2001.
Walters, Suzanna Danuta. "As Her hand Crept Slowly up Her Thigh: Ann Bannon and the Politics of Pulp." *Social Text* 23 (Autumn-Winter 1989): 83–101.
Wartenberg, Thomas E. *Unlikely Couples: Movie Romance as Social Criticism*. Boulder, CO: Westview Press, 1999.
Watts, Julia. *Wedding Bell Blues*. Tallahassee: Naiad, 1999.
Weir, Angela, and Elizabeth Wilson. "The Greyhound Bus Station in the Evolution of Lesbian Popular Culture." In *New Lesbian Criticism: Literary and Cultural Readings*. Ed. Sally Munt. New York: Columbia University Press, 1992.
Weiss, Andrea. *Vampires and Violets: Lesbians in Film*. New York: Penguin, 1993.
Wheeler, Lorna, and Lara Raven Wheeler. "Straight-up Sex in *The L Word*." In *Reading the L Word: Outing Contemporary Television*. Eds. Kim Akass and Janet McCabe. London: I. B. Tauris, 2006.
Whelehan, Imelda. *The Feminist Bestseller: From Sex and the Single Girl to Sex and The City*. Hampshire, UK: Palgrave Macmillan, 2005.
Williamson, Penelope. "By Honor Bound: The Heroine as Hero." In *Dangerous Men And Adventurous Women: Romance Writers on the Appeal of the Romance*. Ed. Jayne Ann Krentz. Philadelphia: University of Pennsylvania Press, 1992.
Wings, Mary. "Rebecca Redux: Tears on a Lesbian Pillow." *Daring to Dissent: Lesbian Culture from Margin to Mainstream*. Ed. Liz Gibbs. London: Cassell, 1994.
Winters, CN. *Contractor for Hire*. Monroe, MI: Baycrest Books, 2004.
Wolfe, Susan J., and Lee Ann Roripaugh. "The (In)visible Lesbian: Anxieties of Representation in *The L Word*." In *Reading The L Word: Outing Contemporary Television*. Eds. Kim Akass and Janet McCabe. London: I. B. Tauris, 2006.
Zimmerman, Bonnie. *The Safe Sea of Women: Lesbian Fiction 1969–1989*. Boston: Beacon Press, 1990.

Websites

www.boldstrokesbooks.com
www.jenniferfulton.com
www.kallmaker.com
www.likesbooks.com
www.radfic.com
www.rwanational.org

INDEX

Agency 88, 104
Ambiguity 30, 33, 35, 46, 49, 70, 74, 103
Appearance 26, 34, 80, 81, 85 148, 177; hero 92–93, 145, 173; heroine 102–103, 104, 173; lesbian 87, 94–95, 145
Attraction 10, 50, 65, 72, 73, 79, 118, 178, 180; between couple 9, 47, 59, 109, 124, 154, 155, 189
Autonomy 64, 68, 74, 94, 99, 184, 195

Bannon, Ann 40, 41, 44–46, 49, 209n.; *Beebo Brinker* 42, 43; *I Am a Woman* 42, 44; *Journey to a Woman* 42, 44; *Odd Girl Out* 41, 44; *Women in the Shadows* 42
Beebo Brinker 42, 43
Behavior 17, 84, 85, 89, 102–104, 112, 114, 115, 117
Brinker, Beebo 40, 44, 53, 95
Brown, Rita Mae 17, 47, 51–53; *Rubyfruit Jungle* 17, 47, 51–53, 105
Butch 15, 17, 26, 82, 90, 95–96, 103, 108, 148, 177, 204n.

Car Pool 18, 151, 155, 156
Careers 17, 66, 83, 90, 152, 154, 156
Children *see* Family
Christabel 206n.
Codes 26, 55, 76, 87, 112; genre 77, 112; social 85, 105
Comic romances 176, 178, 180, 181, 189, 190
Coming out 15, 68–69, 99, 118, 121, 127, 153, 157, 177, 192
Community 15, 26, 29, 34, 41, 43, 53, 62, 75, 106, 126, 139, 151, 153, 160, 189–192
Connection 47, 49, 59–60, 68, 73, 97, 105, 117, 128, 134, 194
Couple 10, 14, 16, 19, 36, 39, 44, 73, 75, 92, 112, 123, 184; heterosexual 11, 63, 64, 92, 108, 187; lesbian 25, 71, 93, 99, 105, 110, 137
Critics of romance 6, 12, 30, 40, 45, 60, 61, 63, 77, 96, 114, 132, 170, 181, 185, 194
Curious Wine 63–70, 72, 75, 83, 99, 130, 139, 177, 186, 192

Dangerous Men and Adventurous Women 6, 12, 64, 77, 101, 126, 171, 184, 200n.
Dark Dreamer 141, 148
Desert of the Heart 2, 47, 49–51, 105
Desire 8, 12, 27, 36, 41, 43, 45, 57, 59, 62, 121, 128, 156, 160, 165; heterosexual 45, 76; lesbian 40, 45, 71, 76; romantic 37, 38, 41, 125, 134; sexual 37, 41, 47, 102, 113, 123, 129, 163
Deviance 26, 45, 87, 105, 107, 205n.
Dress 79, 85

Edge of Twilight 45
Embrace in Motion 151, 152, 156, 158

Family 16, 156, 178, 187, 188
Fantasy 8, 15, 24, 45, 59, 69, 71, 78, 87, 97, 133, 144, 150, 156, 166, 170, 183; heterosexual 15, 24, 49, 182; lesbian 15, 49, 169, 181, 186
Fated Love 160, 163, 167
Femininity 32, 50, 82, 90, 102, 103, 108, 126, 177
Femme 15, 17, 26, 95, 96, 103–104, 108, 145
Forrest, Katherine 63, 70, 71, 72, 139, 178; *Curious Wine* 63–70, 72, 75, 83, 99, 130, 139, 177, 186, 192
The Friendly Young Ladies 17, 26, 35–40, 90
Friendship 26, 27, 47, 71, 107
Fulfillment 45, 58, 65, 71, 111, 114, 127, 144,

217

150; emotional 99, 120, 122, 128; sexual 99, 102, 114, 165, 189, 192
Fulton, Jennifer 18, 142–150, 168; *Dark Dreamer* 141, 148; *Greener Than Grass* 146, 148; *A Guarded Heart* 148; Moon Island Series 146–147, 149, 163; *More Than Paradise* 18, 145–146, 149; *Passion Bay* 147, 169; *The Sacred Shore* 147; *Saving Grace* 144; *True Love* 142–143, 150

Gaze 80; *see also* Look
Gender 39, 40, 41, 65, 68, 74, 82, 95, 103, 169, 174, 179, 185, 209n.
Genre 5, 6, 9, 13, 16, 22, 23, 26, 41, 60, 63, 71, 93, 94, 106, 112, 141, 149, 159, 169, 190n., 207n.; adaptations 13, 23, 84, 148; conventions 23, 141, 152, 202n.
Gesture 57, 69, 74, 79, 80, 81, 104, 110, 143, 203n.
Greener Than Grass 146, 148
A Guarded Heart 148

Hall, Radclyffe 2, 17, 28–35, 70, 87, 139; Stephen Gordon 29, 30–35, 45, 53, 71, 95, 105; *The Well of Loneliness* 2, 17, 26, 28–35, 36
Heterosexuality 29, 36, 47, 68, 70, 76, 121; romance 30, 39, 63, 68, 76, 88, 93, 101, 117, 123, 130, 176, 180
Highsmith, Patricia 17, 46; *The Price of Salt* 17, 46
Homophobia 155, 157
Humor 52, 91, 112, 146

I Am a Woman 42, 44
Image 68, 80, 81, 83, 89, 96 103
Identity 16, 18, 26, 42, 56, 80, 96, 147, 156, 179; lesbian 45, 52, 69, 70, 75, 87, 99, 117, 137, 187
In Every Port 151, 156
Intentionality 30, 33
Intimacy 14, 25, 30, 36, 38, 62, 70, 90, 92, 100, 112, 135, 146, 151; emotional 39, 95, 111; sexual 11, 12, 17, 39, 48, 68, 111, 117, 121, 137, 164, 192
Invert 25, 29, 34, 39

Journey to a Woman 42, 44
Juhasz, Suzanne 8, 15, 48, 71, 126, 169, 181, 186, 187; *Reading from the Heart* 57, 169, 181
Just Like That 152, 154, 155, 157, 158

Kallmaker, Karin 18, 151–159, 168; *Car Pool* 18, 151, 155, 156; *Christabel* 206n.; *Embrace in Motion* 151, 152, 156, 158; *In Every Port* 151, 156; *Just Like That* 152, 154, 155, 157, 158; *Making Up for Lost Time* 151, 153, 154, 157; *Paperback Romance* 153, 158; *Wild Things* 151, 152, 153, 155, 158
Krentz, Jayne Ann 6, 93, 101, 126, 133, 171, 84; *Dangerous Men and Adventurous Women* 6, 12, 64, 77, 101, 126, 171, 184, 200n.

Lack 58
Language 17, 24, 25, 56–70, 106, 110; articulation 26, 45, 55, 57, 59, 62, 65, 73, 161; communication 12, 55–78, 154, 155, 161, 166, 182; content 57, 112; expectations 57, 58, 62, 63, 112, 113; speech 55, 58, 59, 62, 64, 69, 161; terms 56, 64
Look 17, 69, 74, 82, 84, 95, 96, 104, 106
Love 7, 14, 16, 29, 32, 36, 45, 51, 60, 62, 91, 130; definitions 51, 142, 143; expectations 121, 127, 131, 142, 150, 166; *Fated Love* 160, 163, 167
Love's Masquerade 165, 167
Love's Tender Warriors 167

Making Up for Lost Time 151, 153, 154, 157
Masculinity 68, 79, 92, 96, 108, 114, 124, 172, 177
A Matter of Trust 160, 163
Meaning 17, 53, 55, 75, 77, 111, 164; construction 9, 57, 59, 80, 83; interpretation 37, 56, 77, 202n.
Miller, Isabelle 2, 17, 47–49; *Patience and Sarah* 2, 17, 47–49, 71, 105
Moon Island Series 146–147, 149, 163
More Than Paradise 18, 145–146, 149
Mothers/daughters 49, 181–182, 183, 186, 185
Mutuality 11, 47, 68, 113, 125, 126

A Natural History of the Romance Novel 22
Negotiation 13, 79, 99, 101, 105, 129, 144

Odd Girl Out 41, 43, 44

Paperback Romance 153, 158
Partners 69, 73, 92, 130, 134, 137, 155, 158, 184
Passion 18, 60, 65, 76, 80, 90, 101, 115, 117, 128, 160, 162; heterosexual 86, 114; lesbian 45, 118, 123
Passion Bay 147, 169
Passion's Bright Fury 160, 161, 163, 167
Patience and Sarah 2, 17, 47–49, 71, 105

Pathology 30, 33, 39, 49
Performance 96, 103, 183; sexual 12, 113, 127
Power 61, 83, 101, 115, 116, 122, 125, 137, 179, 184, 192; between couple 11, 75, 101, 109, 113, 127; individual 88, 104, 116, 126, 134
The Price of Salt 17, 46
Pulps 2, 13, 16, 26, 28, 40–46, 49, 53, 71, 87, 103, 105, 120, 168

Radclyffe 18, 159–168; *Fated Love* 160, 163, 167; *Love's Masquerade* 165, 167; *Love's Tender Warriors* 167; *A Matter of Trust* 160, 163; *Passion's Bright Fury* 160, 161, 163, 167; *Safe Harbor* 160, 162, 167; *Tomorrow's Promise* 165; *Turn Back Time* 18, 163, 167
Radway, Janice 2, 8, 12, 18, 22, 47, 58, 112, 115, 124, 126, 172, 176, 181, 185, 194, 196; *Reading the Romance* 2, 18, 59, 133
Reader 15, 170–175, 177; engagement 5, 8, 169, 170, 196; expectations 9, 12, 23, 112, 140, 141, 149, 159, 167; lesbian 13, 15, 17, 106, 109, 138, 140, 168, 181, 185, 186, 193, 196
Reading from the Heart 57, 169, 181
Reading the Romance 2, 18, 59, 133
Regis, Pamela 2, 8, 22, 63, 86, 92, 105, 195; *A Natural History of the Romance Novel* 22
Relationships 133, 140, 151, 154, 167, 170, 195; author/reader 7, 8, 13, 22, 46, 54, 80; in text 9, 16, 17, 28, 30, 36, 40, 44, 49, 60, 62, 71, 126, 132, 143, 155, 196
Renault, Mary 17, 36, 70, 87, 90; *The Friendly Young Ladies* 17, 26, 35–40, 90
Representation 18, 25, 30, 40, 80, 83, 85, 108, 117, 203n.
Risk 50, 57, 133, 161, 162; emotional 161; sexual 121
Romance: conventions 9, 15, 16, 23, 26, 30, 63, 70, 71, 108, 178; definition 9, 22, 152, 200n.; happy ending 10, 16, 29, 45, 47, 48, 62, 65, 69, 71, 75, 88, 91, 106, 112, 121, 127, 134, 143, 158, 164, 167, 169, 170, 171, 181, 188; hero 11, 61, 64, 66, 74, 92–93, 98, 113, 115, 122, 131, 134, 148, 171, 173, 176, 188, 194; heroine 10, 14, 23, 61, 64, 67, 93, 99, 102, 113, 115, 126, 131, 171, 173, 176, 182, 188, 194; narrative 9, 16, 22, 26, 59, 63, 90, 104, 134, 151, 167, 185
The Romance Revolution 111, 113, 133

Rubyfruit Jungle 17, 47, 51–53, 105
Rule, Jane 47, 49–51; *Desert of the Heart* 2, 47, 49–51, 105

The Sacred Shore 147
Safe Harbor 160, 162, 167
Saving Grace 144
Self-awareness 8, 10, 50, 53, 59, 99, 101, 118, 126, 134
Settings 59, 60, 63, 77, 79, 84, 86, 146, 163
Sex 8, 11, 17, 111, 114, 121, 125, 136, 143, 146, 164, 196; behavior 17, 119, 120; eroticism 12, 111, 123, 131, 137, 157, 166; expectations 105, 112, 123, 131, 132; experience 122, 126, 127, 129; graphic 113, 116, 132, 161, 193; satisfaction 15, 58, 114, 115, 122, 130, 192
Sexuality 11, 13, 15, 27, 60, 78, 106, 118, 131, 148, 152, 162, 167, 183, 197; femininity 32, 50, 82, 90, 102, 103, 108, 126, 177; masculinity 68, 79, 92, 96, 108, 114, 124, 172, 177
Society 8, 14, 39, 63, 84, 104, 117, 174–175, 179, 187
Spring Fire 41, 44, 46, 120

Thurston, Carol 2, 3, 8, 18, 111, 113, 114, 116, 133, 196; *The Romance Revolution* 111, 113, 133
Tomorrow's Promise 165
Transformation 10, 13, 51, 108, 115, 121, 122, 148, 183
Transgression 15, 51, 75, 82, 96, 105, 179, 187
True Love 142–143, 150
Turn Back Time 18, 163, 167
Twilight Girls 43, 46, 121

The Unlikely Couple 14–15

Value 5, 8, 13, 16, 19, 71, 84, 88, 90, 115, 134, 135, 138, 170, 183, 197, 199n.
Violence 11, 115, 118, 145
Virginity 114, 115, 183

Wartenberg, Thomas 14, 101; *The Unlikely Couple* 14–15
The Well of Loneliness 2, 17, 26, 28–35, 36
Wild Things 151, 152, 153, 155, 158
Women in the Shadows 42

Xena and Gabrielle 107–109, 177, 204n.

www.ingramcontent.com/pod-product-compliance
Lightning Source LLC
Chambersburg PA
CBHW032053300426
44116CB00007B/723